971
.3541
Rob

Robertson, John Ross, 1841-1918.
    Old Toronto, a selection of excerpts from
Landmarks of Toronto. Ed., integrated and
sometimes emended by E. C. Kyte. With an
index and twenty-seven of the original
illustrations. Toronto, Macmillan, 1954.
    xi, 346 p. illus. (Pioneer books)

RELATED
BOOKS IN
CATALOG
UNDER

1. Toronto - Hist. 2. Toronto - Descr.
I. Title.
                                G-9497

OLD TORONTO

YORK IN 1803

OLD TORONTO

A SELECTION OF EXCERPTS FROM

LANDMARKS OF TORONTO

By JOHN ROSS ROBERTSON

EDITED, INTEGRATED AND SOMETIMES
EMENDED

By E. C. KYTE

WITH AN INDEX

AND

TWENTY-SEVEN OF THE ORIGINAL ILLUSTRATIONS

TORONTO
THE MACMILLAN COMPANY OF CANADA LIMITED

PRINTED IN CANADA

ACKNOWLEDGMENT

The Editor's grateful thanks are here expressed: —

To Mr. H. Pearson Gundy, Librarian of Queen's University.

To Dr. Lorne Pierce for kindly permitting quotation from Richard Cockrel's pamphlet on Education, recently re-published by the Bibliographical Society of Canada. (*See* pages 304-5.)

To Dr. C. R. Sanderson, Chief Librarian, Toronto, and to Miss Elsa Loeber, of the Reference Library.

To Mr. C. H. J. Snider for his kindness in reading the type-script of certain chapters and for his valuable suggestions.

To Mrs. J. G. Boyd, King, Ont., for her loan of a set of the *Landmarks*; a very great benefit.

And to certain of the Staff of The Macmillan Company— Miss W. Eayrs and Mr. K. R. E. Dobbs in particular—who have assisted, supported, and at times wrestled with the Editor, to the ultimate benefit of the Book.

FOREWORD

This is not a History of Toronto. It is a mosaic, set with the lives of men, with the matters, scenes and facts that were vivid and actual in Upper Canada (but especially in Toronto) better than a century ago. Or it is a kaleidoscope of many-coloured fragments, a pattern that changes as the reader turns; from splendour to strife—to pathos—to laughter—to horror. The chapters here printed bring together topics that were originally scattered through six large volumes; now presented to inform, to interest, and even to amuse.

Careful search for an integrating motive in the many-paged, haphazard collection of historical fragments entitled *Robertson's Landmarks of Toronto,* brings an impression of almost incredible persistence. Neither war nor pestilence, neither wreck nor arson, prevented the citizens from striving toward a better, fuller, richer life. There is little sign that the City's elected representatives were the leaders in the effort; what we have today is, to a major degree, the summed results of thousands of efforts by thousands of largely obscure men and women.

Few of these names, these achievements, find commemoration here; but the "common man" who built his log hut in Muddy York, who was with Brock at Queenston ("Push on, the York Volunteers"), who helped to shake Mackenzie out of his dreams, who attended a little Methodist church or "sat under" Dr. Strachan, and was married in the Cathedral of St. James—that man made Toronto what it is today and his signature is at the bottom of our picture.

The original material from which this book has been made was first collected, seventy years ago, by reporters for the Toronto *Evening Telegram.* Its publication in volume form spaced out twenty years, 1894-1914. Early in the eighteen-eighties many, perhaps the majority, of the streets and houses, many even of the men, whose story is told, whose lives are chronicled, still had an actual existence. So, with such evidence at hand, the chapters went at a comfortable jog-trot through scenes that were actual then but that now are a dead man's memories of a different world. Yet colour still remains in them, and from below they light up the sober pages of Canadian history: 1812 and 1837; Yonge Street in the making, and the name of Gallows Hill; "murder and sudden death"; the unholy ways of fire and the wayward Don; school-keeping and store-keeping; theatres, performing elephants and popular preachers—all are here, arranged for the interested reader.

A major problem has been that of compression and inclusion: how best to present the essence of forty-five hundred pages. Matters of much importance were deliberately omitted: the story of the Post Office, of the telegraph, of the printing-press—and much military (peace-time) history. Perhaps, later, public interest may call for another volume: it could be worth while.

What has been attempted is a presentation of this city of Toronto in its early years, by means of a series of pictures; so that, it may be, men will recognize here and there a hint of the days to come: a shadow of the time that finds Toronto a living, growing force in the lives of men and in the history of Canada.

E. C. Kyte

A note on the arrangement of the text:

The greater part of this book consists of excerpts from John Ross Robertson's *Landmarks of Toronto:* they are printed the full width of the page. The text of the editor's comments is slightly indented. For greater ease in reading, references to the original volumes of the *Landmarks* have been omitted.

E.C.K.

CONTENTS

LIST OF ILLUSTRATIONS

I. AS IT WAS IN THE BEGINNING

Judged by her juniors (Winnipeg, Calgary, Vancouver) the great city of Toronto has an enviable history. "Enviable" perhaps rather than "envied"; but her eighteenth-century birth certificate, her wholly British origin, her battle honours — a little dim in brilliance, but supreme in sacrifice — her fighting growth, her mighty present and her regal tomorrow, combine to place her in a situation most worthy of praise.

From the day on which Governor Simcoe said, "Here let there be a city" to the day when (Rebellion broken) the Durham Report was accepted as a workable basis for national life, was forty-four years; little more than half a lifetime as men now measure expectancy. Yet by the end of that time Toronto had established a pattern of existence that still persists, had saved Upper Canada by her example (of how not to do things) and was clipping the wings of her aristocracy in order to make them market-conscious. Forty years on did little more than add to her power and wealth, and enable her to wear with embarrassed rectitude the title of "Toronto the Good". This chapter is, and this volume will mainly be, concerned with her infant years.

The first fort (French), the purchase of the site for a city, the early settlers, the opening of Yonge Street, the establishment of justice and society, assessment rolls and taxes — such matters may fitly be noted in these preliminary pages.

We begin with the fact that some time in 1749 a stockaded trading-post, commonly known and described as Fort Toronto, but officially named Fort Rouille (in compliment to Antoine Louis Rouille, Comte de Jouy, Colonial Minister of

France from 1749 to 1754) was established by the Canadian French three miles east of the mouth of the Toronto River. An officer and fifteen soldiers was its first garrison. For a few years it flourished, although its success was gained at the expense of Fort Niagara; but in the Seven Years' War, when the English conquest of Fort Frontenac and the re-capture of Oswego threatened the western forts of the French, the order was given that all available troops should be sent down for the protection of Fort Niagara, and that Fort Toronto should be burned at once if the English made their appearance. It was done: when Lieutenant Francis with thirty men arrived to reconnoitre he found five piles of burned timber and three rows of charred and broken cedar posts.

Fort Toronto was never rebuilt. In 1760 Major Robert Rogers, an officer who had distinguished himself in the war, visited the site of it on his way to take possession of the western forts vacated by the French. He says: "There was a tract of about three hundred acres of cleared land round the place where formerly the French had a fort called Fort Toronto. The soil is principally clay. The deer are extremely plentiful. I think Toronto a most convenient place for a factory," the Major adds, meaning by factory, trading post. Captain Gother Mann, an officer of the Royal Engineers, was instructed in 1788 to examine Toronto harbour, take soundings and look over the whole locality with a view to the establishment of a settlement here. He drew a ground plan of the old French fort, showing the lines of the stockade and the five little parallelograms, in-side being the storehouse, a little in advance of the others, and the quarters for the keepers, officers, soldiers and men employed. Captain Mann entitled his map "Plan of the Proposed Toronto Harbour, with the Proposed Town and Port by the Settlement". He expressed his opinion that the best position for a fort to protect the proposed settlement is the exact spot today occupied by the stone barracks. From this point slantingly across the entrance into the harbour he takes soundings and finds the water to vary from one to four fathoms in depth. Captain Mann also lays out a town on paper, making the town plot exactly square, consisting of eleven equal-sized blocks each way, a broad strip of reserved ground in front, a large patch of commons in the rear and the surrounding country cut up into farms and roads. In the time of Augustus Jones, the land surveyor brought over by Governor Simcoe, the Toronto river had come to have another name — St. John's river. Augustus Jones makes a survey of the broken front concession of York, and from this it is evident that the old French fort stood two chains or 132 feet from the present Dufferin street. Mr. Jones observes the remains of an old forge, and notes that the timber is birch, black oak, beech and hemlock, the soil clay.

During Governor Simcoe's administration a new fort was built and a stockade erected around it, on the west side of Garrison Creek, east of the site of the old fort. In this creek, before the woods were cut down, salmon used to be caught for quite a distance up the valley. The Government common at the water's edge, in the centre of which the fort was built on elevated ground, was originally a portion of a great circle radiating a thousand yards from its centre, the fort. The eastern entrance to the fort was reached by an ascent from the ravine of Garrison Creek. The arched gateway was protected by strong iron studded portals. Within, a sentry and the guard house on the left; beyond, the loop-holed block house on one side and the quarters of the men, officers and commandant on the other. Up to 1849 the buildings on the east side of the enclosure were pretty much the same as in the year 1800.

Why was the name "Toronto" changed?

Frederick, Duke of York, was the second son of George III. He served for a time in the Prussian army, commanded a British corps in the French campaigns of 1793-4, and was made a Field-marshal in 1795. On receiving word of the success of His Majesty's arms under H.R.H. the Duke of York, by which Holland was saved from the invasion of the French, Governor Simcoe determined to change the name of Toronto to that of "York". This was done in August, 1793.

So much for the Old Fort: but to reach the Town we have to go back about seven years.

Stockton in one of his clever sketches humorously tells of a man who started out alone to establish the nucleus of a city in an uninhabited land. Ludicrously absurd is the picture drawn of him digging away on the great lonely plain, and yet how similar is the circumstance to which Toronto owes its existence. The new Governor of a new-created province goes cruising about in a strange country inhabited only by savages, and coming to a region of thickets, marshes and venomous copperheads, draws his sword and exclaims: "Here will be built a great city in the spring!" And surely enough a log house sprang up in the wilderness, and about the log house a hamlet and out of the hamlet a great and prosperous city. Here then, on July 26, 1793, on the schooner *Mississaga* came John Graves Simcoe, Lieut.-General in the British Army, and first Governor of Upper Canada, accompanied by his Executive Council, his Queen's Rangers in their dark green suits, his faithful aides, his surveyor and his canvas tent, which once belonged to Captain Cook, the famous circumnavigator. With a royal salute of 21 guns the Governor inaugurated his administration with a Council in the tent on Saturday, August 3. Meanwhile surveyor Augustus Jones, who was walking about to look at the new town, remarked that nothing was to be seen of it except the site. During the spring of 1794 the Governor built Castle Frank, in the midst of the woods on the brow of a steep high bank overlooking the valley of the Don, at a point just a few yards beyond the fence which now bounds St. James' cemetery at the north. A large portion of the land formerly belonging to Castle Frank is now part of the burying ground. Immediately below the house, on the south, was a deep glen, down which, between hog-back formations, ran a stream named Castle Frank Brook, which flowed into the Don, just above a small island on the west side. The marshes gave way on the right at this point to good land covered with elm, butternut and basswood trees.

Castle Frank was a Chateau, or cottage or summer house.

It was not occupied permanently by the governor and his family, but it was doubtless the scene of nearly all the social life in the little settlement during Governor Simcoe's administration. The building was oblong, of the dimensions of thirty by fifty feet — the former being the frontage, which was toward the south. The façade was much like that of a Greek temple.

CASTLE FRANK

At the gable end, in the direction of the roadway leading from the infant capital, was a door but no windows. The trunks of four large, well-matched, unbarked pine trees answered for columns supporting the pediment or the projection of the whole roof. On each side were four windows with shutters of heavy double planks running up and down on one side, and crosswise on the other, and thickly studded with the heads of stout nails. Of a similar construction was the door. A chimney arose from the middle of the roof. The walls were built of rather small, carefully hewn logs, of short lengths, clap-boarded. They presented a comparatively finished appearance on the outside, but after a time took the weather-stained colour that unpainted wood assumes. Inside, the finish was rough, in fact the interior was never fully completed.

"Frank" was the name of the five-year-old son of Governor Simcoe; and when he died in 1812 at the storming of Badajoz, the house, closed and tenantless, was left to decay. But the infant city, that his father had founded, lived, flourished and expanded. The site on which Toronto stands was sold by the Mississaugua Indians to the English Crown through Governor Simcoe in 1787; one hundred and sixty-seven years ago.

Real estate men were not in evidence in those days, or perhaps the Indians would have fared much better. Indeed, they could not have fared worse when they parted with about 250,000 acres in what is known as the "Toronto Purchase".

There were two palavers with the Government agents before the Crown secured the property of the red men. The first meeting was held at the Carrying Place in September, 1787, and at this meeting the purchase was formally discussed — while at the second meeting on the 1st August, 1805, the bargain was completed.

The entire 250,808 acres were sold for £1,700 sterling, or $8,500, in cash and goods.

The Prince Edward district, now the county of Prince Edward, was settled after the American War by U.E. Loyalists, and by a few English, Irish and Scotch, who emigrated about 1785-90.

When one enters the county from the west, he leaves the village of Brighton behind and crosses a neck of land separating the western extremity of the Bay of Quinte from Lake Ontario. On this road and about ten miles from Brighton was in the olden days a settlement called the "Carrying Place", this being the spot at which the Indians and Indian traders were wont to carry their canoes and merchandise overland from the Bay of Quinte to Lake Ontario and vice versa. From the Carrying Place to Consecon the distance is about 5 miles.

On the 23rd Sept., 1787, Deputy Surveyor-General John Collins, from Quebec, acting on behalf of the Crown, with a couple of French-Canadians, one of whom acted as interpreter, met three Indian chiefs at the Carrying Place on the Bay of Quinte, and bargained for a large tract of land in, around and including a part of the county of York, and all the land now occupied by the city of Toronto.

The sale was not, however, completed for eighteen years. In August, 1805, another meeting was held at the River Credit, on Lake Ontario, thirteen miles west of Toronto, between the Government and the Indians. This meeting was more representative than the former one. In September, 1787, only three Indian chiefs were present. In August, 1805, eight were on hand.

On this occasion the Crown was represented by William Claus, the Deputy Superintendent-General and Deputy Inspector-General of Indians. After the meeting at the Carrying Place two of the Indian chiefs, Wabukanyne and Neace, died. The second meeting and treaty or indenture were necessary as the first did not ascertain or describe the tract of land agreed to be conveyed.

At the second meeting it was agreed that the sum of £1,700 or $8,500 should be given for the 250,000 acres that were required. This includes practically all the land on which Toronto is built, runs back from Etobicoke to Lloydtown and takes in also the counties of King, Vaughan and York. What was paid and how it was paid, what the proportion was of goods to cash is not yet clear. Fifteen laced hats, four dozen black silk handkerchiefs, a gross of butcher's knives with red handles, blankets, scissors, powder, shot — even today Toronto seems cheap at the price. And if the landless men protested afterwards, the answer must have been "So what?"

"Father, while Colonel Butler was our father, we were told our father the King wanted some land for his people; it was some time before we sold it, but when we found it was much wanted by the King to settle his people on it, whom we were told would be of great use to us, we granted it accordingly.

"Father, we have not found this so, as the inhabitants drive us away instead of helping us, and we want to know why we are served in that manner. Colonel Butler told us that the farmers would help us, but instead of doing so when we encamp on the shore, they drive us off and shoot our dogs, and never give us any assistance, as was promised to our old chiefs."

At the end of the meeting, the "business done" appears to have been that of the Indians; but the matter was now on a legal footing and enables us to draw up the following table of dates:—

1787—At the Carrying Place, Bay of Quinte, three Indian chiefs agree to sell the land (called subsequently "the Toronto Purchase").

1788—Captain Gother Mann prepares a map of Toronto (see page 31).

1793—(May) Simcoe takes possession of the site and begins to build the fort.

     (June) The first official plan of York is made by Alexander Aitken, Deputy Surveyor.

1794—York at that time was a small hamlet, numbering about four hundred inhabitants, in close proximity to, and west of, the river Don. (This estimate of population should probably be halved; and even those were mainly officials, based on Newark.) William Berczy brings German settlers and hired axe men to clear out the line of Yonge Street and a part of the lot where York was to be built.

1794-5—Log huts erected in the Old Fort and the Parliament Buildings begun.

1795—The first frame house was built in York by William Smith. It took the place of a log hut built in 1794.

FIRST PARLIAMENT BUILDINGS

1796—David Thomson took up his abode on what was then forest land in Scarboro. He was the first settler there.

1797—Parliament met on May 30, and the Receiver General's Office was opened. The Legislative Buildings were on Palace (now Front) Street, at the foot of Berkeley St.

1798—The Registrar's Office was opened in the Legislative Buildings. Thomas Ridout was the first Registrar. The first Court of Assize was held in November.

1799—The first Town Meeting was held on March 4 to provide for the nomination and appointment of parish and town officers within this province.

1799—One hundred guineas reward was offered for information "as to who has been setting certain places on fire". Much more was to be suffered from the incendiary for the next seventy years.

1800—On January 20th the Court of Oyer and Terminer was opened: "before which came John Small, Esq., indicted for having mortally wounded the late Attorney-General in a duel; after a trial of about eight hours he was acquitted". This verdict means, if words have any meaning, that John Small, Esq., did *not* mortally wound the late Attorney-General.

1800—Toronto's first white baby born in a log hut on Duke St. His name was Andrew Heron and he lived to be eighty-eight.

1800—(Dec. 18) OPENING UP YONGE STREET — On Thursday last, about noon, a number of the principal inhabitants of this town met together in one of the Government buildings to consider the means of opening the road to Yonge street and enabling the farmers there to bring their provisions to market with more ease than is practicable at present. The Hon. the Chief Justice was called to the chair. He briefly stated the purpose of the meeting, and added that a subscription had been lately opened by which something more than two hundred dollars in money and labour had been promised, and that other sums were to be expected from several respectable inhabitants who were well-wishers to the undertaking, but had not yet contributed towards it. These sums would not, he feared, be equal to the purpose, which could hardly be accomplished for less than between five and six hundred dollars, but many of the subscribers were desirous that what was already subscribed should be immediately applied as far as it would go, and that other resources should be looked for. With this in view it had been suggested that a considerable aid might be obtained by shutting up the street which now forms the northern boundary of the town between Toronto street and the Common, and disposing of the land occupied by it. This street, it was conceived, was altogether superfluous, as another street, equally convenient in every respect, runs parallel to it at the distance of about ten rods, but it could not be shut up and disposed of by any authority less than that of the Legislature. To consider of an application to Parliament for the purpose was one of the objects of the meeting. The subscribers present were unanimously of opinion that the subscription should be immediately applied as far as it would go, and that an application should be made to Parliament at its next session for the purpose above mentioned. A paper was then produced and read containing a proposal from Mr. Eliphalet Hale to open and make the road or so much of it as might be required, at the rate of twelve dollars per acre for clearing it where no causeway was wanted, four rods wide, and cutting the stumps in two middle rods close to the ground; and 7s 6d provincial currency per rod, for making a causeway 18 feet wide, where a causeway might be wanted. He undertook to give security for performing the work by the first of February next. Mr. Hale's proposal was accepted.

Hale was a bricklayer and also a contractor. He built the first brick houses in York, and now advertises for "five or six good axemen by the month" to clear Yonge Street.

He was also a boot and shoe dealer, advertising in 1803 that he made "suwarrow, common and half boots etc. the next door north of Alexander Woods". When he died in 1807, he was High Constable for the Home District.

1801—First table of meteorological observations was published, for the month of January. Only on one day, the 3rd, did the thermometer go below zero. On January 11th, it was 49° above at noon. Those good old-fashioned winters! And in the following year on January 3rd, the temperature at noon was 57°. It was the warmest day of the month.

It will be convenient here to discourse of York's assessment rolls; the first of which is dated February, 1798,

and comprises not only the town but also the townships of York, Vaughan and Markham. It was duly prepared and forwarded to the Lieutenant Governor, being signed "errors excepted," by "Thomas Ridout, Clerk of the Peace, Home District." It is impossible to say how much refers to the town and how much to the townships, but the total amount estimated for the home district to produce from one hundred and twenty-seven ratepayers was only £25 16s 3d currency, equivalent to $103.25. The assessors were Thomas Barry and George Playter, and the "magistrates approving" John Small and William Willcocks.

The collector appears to have been Mr. Samuel Heron.

In the following year the number of those assessed was two hundred and twenty-four, the rate being estimated to produce £75 8 0 currency ($301.60). Thomas Stovell succeeded Thomas Barry as assessor, the name of William Jarvis was added to the approving magistrates, and Archibald Cameron was collector.

In 1800 the taxpayers had increased to two hundred and fifty-four, the rate producing £81 5 6 ($325.10). John Ashbridge and Elisha Beman were the assessors; the approving magistrates, with the exception of Willcocks, were the same as the year previous, but the collector was Jacob Herchmer — a very lively time he must have had of it — and the treasurer was Mr. William Allan.

In 1801, though the population of York is given separately, its assessment is not; it was joined for rating purposes with York township, Etobicoke and Scarboro, the total population being only six hundred and · seventy-eight. Of this number there were one hundred and ninety-two rate-payers, whose payments in the aggregate were £97 6s 6d ($389.30). But if the population and income were small, the number of office holders was by no means limited, though it must be admitted that, with the possible exception of the collectors, the work was all done without any remuneration.

The following is a complete list of the officials: —

Town Clerk—Eli Playter.

Assessors—James Playter and Simon McNabb.

Collector—John Cameron.

Overseers of the highway—Elisha Bennard, Robert Lang, J. Ashbridge, John Playter, Ben Davis, John Wilson, D. W. Kendrick, Wm. Jones and William Cornell.

Eli and John Playter were brothers. A son of the latter for many years filled most ably the post of secretary to the York Pioneers. James Playter was another member of the same family.

J. Ashbridge was the man who bestowed his name on the small bay to the east of Toronto Harbour.

D. W. Kendrick was Duke Kendrick, one of several brothers. One of them resided for some years in a small wooden cottage on Bloor street, nearly opposite University avenue.

William Cornell was a Scarboro' man, who emigrated to this country about 1780.

The Poundkeepers were—Alex. Galloway, John Davis, Jas. Everson, Andrew Thomson and W. Jones.

There was probably some small fee expected by these latter officials; that is, if they could get it.

The Townwardens were—Jacob Herchmer and Duncan Cameron.

It will be seen, therefore, that for 192 ratepayers there were no less than twenty officials, a tolerably large number. It cannot be said that matters are much improved in that respect a hundred and fifty years or nearly so, later. Indeed in some respects they are worse, for offices that were honorary then are now remunerative to their incumbents.

Among items that are of interest in the accounts is the following entry: "December 8th, 1800, paid two constables for going up to the Humber to apprehend the rioters, £1 5 0." These rioters were probably some lumberers who had engaged in a drunken quarrel with the fishermen of the neighbourhood.

Again there is this entry: "Paid John Lyons for two wolves' scalps as per Mr. Ruggles' certificate, £2, Jan. 17th, 1801." On March 17th in the same year there is a similar entry of £6 for two wolves' scalps to William Peck and four to John Burk. William Willcocks, J.P., gave the certificate in these cases. Either the collector of taxes was very lax in the performance of his duties, or the taxpayers were determined not to part with their money, for on the credit side of the accounts of the Home District for 1801 is this entry:—"N.B.— No money has been received from the collector appointed from April, 1798 to April, 1799."

So as to show as nearly as possible the amount of cash received in proportion to the amount of rate levied the following accounts from 1798 to April 1st, 1802 are given:—

Rates levied	£ s. d.	Total £ s. d.	Rates paid	£ s. d.	Total £ s. d.
[1] 1797-8 to Feb.	25 16 3		Apr. 23, 1800	23 18 9	
[1] 1799 to Jul.	75 8 -		Apr. 8, 1801	32 9 9	
[2] 1800 to Apr.	81 5 6		Apr. 29, 1801	13 - -	
[3] 1801 to May	97 6 6		June 25, 1801	5 4 -	
			Apr. 1802	22 4 6	
			Apr. 1802	25 13 7	
					149 10 7
		279 16 3	By balance		130 5 8
To balance		£279 16 3			£279 16 3
		£130 5 8			

[1] Includes town of York and Townships of York, Vaughan and Markham.
[2] Includes all the preceding, with Etobicoke, King and Whitchurch.
[3] York, Scarboro, Etobicoke and town of York.

These figures, to borrow a hackneyed phrase, "afford food for reflection."

Of rates levied in May, or up to that period in 1801, only fifty-two and a half per cent had been paid a twelve month later, and so far as the accounts are given in the four years immediately following this period, very little change for the better took place.

This was in a great measure due, not probably to any disinclination on the part of the inhabitants of York to "render unto Caesar the things that are Caesar's" but from absolute inability to find the necessary cash. Taxes could not be paid in kind and the supply of ready money for many long years after this period was exceedingly limited. A son of a resident in Markham in 1794, indeed born there in that year, related shortly before his death, which occurred about twenty years since [i.e., about 1874] how a New England pedlar came through Markham in 1805 and created quite a sensation, not only by paying ready cash for what he required from the farmers, but by being able to take produce from them instead of cash for their purchases from him. This same enterprising American gave one of the boys four pence in coppers. That boy told when he had reached old age how proud he was and how envied by his companions at being the possessor of such great wealth. And strange as it may appear to the inhabitants of Toronto in 1893, probably not a few of the older inhabitants of Markham in 1805 thought four pence "a great deal of money." *Tempora mutantur nos et mutamur in illis.*

As might be expected when the taxes came in so badly, the few paid public servants that the district boasted of in those days got their money equally badly. On March 9th, 1802, occurs this entry, "Paid Daniel Tiers his salary as court keeper, up to the 1st April, five quarters at £8 per annum, £10," and all through the accounts are entries showing how creditors had to be paid cash in instalments on bills that were already overdue.

Pathmasters had to keep the roads in order and were able to call on all householders to do so many days' or hours' work upon the roads; a duty both hated and evaded in every possible way.

Colonel Givins, for instance, in 1809 was "allowed to perform his statute labor for this year *and last* upon the road leading past his house to the Humber." That would be on Dundas Street from the beginning of Ossington Avenue.

1803 — The population of York had increased to such an extent that there was an imperative demand for a public market. Accordingly, Governor Peter Hunter appointed a weekly market day and a place where the market should be held. This was a plot of five acres, bounded by Market, New, King and Church Streets. It was simply a wooden shambles 45 feet long and 30 feet wide, running north and south and situated in the middle of the square. A public well was dug here in 1823 at a cost to the county of £28.1.3; which includes the charge for boring 8 feet, 2 inches through the rock. This well still exists somewhere under the present market. In this square, also, the stocks and the pillory were set up, and public auctions were held.

Oxen were extensively used for purposes of traction, and to some of our readers it may be news that the creatures were shod. Here is a description of the necessary machine.

It consisted of a framework, four feet wide, of strong hardwood bars about four inches square, and six feet long, dovetailed into four posts about five feet high and six inches square, forming the corners of the stand, and resting on a substantial floor of two-inch planks. There were three of the horizontal bars on each side of the frame, and on the top and ends it was held together in its length and width by timber of the same size as the posts. At the upper end of this contrivance, midway between the two corner posts were two perpendicular bars, one fast, the other moving from right to left on a pivot at the bottom, and capable of being made fast by a bolt at the top. When an ox was brought to be shod he was driven into this framework stall, his head secured by the movable bar, and the blacksmith then commenced his anything but agreeable task of shoeing the animal. It was an operation not often performed, and when it was, was attended with a great deal of trouble, not only to the workman, but pretty generally to the ox.

A little earlier a log hut had been erected for the artificers and men at work upon the public buildings. "This hut was used last winter [1802] for the King's oxen." A plot of land at the east end of the town between the first Parliament Buildings and the Don River was enclosed for the benefit of "the King's oxen when employed".

In this year also (1803) notices and advertisements reveal attempts at formation of a public conscience. Consider this one:—

Twenty Dollars Reward will be paid by the subscriber to any person who will discover the man who is so depraved and lost to every sense of social duty as to cut with an axe or knife the withes which bound some of the fence around the late Chief Justice's Farm on Yonge street, and to throw down the said fence. Independent of the above inducement, it is the duty of every good member of society to endeavour to find out who the character is who can be guilty of such an infamous act in order that he may be brought to justice. Robert I. D. Gray.

Two years later, in 1805, it is evident that rewards for lost property were also liberal.

Thirty Dollars Reward. Lost or stolen on or about the 25th ult., from the house of C. B. Wyatt, Esq., surveyor general, three silver tea spoons to be returned and give information against whoever may have stolen the same, so as he or they may be prosecuted to conviction, shall, on application to Mr. Wyatt, or to the printer thereof, receive a reward of Thirty Dollars.

The grammar and syntax are somewhat weak but the reward and the intention are definite.

Now, for purposes of comparison, let us look at Toronto (or York) at intervals of several years, before we go on to individual "firsts" in the second part of this chapter.

The Town Meeting for 1806 made Eli Playter, Town Clerk, and Thomas Mosley, Collector. There were Overseers of Highways, and there were Fence Viewers; there were Pound Keepers — Isaac Collombes was one of them — and it was —

agreed by a majority of the inhabitants that hogs shall run at large in the country. Fences to be five feet high with the stakes and riders; and no more than a space of four inches between the rails to the height of three feet of the same.

Thomas Ridout, Clerk of the Peace for the Home District, announced in August that the Commissioners of the Highways would receive proposals for the first opening and making the road called Dundas Street "leading through the Indian Reserve at the River Credit, and also to erect a bridge over the said river". Thomas Ridout, Clerk of the Peace, had also the misfortune to be concerned with York in war. The taking of the town in 1813 has often been described; and while the *Landmarks* include much about the three-year war, the City's share is not over-emphasized. We reprint three personal narratives — (1) a letter from John Beikie, Sheriff of York County in 1812 (with a feminine postscript), (2) a memorandum from Mr. Thomas Ridout and (3) a "communication" made to the Governor-General by Dr. Grant Powell and Dr. John Strachan.

(1) York, 5th May, 1813. My Dear John, — Early on the morning of the 27th ultimo the enemy's fleet, consisting of fourteen sail, doubled Gibraltar Point under easy sail, and came to anchor off the site of the Old Fort, Toronto. Everyone, you may be sure, ran to prevent their landing; but they sailed in in spite of us, though not without great loss on both sides. As I had no military command I volunteered with the Grenadiers

of the 8th Regiment, and had the mortification to see their gallant leader fall. Captain McNeil was beloved by his men. About this time the enemy were landing in great numbers, and we were ordered to make for the battery. As I did not hear this order, I found myself suddenly with Major Givins at the head of about a hundred Indians.

He desired me to advance nearer the water for fear of being made prisoner; and, in an instant afterward, everyone fled the best way he could. I got safe to the Government House Battery, and thought everything coming on well, when I heard a dreadful explosion, and then cheers. But alas! it was the blowing up of about thirty of our poor fellows and the enemy gaining possession of our battery. From this moment every heart was dismayed; the enemy were rushing on; the General ordered a retreat, and fire to be set to the magazine. This was the grandest, and at the same time, the most awful sight I have ever seen.

The only thing then to be done was for the town to capitulate, which was done. Then the business of plundering and burning commenced and did not cease until the evening of the 1st inst., when they all went on board their vessels, where they yet remain at anchor in the harbor. They have burnt the Government House, the two block houses, one barracks for soldiers and other buildings. They have broken every door and window in the council office, which was Elmsley House, and burnt a schooner belonging to an inhabitant of York.

They have carried off the *Gloucester,* which was undergoing repairs, and was to be converted into a transport, being too old for a ship of war. The new ship on the stocks we burnt ourselves, for otherwise, I dare say, they would have done it.

Thank God, I escaped unhurt. A rifle ball struck and passed through the upper part of the cape of my coat, under my ear. The American commander-in-chief, Pike is. killed. General Dearborn now commands.

I remain always,
Your affectionate brother,
JOHN BEIKIE

Never did I pass so awful a day as the 27th of April, with my two poor fellows in the heat of the battle. I never prayed more fervently, or said that beautiful psalm (He that dwells in the help of the Highest shall abide in the protection of the God of heaven, etc.) more devoutly since that day.

It is a beautiful psalm, and He who strengthens the weak gave me more strength and fortitude than all the other females of York put together, for I kept my castle when all the rest fled; and it was well for us that I did so — our little property was saved by that means. Every house they found deserted was completely sacked.

They so overloaded their vessels that I am told they have thrown quantities of pork and flour into the lake. I really attribute this visit to the vengeance of Heaven on this place, for quantities of stores, farming utensils etc., sent from England in the time of General Simcoe, were allowed to remain in the King's stores, and nothing of them did they [i.e., the troops] ever get. Now, our enemies have them, to do with them as they please. I think we deserve all we have got. Keep up your spirits, my dear John, for God seems to be on our side.

Your affectionate sister,
PENELOPE BEIKIE

In the circumstances, a somewhat feminine attitude on the part of both sexes is understandable.

(2) Mr. Thomas Ridout writes of the latter half of the U.S. occupation of York.

I left York on Sunday the second instant, at noon, at which time the American fleet, consisting of the *Madison, Oneida,* and ten schooners with the *Gloucester* were lying at anchor about ten miles from the Garrison, wind-bound by a south-east wind. All their troops were embarked the evening before, excepting a small party who burned the large block house, government house and officers' quarters. At nine in the morning a naval officer came down to town and collected ten men out of the

taverns where they had been all night. The commissariat maga-
zines were shipped the preceding days and great quantities of the
provisions given to our country people who brought their
waggons down to assist the Americans to transport the public
stores found at Mr. Elmsley's house and at Boulton's barn. The
lower block-house and government buildings were burned on
Saturday. Major Givins' and Dr. Powell's houses were entirely
plundered by the enemy and some persons from the Humber.
Jackson and his two sons and Sudden, the butcher, had been
riding through the country ordering the militia to come in and
be put on their paroles, which caused great numbers to obey
voluntarily and through fear. Duncan Cameron, Esq., delivered
all the monies in the Receiver-General's hands, to the amount,
as I understand, of £2,500, over to Captain Elliot of the
American navy, the enemy having threatened to burn the town
if it was not given up. On Friday the 30th the Chief Justice,
Judge Powell, my father, Dr. Strachan and D. Cameron called
upon General Dearborn, requesting he would allow the magistrates to retain their authority over our own people. Accordingly
he issued a general order, saying it was not his intention to
deprive the magistracy of its civil function; that they would be
supported, and if any of the United States troops committed
any depredation a strict scrutiny into it should follow. The
gaol was given up to the sheriff, but no prisoners. The public
provincial papers were found out, but ordered to be protected,
so that nothing was destroyed, excepting the books, papers,
records and furniture of the Upper and Lower Houses of
Assembly. It was said they had destroyed our letters and taken
away the cannon. The barracks were not burnt. The American
officers said their force on the 27th was three thousand land
force and one thousand seamen and mariners, and that their
loss was five hundred killed and wounded. T. G. Ridout,
Kingston, May 5, 1813.

Kingston naturally was a refuge for displaced citizens of
York; and even for generals. What an illumination the
sentence about the activities of Jackson and Sudden the

butcher throws upon the wavering loyalties of many inhabitants. Note that this action immobilized the militia when the
enemy's fleet of twelve sail returned at the end of July. Though
merely the cat coming back to make sure that the town was
still its mouse, there was menace and grief and loss in the
proceeding, and another opportunity for traitors.

(3) We beg leave to state, for the information of his Excellency the Governor-General, that about eleven o'clock on Saturday morning the enemy's fleet of twelve sail were seen standing
for the harbour. Almost all the gentlemen of the town having
retired we proceeded to the Garrison about 2 o'clock and watched
until 3 o'clock, when the *Pyter,* and *Madison* and *Oneida* came
to anchor in the offing, and the schooners continued to pass up
the harbour with their sweeps, the wind having become light,
then coming to abreast of the town, the remainder near the
Garrison. About 4 o'clock several boats full of troops landed at
the Garrison and we, bearing a white flag, desired the first officer
we met to conduct us to Commodore Chauncey. We mentioned
to the Commodore that the inhabitants of York, consisting chiefly
of women and children, were alarmed at the approach of the
fleet, and that we had come to know his intention respecting the
town; that if it were to be pillaged or destroyed we might take
such measures as were still in our power for their removal and
protection. We added that the town was totally defenceless,
the militia being still on parole, and that the gentlemen had
left it having heard that the principal inhabitants of Niagara
had been carried away captive, a severity unusual in war. Commodore Chauncey replied that it was far from his intention
to molest the inhabitants of York in person or property; he
was sorry that any of the gentlemen had thought it necessary to
retire, and that he did not know of any person taken from
Niagara of the description mentioned. Colonel Scott, the
commandant of the troops, said that a few persons had certainly
been taken away. The Commodore told us that his coming to
York at present was a sort of retaliation for the visits our fleet
made on the other side of the lake and to possess himself of

the public stores and destroy the fortifications, but that he would burn no houses. He mentioned something of Sodus and the necessity of retaliation should such measures be taken in the future. He likewise expressed much regret at the destruction of our public library, April 27th, informing us that he had made strict search through his fleet for the books; many of them had been found which he would send back by the first flag of truce.[1] He then asked what public stores were here, a question which we could not answer. In parting both the Commodore and Colonel Scott pledged their honour that our persons and property should be respected, and that even the town should not be entered by the troops, much less by any gentleman there. As we were quieting the minds of the inhabitants the troops took possession of the town, opened the jail, liberated the prisoners, taking three soldiers, confined for felony, with them; they visited the hospitals and paraded the few men that could not be removed. They then entered the stores of Mr. Allan and Mr. St. George, and secured the contents consisting chiefly of flour. Observing this we went to Col. Scott and informed him that he was taking property. He replied that a great deal of officers' luggage had been found in Mr. Allan's store, and that all the private property was to be respected. Provisions of all kinds were lawful prizes, because they were the subsistence of armies; that if it prevailed in the contest the British Government would make up the loss, and if they were successful their Government would most willingly reimburse the sufferers. He concluded by declaring that he would seize all provisions he could find. The three schooners which had anchored abreast of the town towed out between 11 and 12 o'clock on Saturday night, and we supposed that the fleet would have sailed immediately, but having been informed by some traitor that valuable stores had been sent up the Don, the schooners came up the harbour yesterday morning. The troops were again landed, and three armed boats went up the Don in search of the stores. We have since learned that through the meritorious exertions of a few young men, two of the name of Playter, everything was conveyed away before the enemy

[1] For further information concerning this library see page 337.

reached the place. Two or three boats containing trifling articles which had been hidden in the marsh were discovered and taken, but in the main the enemy were disappointed. As soon as the armed boats returned the troops went on board, and by sunset both soldiers and sailors had evacuated the town. The barracks, the wood-yard, and the storehouses on Gibraltar Point were then set on fire, and this morning at daylight the enemy's fleet sailed.

It was the opinion of Candide that "a modest woman may be once outraged, for her virtue is greatly strengthened thereby"; and even the double outrage in April and July failed to destroy the virtue of Little York. Once on her feet again she resumed her former way of life; and there was nothing meretricious in her welcome to new, or old (from Kingston), inhabitants. But the period of her childhood was definitely over.

II

The *Upper Canada Gazette* and *American Oracle* was first published on April 18, 1793, in the old town of Niagara, then called Newark. Louis Roy, its first printer, sold out in the following year to Gideon Tiffany, who gave place in 1797 to Titus Geer Simons and his partner William Waters. On the 4th of October, 1798, the *Gazette* was published for the first time in "the new capital — York"; and for the next forty-eight years news of general and local importance appeared in its pages. Also advertisements; and today these give us the growing measure of the infant city. We cannot say, of course, that every new tradesman advertised in the *Gazette* (or, rather, in the *American Oracle,* its supplement), but enough of them did so to make an interesting gallery of "Firsts". We naturally begin with a bricklayer, Mr. Eliphalet Hale, who was to become a contractor, open up Yonge Street, and die in 1807 as High Constable for the Home District.

In 1799 he respectfully informed the inhabitants of York that he would attend there ready to "commence bricklaying, lathing and plastering in the first part of April". The work would be "faithfully and timely executed" — an assurance that all succeeding tradesmen offer in various phrase. There is Evean Eveans, a fashionable "taylor and habit maker (from London)", who has "taken a room in a small building for the purpose of prosecuting the duties of his trade" in 1799. Two years later comes competition from Hugh McCaul, who "hopes by the goodness of his work, the reasonableness of his charges, and his punctuality in executing all orders to merit a preference". By 1815 there were four tailors in York.

In April, 1800, we have the first watch-maker, Elisha Purdey, who "repairs and cleans watches of all kinds, in the best manner and on the most reasonable terms". He had a room in the house of Mr. Mathers, and was soon to have a competitor in the person of Jordan Post. In 1800, also, an auctioneer is found.

William Cooper begs leave to inform his friends and the public in general that he has lately received License as Auctioneer for this Town. That he has appropriated a part of his house in Duke street for the purpose of an auction room, which will be made as commodious as possible; where every attention will be paid to such articles as his friends may be pleased to honor him with the disposal of. He flatters himself that the tenor of his conduct heretofore will entitle him to the confidence and patronage of the public; secrecy will be strictly observed on his part. York, September 13th.

He will sell by auction at the house of Mr. John McDougall between the hours of 11 and 12 o'clock on Monday, the 22nd instant, 4 barrels of prime tobacco, 1 do. of pork, a well assorted library of books in different languages; some of the most fashionable colored fine and refine cloths, together with sundry other articles too tedious to mention.

The last phrase is pleasant; so too is the assurance that secrecy will be observed. William Cooper, one of three brothers, had settled in York about 1795. He was a wharfinger in 1805: "Cooper's Wharf" was well known. He also was a prominent Anglican who sometimes, in the absence of George O'Kill Stuart, read the service to the congregation of St. James. Cooper's competitor, Thomas Mosley, who died in 1827, had no legs but advertised proudly that he had a serviceable tongue. We shall meet him again.

Paul Morin begs leave to inform his friends and the public that he has declined carrying on the baking business for Mr. Beaman and now carries it on in all its branches on his own account, at the house formerly occupied by Mr. Beaman, where they may be supplied with bread at the rate of four lbs. for a shilling; biscuit, buns, cakes etc. He hopes by assiduity and attention to his business to merit encouragement.

N.B.—Any person sending flour to be baked by him will receive seven lbs. of bread for every six lbs of flour.

In this case a shilling would probably mean Halifax currency, or twenty cents.

Elisha Beaman was one of the two Assessors for York in 1800, but he is not known as a baker. We can follow Paul Morin a little further. In April, 1808, the following notice appeared in the *Gazette*.

Died, on Tuesday morning last, Mr. Paul Marian, baker and innkeeper, of this town, an honest, industrious and respectable man, whose death will be felt by his family and the inhabitants of this town as an afflicting private loss and a real public one.

And in March, 1828, his son advertises:

William Marian respectfully acquaints his friends and the public in general, he has recommenced the baking business in the house formerly known as the York hotel, and solicits the patronage of the public.

Readers will have noted the anglicizing of *Morin*. We wonder where William had been during those twenty years. Jordan's York Hotel was "the first class hotel, not only of the town but of all Upper Canada"; and in its ballroom the Parliament of Upper Canada sat for one session. And considered themselves in luxurious quarters. Before the hotel was erected Paul Morin had built his "large dome-shaped structure of brick for a bakery"; and in 1804, Paul Belcour, another Frenchman, was competing, and offering to return one pound of bread for every pound of flour sent him.

When Jordan's hotel was built Marian's oven fell into disuse, but after the abandonment of the hotel it was repaired and enlarged and in it was baked much of the bread supplied to the soldiers in 1838-9. The first stone pavements laid in York were on the sidewalks about Jordan's. They were flat stones from the lake beach, of irregular shapes and surfaces and made a very uneven footpath.

Many housewives, of course, baked their own bread.

After the baker comes the barber or, to give him the style that he prefers, "Ladies' and Gentlemen's Hairdresser". Mr. Thomas Seaton Peacock announces in 1802 that as soon as he can get away from regimental duties "he means then to settle here and follow said business". In a very short time there were four barbers in the little city: and a chairmaker, Donald Tiers, who advertised that he made "armed chairs, settees, and dining ditto; fan back and brace back chairs". When he gets some paints "it will then be in his power to finish his chairs in the best manner".

In January, 1803, the first church was begun, with the proviso, from those who contributed to its erection, that not more than six hundred pounds should be expended in the first instance; and that sum was "to be laid out in such manner that Divine Worship can be performed with decency in the church". Four years later a rather peevish gentleman complains:

Shortly after my entrance I was not a little surprised at finding there were no pews, benches or any other such necessary appendages for strangers or transient persons of decent appearance, and was therefore reduced to the uncomfortable necessity during the service, either of standing as a public spectacle, or of seating myself among the military who compose the garrison.

He concludes "a number of years will elapse before I revisit your place", by which time probably St. James's Church had been burned down.

There were still openings for tradesmen; in 1805 the first hatter arrived:

Prior to this hats were bought at the general stores but henceforth there would be a hat shop.

Samuel Jackson informs his friends and the public in general that he is commencing the hatting business opposite to Thos. Ridout, Esq., in the town of York, where he will take all kinds of furs, lamb's wool and country produce, or cash itself will be received for hats, but no credit need be asked.

Mr. Joseph Cawthra, on the road to being a universal provider, "has opened an Apothecary's store in the house of A. Cameron, opposite Stoyles' Tavern in York, where the public can be supplied with most articles in that line". An up-to-date drug store evidently; you could also buy shoes, hats, table knives and bed ticks, "a few casks of fourth proof Cognac brandy, and about twenty thousand whitechapel needles".

After the druggist came the doctor, in 1807. Dr. Glennon, formerly "at one of the first colleges in Europe" (but he doesn't say which) commenced business at the house of Mr. Paul Marian — our baker. "He has on hand an assorted stock of genuine medicines", was the first M.D. who gave his whole time to civilian practice, and stayed here about five years.

The first practical saddler and harness-maker, Calvin Banister, arrived in 1807; a cabinet-maker and joiner came in 1815 — his name Harvey Gilbert; and with the war at an end, tradesmen began to flock to York. A few years later we find an advertisement which gives us the measure of the city at that time and with which this chapter may fittingly conclude.

PIANOFORTES — T. Browning, pianoforte manager, begs to inform the nobility of York and its vicinity that he has brought from London a few superior instruments, grands, cabinets and squares, which will be sold at a very low price. N.B. — Instruments repaired and tuned. Applications, if by letters postpaid, at Mr. Mills, No. 187 King street, York.

II. CITY PLANNING

Toronto has excellent claims to the title of a Planned City. She first appears in 1788 as an engineer's dream, before even one log hut asserted the domination of humanity over the wilderness; and sixty-six years later, sixteen other plans had been produced to illustrate her growth. That the first three plans were of a city unseen only again proves true that "as imagination bodies forth the forms of things unknown, the poet's pen turns them to shape and gives to airy nothing a local habitation and a name". Poet — engineer — architect; the seeing eye is what matters.

Five years ago, during a search in London for documents bearing on the boundary of the Province of Ontario, a map of Toronto harbour and a plan of a proposed settlement on it were found, which had been executed in 1788 by Captain Gotherman, an English officer, whose name is also found in a document dated London, November 23, 1791, relating to the defences of Canada in the direction of Lake Champlain. This map is entitled, "A plan of Toronto Harbour, with the proposed Town and part of the Settlement. Quebec, 6th December, 1788. Gotherman, Capt. Commanding Royal Engineers". Along with this plan was a report submitted by J. Collins, Deputy Surveyor-General, to the Right Hon. Lord Dorchester, Governor-General and Commander-in-Chief in British America, on the military posts and harbours on Lakes Ontario, Erie and Huron.

It will be noted that the name of the engineer is spelled "Gotherman"—one word.[1] When or why the separation took place is not known.

[1] On all subsequent maps and reports it is printed as Gother Mann.

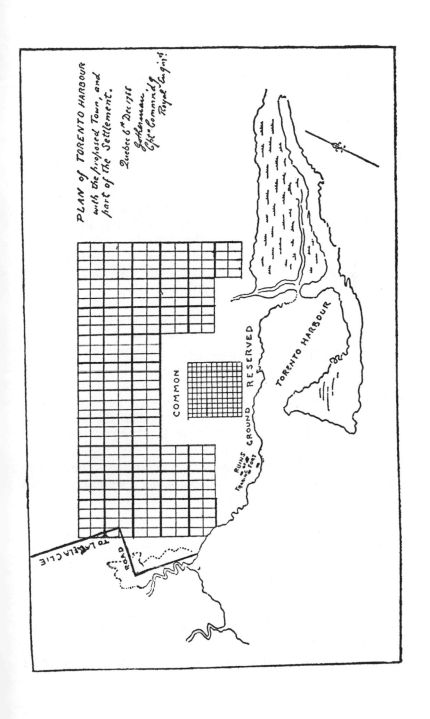

PLAN of TORENTO HARBOUR with the proposed Town, and part of The Settlement.

Quebec 6th Decr 1788

Gother Mann,
Capt Commandg
Royal Engineers

TORENTO HARBOUR

COMMON

GROUND RESERVED

RUINS of the TRADING FORT

ROAD

To LA TRANCLIE

This map of Captain Mann's is the first made of the harbour and site of Toronto. From the destruction of Fort Rouille or Fort Toronto in 1759 there had been no settlement here. Still it is evident from occasional mention of the location that it was regarded as the probable site of a settlement at some future day, and at the time of the division of the Province of Quebec into two Governments there were men at Quebec who expected that a settlement would spring up here, as is seen from the fact that M. Rocheblave, Captain La Force and Captain Bouchette endeavoured to secure large grants of land in this locality, but unsuccessfully, because of the transfer of the land granting power from Lord Dorchester's Government to that of the new province of Upper Canada. This explains sufficiently why Captain Mann took the trouble to sketch out this city in 1788.

Lac le Clie is probably Lake Simcoe, and that the engineer spelled the name of the future city "Torento" only proves that he was unfamiliar with the word.

Captain Mann's map is a wholly ideal one, but it is the earliest map of the projection of a town where the city of Toronto now stands, and it is curiously like the plan really adopted in the laying out of the town in 1793. In the journal of Mr. Chewett, chief draughtsman in the first Surveyor-General's office of Upper Canada, is an entry of a plan sent to him by Lieutenant-Governor Simcoe, of the town and township of Toronto.

In 1793, Governor Simcoe came to Toronto Harbour, said, "Here let there be a city", and then returned to Niagara. He then ordered a plan to be made by Mr. Alexander Aitken, deputy surveyor.

This plan was in the Surveyor-General's office till 1796, but was taken to England by Governor Simcoe as a souvenir of the founding of York.

No trace of it was found until 1905, when it was discovered

by the writer of this landmark in the Record Office at London. Its existence was known, but Mr. Aitken, who lived during the last years of his life at Kingston, said that he had never seen it after he had handed it to the Surveyor-General. The Crown Lands Departments at Quebec and at Toronto were searched, but without success, and the archives of the Old Parliament of Canada as well as those of the Dominion.

Then, by accident, while looking for other historical information, it was found. It appears that it was given to Governor Simcoe when he left Canada in 1796, and was by him about 1797, before he went to St. Domingo, sent to the Colonial Office, London, where it remained until 1842, when it was, along with other colonial maps, placed in the Record Office, where it has lain unasked for by anyone for sixty-three years, in fact the map had never been sought for either at the Colonial Office or the Record Office for a hundred and seven years.

The "Plan of York Harbour" is that "surveyed by order of Lieut.-Governor Simcoe by A. Aitken". The scale is 20 chains, or 1,320 feet, to an inch.

The plan shows from a point 2,640 feet east of the present Woodbine avenue, to a point 1,320 feet west of Bathurst street, and from the Bay on the south to what is now Bloor street on the north.

The site comprises ten blocks, five south and five north of King street, the west boundary being George street, the east Parliament (Berkeley), the north Duke street, and south Palace (Front) street. Although the streets were not marked, the plan shows the location of the present George, Frederick, Sherbourne (Caroline), Princess, Ontario and Berkeley (the first Parliament street), all running from the south to the north, and Palace (Front) street, King and Duke, all running from the west to the east.

In 1794 Toronto began its actual existence in the form of a few buildings constructed of hewn logs or framed lumber; bricks and mortar being used solely in the erection of chimneys, and in a basement or two where greater or future importance was sought. A sketch map of York drawn in 1794 by D. W. Smith, surveyor general of the new Province, shows the entire site of York from the east limit at the Don to the west limit at the Garrison. It also shows the site of Castle Frank with a Government Park, Scadding's farm and bridge over the Don, the Garrison and Western Block House, Russell square (Upper Canada College grounds), Simcoe place (Government House grounds), and the north boundary which to-day would be about a mile north of the Davenport road. This map also shows the harbour and peninsula, for in those days the eastern entrance had not been formed. The town plot is marked "City of York."

As originally laid out and defined in 1794, the town plot of York was a compact little parallelogram, bounded on the south by Palace street, on the east by Parliament street, on the north by the present Duke street, or, as it then was, Duchess street, and on the west by Jarvis street. Comprised within these boundaries were twelve squares, each of about two and a half acres. The land lying between Palace street and the bay front was set aside as a Government reserve.

No maps or records are in existence showing the first possessors and the amount possessed by each of the land within these narrow boundaries. Not until two years later do definite records exist of the divisions of property, and these not of the original town plots, but of the lots included in the first extension of York ratified by the Council, June 10, 1797, and of the park lots, which were simply farms of 100 acres each, stretching westward from the Don, with Queen street as their southern boundary line.

It is interesting to note that in a *Gazetteer* compiled by D. W. Smith (who was then called *Smyth*) and published in 1799, York Township was called "Dublin Township"; and a plan of the harbour dated 1796 was lettered "Front line of the Township of Dublin, now York". How the Irish got in and who turned them out is not stated. In 1797 His Honour the President (Peter Russell) ordered a plan to be made for "the enlargement of York . . . projected in lots containing an acre, more or less". Here are the names of the owners of the lots; and here are squares of about six acres each, reserved for "Hospital, School, Gaol, Church, and Market". Ten acres are "submitted for a college" on Lot (now Queen) and Peter Streets. Yonge Street does not appear.

Although this great northern road, now a crowded thorough-fare, then but a straggling waggon track almost impassable to vehicles, was laid out by Augustus Jones as early as 1793, it was not carried out down to the bay by the first projectors of the town, nor did those who laid out the new town shown in the map, that is the region westward of primitive York, expect Yonge street to descend to the water's edge. In the plans of 1800, Yonge street stops short at Lot street, and it was after this date that it was carried through to the bay. In the map of 1800, a range of lots blocks the way of Yonge street from Lot street, immediately to the south. The traffic coming down Yonge street from the north turned to the eastward at Lot street, and from that road came down into the town by Toronto street, shown in the map three chains and seven links to the east of the line of Yonge street. When Yonge street was extended to the water, Toronto street was shut up, and the proprietors of the land through which the northern road now ran received in exchange for the space usurped proportionate pieces of the old Toronto street. In 1818 deeds for these fragments were given to the owners. At a later period Upper George street, formerly so-called, now known as Victoria street, was opened a little to the east of the vanished Toronto street, and then the present short Toronto street, which accounts for the little jog between these two streets at Adelaide street. Closing a street at the time of which we are speaking was not a very great undertaking, as the streets were nothing more than waggon tracks across vacant lots and open grounds meandering by the most convenient route and by no means presenting in appearance the modern city street, as might be inferred from the map lines.

In April 1801, we have the plan of "Mr. John Stegmann, a well-known surveyor."

This plan shows the first extension of the Town of York westward, with Peter street as its west boundary, while on the east was the thoroughfare now known as Victoria street.

The other streets were John street, Graves (Simcoe) street, both named after Gov. John Graves Simcoe, with York street and Bay street, all running north to Lot street, now Queen.

The streets running east and west were Front street, with "Simcoe Square," the site of the old Parliament Buildings, between John and Simcoe, demolished in 1903, Market (Wellington) street, King street, with Russell Square, bounded by King, John, Graves (Simcoe) and Newgate (Adelaide) streets — Old Upper Canada College grounds.

Yonge street was still not open south of Lot (Queen) street, so that vehicles, as already stated, to reach the market, turned east at Yonge by Lot (Queen) street a few hundred feet and drove down Upper George (Victoria) street, which ran from Lot (Queen) street to Newgate (Adelaide) and then down the present Toronto street to King.

There was originally a cut-off, as shown in the plan, at the north-west corner of Front and Toronto streets, which originally was intended to run south to Market (Wellington) street.

A rather unhappy plan shows the place of the American landing in 1812, west of old Fort Rouille; together with the former place of the ships and stores that were burned, the Garrison magazine that was fired, and "the business part of York" — three blocks. A plan made in 1816 mentions "The new Fort now constructing" (it was "A Redoubt with block houses and barrack"), shows the House of Assembly to the east but gives no detail of the town. Another plan in the same year, signed "G. Nicolls, Lt.-Col. Royal Engineers", though it devotes major attention to the Battery and the Harbour, does give a plan of the town; in which plan we see Yonge Street running north beyond the limits and coming south to water's edge. The idea seems to have been to lay the town out in fifteen blocks: Parliament Street on the east, George on the west, Lot (Queen) on the north; though actually, Lot Street did not run east of Yonge until some years later. This 1816 plan may be described as sympathetic to York's idea of growth. A survey made in May, 1818, by Lieut. George Phillpotts, Royal Engineers, is careful and actual and shows the town and military reserve from the west boundary of the latter, which is the present Dufferin Street, to the east boundary of the town at the Don River; and north to a point 900 feet south of what is now Bloor Street — or about the present line of St. Mary Street. From Queen Street to Bloor Street is the first concession of the township of York, one mile and a quarter in depth.

And now we come to the very valuable plan of York that was produced in 1820: "painted on the spot by Mr. Irvine (or Irving) — a Scotch artist". (The nationality may have been added as a guarantee of the plan's accuracy.) It shows the Old Fort to the west, then two huts and a long empty shore line. Then "Peter Street, west limit of town", and a large house, the "Residence of Hon. George Cruickshank". From there to Parliament Street, the eastern limit, 29 buildings are shown. That was York. Of these buildings two are "residences" (the dwellings of Bishop Strachan and of Samuel Peters Jarvis), several are stores, Major Hillier has a "cottage" and the Attorney-General (Robinson) has an office. Near the centre of the picture is the southern end of Yonge Street. The description in Volume 3 of the *Landmarks of Toronto,* published in 1898, is of sufficient interest for the reprint of its early paragraphs.

One of the most interesting of the early views of the town of York, now Toronto, is an oil painting, made by Mr. Irving, a Scotch artist, who, prior to 1821, was a visitor in York and a guest of the late Hon. George Cruickshank, who resided at the north-east corner of Front and Peter streets. No views have been found of the entire front of the town of York prior to 1821, and this fact enhances the value of Mr. Irving's work. Mrs. Simcoe made a small sketch of the Garrison or Old Fort, as in 1796, with a bit of the harbour adjacent to the fort, and in 1803

an English officer made a drawing of the east end of Palace
street, now called Front street, from the north-west corner of
what is now West Market or Jarvis street, to within a few feet
of the Don river. Lossing gives the blockhouse at the Don in
1800-13, with a few of the houses in the neighbourhood of
Palace street. In 1820 Mr. Irving made an oil painting from a
point on the Island near the lighthouse, which gives an absolutely
correct and artistic view, with the locations of all the houses
on Front street from a hundred yards west of the Old Fort and
Garrison to the second Parliament buildings, which stood in
1816-24 on the site of the jail, built in 1841, at the east end
of what was then Palace street, but what is now Front street.
The site is now occupied by the Gas Company. The buildings
in Irving's sketch are given with so much detail as to be recognizable, and it is evident that the artist, before finishing his
oil, strolled, pencil and pad in hand, and made an outline of
the buildings that he proposed to show in his painting.

The pen and ink sketch given with this landmark is made,
through the courtesy of Mrs. Stephen Heward, of Peter street,
from the original oil, by her son, Mr. Stephen Heward, the
architect, a grand-son of the late Mr. Cruickshank. The artist
has skilfully traced the oil painting, and every building shown
is as in the original. The proof of the accuracy of Mr. Irving's
oil is shown in Mr. Heward's sketch, for some of the buildings
given such as the Old Fort, west of Bathurst street; the Cruickshank house, north-east corner of Front and Peter; the Greenland
Fishery tavern, north-west corner of John and Front, Hon.
George Markland's house, on Market (Wellington) street; the
McGill cottage, where the Metropolitan church now stands, are
familiar to many people in Toronto of to-day. The original oil
gives the Island, the lighthouse and the bay; but for the purposes of reproduction the foreground of the picture has been
omitted, so as to give a better and closer view of the old town.

Where any doubt existed as to the location of the buildings
or the names of owners or residents, careful enquiry has been
made amongst old residents, such as Mr. William Helliwell, of
Highland Creek, who arrived in Toronto in 1818, and also from

Rear View of the City Hall, 1849

Mrs. Charles Seymour, a daughter of Dr. Grant Powell, a resident from 1811. Mrs. Seymour was born in 1806, and came with her father to Toronto in 1811. Her memory of the capture of Toronto by the Americans, of the burning of the first Parliament Buildings on the site of the old jail, and her recollection of the residents of the entire front of the city, and every house from 1811 to 1860, is perfect. In an interview at Ottawa Mrs. Seymour, now (1896) ninety years of age, recounted to the writer the names and locations of all the houses on Front street, with the names of the residents, prior to 1820, from the Old Fort to the Don.

The key gives the location of the houses on Front street, which ran from the garrison on the west to the north-east corner of what is now Front and East Market square, a conjunction of New (Nelson and later Jarvis) street and Palace (Front) street.

The key also gives the location of houses on Market street, now known as Wellington street, for these houses could be seen from the bay, there being then but few houses between the present Front street and Market street, and in some places the houses on King street could be seen from the bay front.

From west to east, counting fort, streets, houses, stores and hotels, fifty-four numbers sufficed in 1820. It is a striking manifestation of the growth of York that in 1828 a similar picture went to 91. We begin with the Western Battery and the house of Colonel Givens; we pass the small clearing in the then thick brush wood, a military cemetery where lies Governor Simcoe's child; and we note that No. 10, is nearly three miles from the water's edge — the home of Baldwin of Spadina. Here is no ribbon development, this is a city. Several prominent men were still living in the buildings they occupied eight years previously; some houses had other tenants. The ruins of the Parliament Buildings burned (for the second time) in 1824, are shown; and we quote the descriptions for the last three numbers.

89. Forks of the Don river. There were two bridges built

here about 1823. There were two streams, designated the Great Don and Little Don.

90. Scadding's house, built in 1796. In that year Mr. Scadding received a grant of land from the government consisting of 280 acres on the east bank of the River Don, and built a house about where the present jail building stands. The Scadding farm consisted originally of the whole of lot No. 15, extending from the water's edge of the bay north to the present Danforth avenue, bounded on the east by Broadview avenue (formerly known as the Mill Road) and on the west by the Don River.

91. Mr. Scadding left Mr. George Playter in charge of the property. Mr. Playter lived in a log cabin on the east side of the river, just south of the Kingston Road. This cabin can now be seen at the Exhibition grounds. Mr. William Smith bought Mr. Scadding's property south of the Kingston Road in 1819. He then bought the house of John Playter and moved it across the road to his tannery, Mr. Smith preserving his residence at the corner of King and Sherbourne streets, where he lived until 1832. In 1879 Mr. Smith had the log cabin that was built by Mr. Scadding in 1796 removed to the Exhibition grounds, where it now stands.

In 1834, when the population of the city was about 8,000 people, the picture starts from the east at the celebrated windmill of Gooderham and Worts. It was situated in Vale Pleasant, and its owners lived half a mile to the east on the Kingston Road. The first house west of the mill was that of Enoch Turner, the brewer. The picture is in depth, going back to Osgoode Hall and "the Hon. John Boulton's elegant newly-erected Gothic Mansion" on York Street; it also takes in the Harbour, and number 46 is "Horse boat. Boat propelled by four horses. It was called 'Sir John of the Peninsula.' Ran every day from Steamboat wharf to the peninsula or island across the Bay. Fare to and from the island was 1s. 3d." (For more information turn to page 267.) It may be of interest here to make brief mention of Toronto's assessment

rolls, in this first year of her incorporation. We quote from
the *Landmarks,* Volume I:

In 1833 the population of the town of York was 8,731, distributed as follows: — The town proper, 7,473; Macaulay
Town, a district included in the parallelogram bounded by the
modern Queen, Yonge, Edward and Chestnut streets, 558; the
region from Osgoode Hall, where Macaulay Town ended, to
Farr's brewery on Queen street, 400; and the region from the
east end of King street to the Don bridge, 300. Up to this
time the people of the town had acted in an isolated way in
regard to matters pertaining to the public health, comfort and
convenience, and consequently but little had been done in such
matters. Now the community had grown to such a bulk that it
was found necessary for the inhabitants to combine under a
magistracy of their own and a union of interests. In February,
1834, a bill was introduced into parliament by Mr. Jarvis, the
member for the town, asking for a charter of incorporation.
The measure was carried, and on Thursday, March 6, of the
same year the bill became law. It was a long act, containing
ninety-seven clauses, enacting that the town of York should be
constituted a city under the name of Toronto, and should be
divided into wards, with two aldermen and two common councilmen for each ward, elected by the inhabitants, and a mayor
chosen from among the aldermen and councilmen by themselves. By the third of April the elections had taken place.

The first assessment showed a rateable value of £186,882,
which yielded, at three pence in the pound, a revenue of
£2,333 0s. 6d. At any rate, it was enough to get the Council
out of debt. The Mayor, William Lyon Mackenzie, had a
town lot, a frame house under two stories and two additional
fireplaces. He was assessed at £95 (that is, he had to pay one
pound, three shillings and nine pence), and he also had to
do five days of statute labour on the roads. Mackenzie then
lived on March Street between Richmond and Newgate Streets

and near the school reservation. Streets and names alike were being altered during these years, 1835-37.

Richmond street, prior to 1834, commenced at New (Nelson) street and ran west to Yonge street and ended there. The continuation of Richmond street to its west limit at Peter street was called Hospital Street, probably because it led to the General Hospital, which was situated in the block bounded by Newgate (Adelaide), John and King streets.

Church street, the *Directory* of 1834 says, "commences opposite the landing place and wharf on Front street and runs north." It crossed Richmond street and then crossed "a street intended to be a continuation of Lot street, but intercepted by land to the east [now Queen street] belonging to the Hon. G. W. Allan and S. P. Jarvis, Esq."

The *Directory* of 1834 also says, "Lot street east commences in Yonge street opposite here, but is intercepted by the grounds of Capt. McGill, S. P. Jarvis, Esq., and the Hon. G. W. Allan; past them it is open and extends to the Catholic church, intended to be a continuation to the Don bridge."

All this means that Church street ran to the north line of Richmond street, and that Lot street (Queen) *did* run east of Yonge street, but was not opened from the present Bond street to Church street. The first property east of Bond was the McGill property (Metropolitan square), further east from Church to Jarvis was the S. P. Jarvis property, and east to Caroline (Sherbourne) was the Allan property, and the next lot east was the Ridout property, extending to Seaton street. The Catholic church referred to was old St. Paul's, on what is now Power street.

There is an interesting sketch of the east end of the city which, for technical reasons, we are not able to reproduce.

This picture shows the old blockhouse which stood near the Windmill, and some of the old houses of the north-east water front, near the Don River. It is an accurate picture of To-

TORONTO IN 1828

ronto made in 1837. The artist, Mr. J. R. Lumley, a lieutenant in the 15th Regiment of Foot, stationed at Toronto in 1837, was an uncle of Mr. P. H. Drayton, barrister, of Toronto, who is the owner of the original sketch. This picture is important, being one of the only two pictures in existence showing this part of the water front.

The pictures of Toronto which precede this picture are those of 1793 by Mrs. Simcoe, one of 1818-20 by Mr. Irvine (previously noted), one of 1825 made by a military officer, name unknown, and another made in 1828 by J. Gleadhill, of London, England. The pictures of 1793, 1820 and 1828 have been reproduced in oil, and were presented recently to the city corporation. A picture made in 1834, and showing the windmill, was also presented. It is a better view than that of 1837, as it takes in more of the city west of the windmill.

The artist evidently made the sketch of 1837 while sitting in a boat, which was at a point on the bay south-west of the south end of Frederick street, about seven or eight hundred feet from the shore.

This sketch is unique in one regard, as it gives the blockhouse at the east side of the Windmill. It is the only drawing extant which shows the old fortification.

A blockhouse was erected on this spot prior to the war of 1812. It was destroyed by the Americans on the 27th April, 1813, but after the invaders left the people of York "built another blockhouse." (Lossing, p. 591.) And this is the blockhouse shown.

From now onward Toronto can be said to have come of age as a planned community. The beautiful plan of James Cane, dated 1842, extends from the wharves of the Harbour to the university; shows the Race Track and the Cricket Grounds (now covered with houses); stretches from the Don to Wilton Park; but is still dominated by the uncompromising line of King, Adelaide and Richmond Streets. *There* was the population, living where their money was made.

A sketch made in 1854 by an American named Whitefield is valuable as showing how well built up the east end of the city had become. It is taken from Palace (now Front) Street, with Berkeley Street as the eastern limit. There are the wharves and the ships, "and the spring tides tossing free": there are the churches, in a commanding group: St. James' (6); St. Andrew's (8); Knox Church (11); and Holy Trinity (13). And, looking at the key for numbers (1) and (2) you find that (although not of course in any other way related) they are the City Hall and the Lunatic Asylum.

III. MAIN STREETS AND NOTABLE HOUSES

Readers of the preceding chapter will have noticed that the basic plan of Toronto — the embryo — was fixed before the first sod was turned. We have a grid, with six roads running south to north, and three roads east to west. In theory, all the nine could have been produced to infinity but in practice only Yonge Street has achieved this. We note also that for some years Yonge Street came no farther south than the line of the First Concession; that is to say, it ended at Bloor. The street that led to it from the Bay was first called "the road to Yonge Street", afterward Toronto Street, and later was closed. Streets running from east to west were Front Street, King Street and Lot Street which is now named Queen Street. In 1834 the western limit of the city was Peter Street and the northern limit was Lot. Richmond was then Hospital Street and Adelaide was Newgate Street (because it was to have led to the gaol). In 1801, according to John Stegmann's map, Yonge Street had been produced south as far as Lot. Toronto Street, one block east, led up to it from the Bay. Next on the west was Bay Street; then York, Graves, John and Peter Streets. Peter was the western limit; beyond it was the Garrison and the wilderness. If we move on 45 years toward the future and consult John G. Howard's plan of 1846, we find that Toronto has widened and deepened. A little east of the old Garrison reserve and "Government Creek", Bathurst Street comes down to the Bay. Portland Street and Brock Street succeed, then Peter. Graves Street is now Simcoe, and beyond Yonge Street, still going east, is Scott Street (now Victoria) and Church Street. Then come Market Street and Nelson Street on either side of the market, then George, Frederick, Caroline and Princes Streets. Be-

THE ROSEDALE HOMESTEAD

yond were Berkeley and Parliament Streets, with the gaol
south of and between them, at the edge of the bay. After
which came Trinity Street, the Windmill and Gooderham's
wharf, the end of the town. Going north, the continuation
of Bathurst Street is known as Crookshank's Lane; and
Brock Street carries on as Spadina Road. College Avenue,
now University, is a lane of many trees. Osgoode Hall stands
in isolation and east of Yonge are Victoria, Bond, and
Church; mere urban expressions of intention with hardly a
house to be seen. What is now Shuter Street was there spelled
Shutter.

It would be easy to fill the remainder of the volume with
passages collected for this chapter. So much must be omitted:
what is essential? First, evidently, the Parliament Buildings
and Osgoode Hall; then a glance at the houses of John
Strachan and Jesse Ketchum, at The Grange, at Berkeley
House and Beverley House; some houses on, and aspects of,
Yonge Street, King and Queen. Then, to conclude, Dundas
Street's tolls and a note on a few street names.

The first Legislature or Parliament of Upper Canada met
on the 17th September, 1792, at Niagara. There is no certainty
as to the building in which this body of men assembled, but
it was probably in Navy Hall, the residence of Governor Simcoe.
Some think that it met in the Freemasons' Hall, a building at
the east end of the town near the river, and this is not improbable. The Freemasons' Hall was convenient to Navy Hall,
and it contained two rooms of reasonable size for such purposes.
The lower room was for public meetings, such as those of the
Agricultural Society, and the upper rooms were occupied by the
Craft of Masons. This was from 1792 to 1796.

In June of 1796 the Legislature met in York. The meeting
place was in the Parliament Buildings, which stood on the
south side of Palace (Front) street, between the street and the
bay, and on the site of the old jail. These buildings were
destroyed by fire on the 27th April, 1813.

It is stated in Dr. Scadding's book on "Toronto of Old"

that the first Houses of the Legislature were "humble but commodious structures of wood, built before the close of the eighteenth century."

We have the exact location of these buildings and a small
drawing of the front, looking towards the west, in a picture
of the east end of the harbour and town, made in 1803 by an
English officer. The buildings were on the site of the present gas
works, and the elevation of the buildings as given in modern
reproductions is accurate, but the description is inaccurate, in
that the buildings were not of wood, but of brick. Heriot, in
his "Travels in Canada in 1806," published in 1807, states
that he visited "York, or Toronto, the seat of Government in
Upper Canada." He then describes Gibraltar Point, now Hanlan's Point, and refers to the Garrison and the house in which
the Lieutenant-Governor lived. With regard to the Parliament
Buildings he wrote: "Two buildings of brick at the eastern
extremity of the town, which were designed as wings to a centre,
are occupied as chambers for the Upper and Lower Houses of
Assembly."

Such evidence admits of no controversy. Then, as late as 1819,
Peter Robinson and Grant Powell, who were "managers of
public buildings," reported to the Legislature concerning the
erection of two new buildings, stating that "they proceeded
without delay to close with the lowest proposals for such a
building, together with the old brick buildings repaired," and
that some progress had already been made "in the repairs of the
old buildings."

This should settle all doubts as to the question of brick or
wood in the original buildings. The Upper Canada Gazette of
July, 1794, contained an advertisement which read: "Wanted,
carpenters for the public buildings to be erected at York," but
this does not indicate, as some would have it, that the buildings
were of wood.

The statement that the first home of the Legislature was of
brick having been sustained, the assertion that the first brick
building in York was that of the Canada Company, on the north-

east corner of King and Frederick streets, is disposed of. It was the second brick building in York.

After the fire the Legislature met in 1814, at Jordan's Hotel on King street east. One session was held in Jordan's, and for several years a rough-cast commodious cottage building on the north-east corner of Wellington and York streets, served as a legislative home. It was the residence of the Hon. George Markland, and afterwards that of the late Chief Justice Draper.

In 1818, new buildings, also of brick, were erected immediately adjoining the exact site of those destroyed in 1813, at the east end of the city at the foot of Berkeley street. These buildings were two in number, two storeys in height, and are shown in a painting of York in 1819-20. The north building was used for Government offices, the south building as the Legislative Chambers. This latter was destroyed by fire on the 20th December, 1824.

The sessions of 1825-8 were held in the Toronto General Hospital building, on the north-west corner of King and John streets, a site later occupied by the rear part of the Arlington hotel, King Street. The hospital building was required for its original purpose in 1828, and the Court-house on Church street, near the north-west corner of King and Church streets, was occupied in 1829-32.

In 1832-41 the buildings on Front street, between John and Peter streets, were occupied by the Legislature. From 1841 to 1848 the buildings were utilized for university purposes; in 1848-9 as an asylum for the insane, and in 1849-51 the House was again re-opened for the sessions of Parliament for the united provinces. From 1856-59 the sessions of the United Parliament were held in the building, in 1861-66 it was used as a military barracks, and from 1867-92 by the Legislature of Ontario, when removal was made to the buildings in the Queen's Park.

In 1826 the southern part of the third park lot west of Yonge Street became the property of Sir John Beverley Robinson, Attorney-General.

Of this land he gave to the Law Society of Upper Canada six acres for the erection of a building for law courts. The Law Society of Upper Canada was incorporated in 1797. The six acres given by Sir John Robinson are now contained between Queen street on the south, Osgoode street on the north, Chestnut street on the east and University street on the west. In the midst of this plot, facing Queen street, and commanding a view down York street to the bay, stands "The Hall" as it is commonly called by members of the legal profession, one of the most stately and imposing edifices in the city and architecturally one of the finest temples of justice on this continent. The oldest portion, consisting of the east wing of the present building, was begun in 1829 under the supervision of Dr. William Warren Baldwin, at that time treasurer of the Law Society. It was not completed until 1832 when the first convocation of benchers within its walls took place on the 6th of February. It was a plain square matter-of-fact brick building two and a half stories in height. In 1844-46 a corresponding structure was erected to the west and the two were united by a building between, surmounted by a low dome. In 1857-60 the whole edifice underwent a renovation; the dome was removed; a very handsome façade of cut stone was put up; the inner area of Caen stone, reminding one of the interior of a Roman palace, was added with the court rooms, library and offices all on a scale of great beauty and dignity. Since the completion of the front in 1860 further additions at the rear and various improvements have been made, and the building is now the headquarters of the Superior Courts in this province. In accordance with the wish of the donor of the land this temple of Themis was named Osgoode Hall in honour of the Hon. William Osgoode, first Chief Justice of Upper Canada.

He was born in England, 1754, was called to the Bar in 1779, received his appointment direct from the Crown and came out with Governor Simcoe in 1791. On the 24th of February 1784 he had been appointed Chief Justice of Lower Canada; but he probably never saw Toronto, for he returned to England in 1801 (after seven years in Quebec) and died in 1824, aged 70. The law that he administered is still the Law of Canada.

As a kind of parenthesis let us now go back to the beginning and rob Chapter One of an honour.

Up to about the year 1882, when it was torn down and used for firewood by the occupants of a neighboring house, there stood in the north-west part of the city an old log cabin interesting historically for many reasons. It was one of the first buildings erected in York, and was for a time the residence of the Duke of Kent on his visit here. In January, 1792, when Governor Simcoe was on his way to his new government his wonder and admiration were excited by a gallant and daring exploit of Captain Aeneas Shaw, who marched in the depth of a rigorous winter from New Brunswick to Montreal on snowshoes at the head of his division of a regiment known as the Queen's Rangers. So great did the achievement seem to the Governor that he reported it in terms of praise to Sir George Yonge, who was then Secretary of War, and after whom Yonge street was named.

In recognition of his services Captain Shaw was rewarded with grants of lands in various parts of the province, and among others 500 acres north of the garrison at Toronto. Here, in the midst of a forest, altogether remote from any other building, he erected a log cabin a little less than half a mile north of what is now Queen street, and several hundred yards northwest of Trinity College. Here, on the completion of his new home, he took up his residence with his family.

And when Prince Edward (Duke of Kent, and father of Queen Victoria) visited York in 1802, in this log hut he was entertained and here for a while he resided.

The next notable house is that which the Rev. Dr. John Strachan built for a private residence, but which was usually called "the Bishop's Palace".

It is not strange that it should have received this high sounding appellation. In the first place it was a palace compared with the other buildings of York at the time of its erection, and then Dr. Strachan came to be bishop, although twenty years later. But the building never was a palace; never was anything more than a private residence. In 1818 Dr. John Strachan, rector of St. James' Church and master of the District Grammar school, built in a large yard where now is No. 130 Front street, a residence of capacious dimensions, with extensive and complete appurtenances. It is a two-storey building with a gable, facing the south, and is not unlike the Grange in general design, but differs with that structure in that no additions to it have been made. It remains now as when built. The bricks used in the construction of the house were manufactured on the spot, and it has the distinction of being the first building erected in York from bricks made here.

The year after the building of the house, and just as the family was nicely settled in it, James Strachan, a book-seller of Aberdeen and a brother of the doctor, paid him a visit. James had not seen his brother since one day twenty years before, when he set out with a slender purse from Scotland to become a schoolmaster in Canada. One can easily conceive the worthy Scotchman's astonishment as passing along the rough streets, past the scattered little frame buildings of the town, with the memory of his brother's former poverty in his mind, he suddenly comes upon the imposing façade of the new mansion, surrounded by its large and handsome grounds. No wonder he pauses and, gravely addressing his brother, says, "I hope it's a' come by honestly, John!" On his return James Strachan published "A Visit to the Province of Upper Canada in 1819," a book now very rare, and much sought after by collectors. In this book, speaking of the society of York at the time, he says: — "The society, both as it respects the ladies and gentlemen, is very superior, and such as few towns of England can furnish. The judges, the Crown officers, the heads of the different departments, several professional gentlemen, merchants, and officers on half-pay, all living with their families in the greatest harmony, cannot fail of rendering York exceedingly agreeable and to strangers interesting." Dr. Bethune, who came to York the same year, gives a similar account of the society of the town. He says: "There were a few scattered houses on King street as far up as the residence of the Lieut.-Governor, and on Front street, at long intervals, they reached nearly to the old garrison. There were also a few on Duke, Yonge and Queen streets. There were but three brick edifices in the town, and, exclusive of the military, the population was about 1,200. Though inferior in size and condition to many of our present villages York took a high rank as to social position. From its being the seat of Government the society was excellent, having not less than twenty families of the highest respectability, persons of refinement and many of high intellectual culture. To these were added a small sprinkling of military. For the size of the place there was a large amount of hospitality exercised, and on a handsome and bountiful scale." The three brick houses of which Dr. Bethune speaks as being the only ones of the kind in town were Dr. Strachan's house, the building erected by Quetton St. George at the north-east corner of King and Frederick streets, now occupied by the Canada Company, and the building directly opposite on the south-east corner of the same streets, afterward the first Bank of Upper Canada. Among the hosts of that day none was more lavish in his hospitality than Dr. Strachan. Not without interest will be found a sketch of the life of this extraordinary divine, who lived in the finest house in the town, gave entertainments that outshone those of the Lieutenant-Governor himself, rode about in a grand coach with a hemispherical top, and was at once priest, soldier and diplomatist. In stature he was slightly under the medium height, with a Milton-like head. John Strachan was born at Aberdeen, Scotland, April 12, 1778. At the age of nineteen he began his career as a teacher at Kettle. With the execution of Governor Simcoe's scheme to have a grammar school in every district of the Province, and a university at the seat of Government, young Strachan was selected as a teacher. He accepted the offer and sailed from Greenock in August, 1799. He first went to Kingston, where he studied divinity under the Rev. Dr. Stuart, the rector of the town, and in the spring of 1803 was admitted deacon. In the early summer of the next year he was consecrated priest, and appointed to the mission at Cornwall where he built up a famous school. He married Mrs. McGill, nee Miss Wood, one of the prettiest girls in Cornwall, in 1807. In 1812, through the efforts of General Brock, he was transferred to York to succeed Dr. Stuart. He arrived in August of that year, and preached his first sermon at the parish church before the legislature, on the war. In 1813 by his remonstrances with General Dearborn and his threats he saved York from being burned. At York he established the famous District Grammar School. In 1818 he was appointed member of the Executive and Legislative councils, remaining in the former until 1836, and in the latter until 1841. To his exertions are due the establishment of the University of Toronto and of Upper Canada College. He laid the corner stone of Trinity College. When the diocese of Quebec was divided in 1839, the Honourable and Right Reverend John Strachan, D.D., LL.D., was made first bishop of the See of Toronto and was consecrated by the Archbishop of Canterbury. He died at his Front street house, November 1, 1867. The pall bearers at his funeral were all old pupils of his York school. They were Ven. Archdeacon Fuller, Rev. Dr. W. MacMurray, Vice-Chancellor Spragge, F. H. Heward, William Gamble and John Ridout. He lies buried in the chancel of St. James' Cathedral, a great monument to a great man.

Dr. Strachan and Jesse Ketchum were contemporaries for years, but the latter built his house of wood.

Among the early settlers of York was a quiet, shrewd man of average stature, homely in appearance and in manners, who came to the infant capital from Buffalo somewhere about the beginning of the century to attend to the affairs of an older brother who had previously settled here and built a tannery. The name of the new comer was Jesse Ketchum, and for nearly half a century he was one of the most prominent citizens of the place. The Gazette of June 11th, 1803, speaks of the death of his father, Joseph Ketchum, as occurring on Wednesday, June 8, at the advanced age of 85 years, and mentions the fact that the burial of the remains took place the following day. On his arrival here Jesse assumed the management of the tannery which was located at the south-west corner of Newgate (now Adelaide) and Yonge streets. It stretched along the south side of the former street nearly over to Bay street; and along the west side of Yonge street almost down to King were ranged high stacks of hemlock bark. He owned the property up to Queen street, beyond which stretched the woods. Across from his tannery he built a residence; a mansion in those days of Little York. It was a large frame building, painted white, and stood at the north-west corner of Yonge and Adelaide streets. The illustration represents it very accurately.[1] Dr. Scadding describes it as a dwelling in the American style, with a square turret bearing a railing rising out of the ridge of the roof. Jesse Ketchum may be credited as being one of the first to introduce sidewalks into the embryo city. The streets were in a deplorable condition at certain seasons of the year on account of the mud; Yonge street was particularly bad, and it was with the greatest difficulty that loads could be drawn along it. The sidewalks which Mr. Ketchum laid out were of tan bark, clean and dry. The exact date of the building of his house is not known, but it was probably in 1813 or 1814. It was destroyed about 1838 or 1839 and the land cut up into building lots. The house did not come down to the corner, but stood a little distance back from both streets; about it was a cluster of out-houses. In the early days of York Jesse Ketchum was one of the most liberal of its citizens, especially in all matters pertaining to secular education and religious instruction, and to his gener-osity is due the fact that the quadrilateral bounded by Queen, Adelaide, Yonge and Bay streets is filled to a remarkable degree with churches and religious and educational institutions. Hospital street, now Richmond street, passed through his land and he opened and named Temperance street. The Bible and Tract

[1] Not reproduced.

Society obtained its house on Yonge street from him on condition that it should distribute books to the amount of the ground rent in the public schools every year, an agreement which is still faithfully carried out by the Society, which also secured the ground rent of an adjoining building under the proviso that books should be given to Sunday schools in a similar manner. He gave a site for a temperance hall, also several acres for a children's park at Yorkville, and this public school on the Davenport road, a little way from Yonge street, now bears the name of "The Jesse Ketchum School." The ground is named the Jesse Ketchum Park. In 1820 among the contributions to a common school was Mr. Ketchum's subscription, unusually large for that time, of $100. Other subscriptions were: Jordan Post, £17 6s. 3d; Philip Klinger, £2 10s, and Lardner Bostwick, £2 10s. From these names it would appear that not all the York pioneers were of English or Scotch extraction. In April 1822 Mr. Ketchum's name is down for a subscription to build a bridge over the Don to cost £325. At the annual town meeting of 1806 he was appointed one of the overseers of highways and fence viewers. In 1800 Yonge street did not extend down to the bay, but stopped at Queen street, the land south of this to the water's edge being simply vacant lots. When Yonge street was cut through, a street further to the eastward was closed and the owners of the land received proportionate pieces of it for the ground taken to lay out Yonge street, and in 1818 the names of Jesse Ketchum, William Bowkett, James Miles and William Richardson, appeared as being entitled to such divisions of the closed thoroughfare. On the east Mr. Ketchum's property was bounded by what was formerly called Upper George street. Mr. Ketchum was a pew-holder in St. James' Church. He was a house-holder, and continued to reside here until he returned to Buffalo in 1845.

Next to be viewed is one of the best loved houses in the city.

At the head of John street, looking down to Queen street, surrounded by spacious grounds, stands one of those low, roomy houses which afford the best type of a gentleman's residence. It is a solid, substantial two-storey structure of brick, with wings at the west and a conservatory extension at the east. A columned porch and a gable with an oeil de boeuf window at the south relieve the main part of the house from the severe simplicity which the facade would otherwise present. The general aspect is that of an English mansion, which evidently furnished the model. This is "The Grange," one of the finest places and one of the best known houses in the city. The main building was erected about 1820 by D'Arcy Boulton, eldest son of Justice Boulton. Justice Boulton lived in the house, and his three-cornered hat, made by "Rogers, York," still hangs in the hall. A wing and the conservatory are later additions. The Grange gate, now crowded back to the head of John street, was originally on Queen street and the house was reached by a sweeping drive through the grounds beginning at the east side of McCaul street. Justice Boulton was a great lover of horses. He drove a pretentious phaeton, and his team, Bonaparte and Jefferson, were the crack pair of the day in York. Of these two horses a curious story is told. Bears were common about the town in its early days, and it is said that Bay street was originally named Bear street from the fact that a bear was once chased down it to the water. In 1809 Lieutenant Fawcett of the 100th Regiment came upon a large bear in Yonge street and cut the animal's head open with his sword. A large bear once strayed upon the Grange pasture a little to the west of the house. Bonaparte and Jefferson saw the monster and at once attacked bruin by plunging at him with their fore feet. The Grange is probably the finest specimen of the beginning of the brick era at York, and as such is particularly interesting, although rendered additionally so from its associations. From its erection up to the present time it has always played an important part in the social life of York and Toronto, and many are the tales its walls could tell of balls and routs and dinner parties, of fair women and notable men. Lord Elgin, when Governor-General of Canada, was the guest there of William Henry Boulton, who was Mayor of Toronto at the time. Mr. Clarke Gamble, who breakfasted with Lord Elgin on this occasion, was greatly impressed by the

Earl, and he describes him as a man out of ten thousand. This is a historical association with the building, memorable from the great public services of Lord Elgin afterward in China and India. The Boultons were very hospitable people and entertained largely. D'Arcy Boulton was a gentleman of polished manners, and his father, the Justice, was a type of the old school English gentleman. D'Arcy was one of the first men called to the Bar in Upper Canada, but he abandoned the law for commercial pursuits, and at length retired, leaving his business in the hands of Wm. Proudfoot. As was almost invariably the custom in those days, the Grange was built in the centre of a hundred-acre park lot. On its completion Mr. Boulton named it the Grange after a family estate in England, and it has since borne the name. Mr. Boulton lived at the Grange until his death in 1844, after which his widow continued her residence there with her eldest son, William Henry Boulton.

Later the house was the resting place of Professor Goldwin Smith. All the wood work was of black walnut, and the rooms were crammed with fine furniture, old china and cut glass. The Grange still serves notably as a centre of art and general culture for Toronto.

The Boulton influence is continued in the next "exhibit"; at one time the temporary home of Poulett Thomson, Lord Sydenham.

The oldest part of Beverley House was built sometime about the war of 1812, by D'Arcy Boulton, eldest son of Judge Boulton, brother of Henry John Boulton and father of William Henry Boulton. At first it was a small brick cottage, and up to 1820 was the only building on the square bounded by John, Simcoe, Richmond and Queen streets, and stood near the southwest corner of this enclosure. D'Arcy Boulton lived here until 1816, when he moved to a large frame dwelling on the west side of Frederick street, just south of King street, and opposite the old post-office.

From the Frederick street house Mr. Boulton moved to the

Grange. On his giving up the cottage at the corner of John and Richmond streets, Attorney-General, afterward Chief Justice John Beverley Robinson, took it. He first added a wing to the westward, then raised the whole building, put on a verandah, built stables to the north-west, and these alterations and additions changed it from the modest little brick cottage into the dwelling house as it now appears. Chief Justice Robinson, who was made a baronet, and whose eldest son was Sir Lukin Robinson, lived here until his death. Sir J. B. Robinson was one of the pew-holders in St. James' Church from its commencement. During the war of 1812 he was a lieutenant of volunteers, and it was the death of Attorney-General Macdonell, who was killed at Queenston Heights while acting as General Brock's aide-de-camp, that made the vacancy which Mr. Robinson at an unusually early age was appointed to fill. Sir John Robinson gave the site of Osgoode Hall, six acres, to the Law Society and the name which the building bears was his suggestion. Beverley House was temporarily the residence of Poulett Thomson, afterwards Lord Sydenham, while Governor-General of the Canadas in 1839-40. It is said that he built the kitchen range connected with the house and that this was the indirect cause of getting the Union measure through the Upper Canada Parliament.

The indirectness is evident; we present the conundrum to university historians.

Major John Small accompanied Governor Simcoe from England to Niagara in 1793; and subsequently came to York where he built a house, in the spring of 1794. This house was at the south-west corner of an acre of ground between King and Front Streets. Again to quote from Dr. Scadding —

Mr. Small's originally was one of the usual low looking domiciles of the country with central portion and two gable wings, somewhat after the fashion of many an old country manor house in England. The material of Mr. Small's dwelling was hewn timber. It was one of the earliest domestic erections in York. When reconstructed at a subsequent period Mr.

Charles Small preserved in the enlarged and elevated building now known as Berkeley House, the shape and even a portion of the inner substance of the original structure.

This piece of ground was apparently enclosed and occupied before any building lots were set apart by authority.

Before the erection of the Government buildings the meetings of the Executive Council were frequently held in Berkeley House, and Governor Simcoe as well as all the other notables of the day were frequent visitors, for it was a well known fact that Major Small kept open house. He would stand in the doorway and call out to any acquaintances who might pass by, "Come in, I have got a good dinner for you to-day." Major Small died here in 1829. His wife also died in the same building. About 45 years ago, Charles Small, the son of Major Small, rebuilt and enlarged Berkeley House, giving it the appearance it now has.

Twenty years ago when the present Mr. John Small was making some alterations in the house the workman came upon the logs used in the construction of the original building. In recent years the old house has been converted into three houses, numbered 299, 301 and 303 East King street. The central one of these contains the remains of the log house erected by Major John Small, and it was here that he lived and died. Like most homesteads Berkeley House has its share of heirlooms, not the least interesting of which is the great dining table, at whose polished sides fifty persons have frequently sat down.

The above was written more than seventy years ago and little now remains above ground to recall the fame of Berkeley House.

There are notable houses on other streets, or the sites on which they were built and their shape in the memories of elderly men. Front Street, for instance (along which, a century ago, anyone might have strolled the length of the city — east to west — without meeting more than a score or so of people in the entire promenade), Front Street had the

No. 1—FRONT STREET IN 1800 FROM PETER TO JOHN STREET

Showing the Cruikshank House, the Beikie House, the Military Storehouse, and the Halfway House.

wharf and the storehouse, the mill and the residence of the famous Mr. William Gooderham. He came to Toronto in 1832, accompanied by fifty-four other relatives and nearly $15,000 in cash, a large sum at that time. Worts and Gooderham started work as millers and were very successful; but apart from this residence, that of Dr. Christopher Widmer, and Russell Abbey where lived Peter Russell, President of Upper Canada, there are no notable houses here.

Better turn north up Yonge Street, noting as we do so that on the wharf at the foot of the street stood, in 1836, Mr. Peter Freeland's soap factory. Many tales are told of that astute merchant and his way of life.

The bay was full of wild ducks in the early days, and [they] were so plentiful around the wharf that Mr. Freeland used to shoot them from the factory door or windows. Mr. Richard Tinning was one day walking along the shore, when some ducks flew up from the water. He fired at them without looking where the shot was going, and it crashed into the windows of the factory. Mr. Freeland ran out, with a number of men, to repel the invaders. In the factory was a tame muskrat that used to dine on fish caught by the men. The fishermen dried their nets alongside of the factory, and one day the muskrat got into the net and was being hauled in. He swam around inside of the wooden floats trying to make his escape; finding that he could not dive under them, he suddenly sprang over and thus made his escape.

The Indians used to catch large quantities of muskrats on the Island, and would land their canoes and cargoes of muskrats' skins on the beach, which was very wide at this point.

During the war of 1837 labour was so scarce that Mr. Freeland could not get men enough to cut the soap into bars. He then ran the soap into boxes, and sold it in one solid mass, as the boxes formed it into shape.

After work was done the men employed in the factory would sit around the kitchen fire moulding bullets.

Mr. Freeland lived in rooms fitted up in the factory at the

time, and coming home late one cold winter night, he found
a soldier lying on the snow, under the influence of liquor. He
sent some men who were working late to bring him in. They
wrapped him in buffalo skins, and left him in the factory.
After a while he awoke, found himself in darkness, and
creeping about came to one of the large soap kettles, about
twelve feet deep. Seeing the window on the other side, he
thought the kettle was a barrier to his further progress, and
trying to get over it, or around it, he fell into it; fortunately it
was empty. The servants, aroused by the noise he made, came
upon the scene with lights, but thought he was safer in than
outside of the kettle, so he stayed there until morning, when
Mr. Freeland put in a ladder and fished him out. Then he stole
along the shore, trying to avoid observation, and thus reached
the Garrison.

But these evidences of vigorous life must not conceal the
fact that above the junction of Yonge and Queen was "a
fine stretch of forest land", and that just to the north of
what is now Grosvenor Street "subterranean springs and
quick-sands rendered the primitive road maker's occupation no
easy one."
Work upon Yonge Street, of course, continued all the time.
It was York's life-line, by which farmers brought necessities
to her markets; and in spite of this there were times when the
road was almost impassable.

The perils and horrors encountered every spring and autumn
by travellers and others in their ascent and descent of the precipitous sides of the Rosedale ravine at the point where the
primitive Yonge street crossed it were a local proverb and a
by-word, ranking for enormity with those associated with the
passage of the Rouge, the Credit, the Sixteen and other deeply
ploughed watercourses, intersected by the two great highways
of Upper Canada. The ascent and descent of the gorge here
were collectively spoken of as the "Blue Hill" from the fact

that strata of a bluish clay might be observed at the summit on both sides.

Later this blue clay was utilized for the making of bricks. Just on the right of the road as we continue north, stood famous Rosedale House, the old home of Stephen Jarvis, Registrar of the Province. It was perched on the crest of a precipitous bank overlooking the deep winding ravines of Rosedale, notable at that time for the lawless gangs that lurked there.

Just beyond the Blue Hill ravine on the west side stood for a long while a lonely unfinished frame building with gable towards the street and windows boarded up. The inquiring stage passenger would be told good humouredly by the driver that this was Rowland Burr's Folly. It was to have been a carding or fulling mill worked by peculiar machinery driven by the stream in the valley below, but either the impracticability of this from the position of the building or the as yet insignificant quantity of wool produced in the country made the enterprise abortive. Mr. Burr was an emigrant from Pennsylvania in 1803 and from early manhood was strongly marked by many of the traits which are held to be characteristic of the speculative and energetic American. But unfortunately for himself, he was in advance of his neighbours. A canal to connect Lake Ontario with the Georgian Bay of Lake Huron via Lake Simcoe and the valley of the Humber was pressed by him years ago and at his own expense he minutely examined the route and published thereon a report. He was a born engineer and mechanician. He built on his own account or for others a number of mills and factories, providing and getting into working order the complicated mechanism required for each and this at a time when such undertakings were not easy to accomplish from the unimproved condition of the country and the few facilities that existed for importing and transporting inland heavy machinery. The mills and factories at Burrwich in Vaughan originated with him and from him that place takes its name.

Chestnut Park on the right was erected at a comparatively modern period by Mr. Mathers, an early merchant of York, who before building here, lived on Queen street, near the Meadows, the residence of Mr. J. Hillyard Cameron. Chestnut Park was afterwards taken by Mr. Macpherson. At the left glimpses are obtained of Oaklands, Mr. John Macdonald's residence, Rathnally, Mr. McMaster's abode and Woodlawn, the home of Chancellor Blake and built by him, but afterwards occupied by Justice Morrison. Summer Hill, seen on the high land far to the right and commanding a noble view of the wide plain below, including Toronto and the lake far distant, was built by Charles Thomson, whose name is associated with the former travel and postal service of the whole length of Yonge street and the Upper Lakes. Summer Hill was greatly improved and enlarged by Larratt Smith, its subsequent owner.

The primitive waggon track of Yonge street ascended the hill at which we now arrive a little to the west of the present line of the road. It passed up through a narrow excavated notch. Across this depression or trench, a forest tree fell without being broken and there long remained. Teams on their way to and from town had to pass under it, like captured armies of old under the yoke. To some among the country folk it suggested the beam of the gallows-tree. Hence sprang an ill-omened name long attached to this spot. Near here at the top of the hill were formerly to be seen the remains of a rude windlass or capstan used in the hauling up of the North-West Company's boats at this point of the long portage from Lake Ontario to Lake Huron. So early as August 3, 1799, the *Niagara Constellation* announced that it was informed on good authority that the North-West Company had it seriously in contemplation to establish a communication with the Upper Lakes by way of York through Yonge street to Lake Simcoe, a distance of thirty-three miles. The *Constellation* adds that the Government has actually begun to open Yonge street for several miles, which example will undoubtedly be no small inducement to persons who possess property on that street and its vicinity to exert themselves in opening and completing what may justly be considered one of the primary objects of attention in a new country, a good road. In these early days the cavalcade of the North-West Company's boats mounted on wheels pursued their way up Yonge street. It used to be supposed by some that the tree across the notch through which the road passed had been purposely felled in that position as a part of the apparatus for helping the boats up the hill.

The tableland now attained was long known as the Poplar Plains, and Stegmann uses this name in his report. A by-road that ascends this same rise near Rathnally is still known as the Poplar Plains road. To the left of Yonge street at the point now reached and lying slightly back stood until recently the house of Mr. J. S. Howard, known as Olive Grove.

Above what is now St. Clair we come to Deer Park where Christ Church will not be built for more than thirty years.

As we reach the higher land after crossing the dam of Whitmore's Mill and returning with the more direct line of the street some rude pottery works meet the eye. Here in the midst of woods the passer-by saw on one side of the road a one-horse clay-grinding machine laboriously in operation and on the other, displayed in the open air on boards supported by wooden pins driven into the great logs composing the wall of the low, windowless building, numerous articles of coarse, brown ware, partially glazed, pans, crocks, jars, jugs, demijohns and so forth. These works were carried on by John Walmsley.

A tract of rough country was now reached, difficult to clear and difficult to traverse with a vehicle. Here a genuine corduroy causeway was encountered, a long series of small sawlogs laid side by side over which wheels jolted deliberately. In the wet season, portions of it being afloat would undulate under the weight of a passing load and occasionally a horse's leg would be entrapped and possibly snapped short by the sudden yielding or revolution of one of the cylinders below. To the right of this tract was one of the church glebes reserved in every township in the original laying out of Upper Canada, one lot of two hundred acres in every seven of the same area. A relic of this arrangement, now broken up, but expected to be permanent when the Quebec Act was passed in 1780, remained down to a late date in the shape of a wayside inn to the right near here styled on its sign the "Glebe Inn," a title and sign reminding one of the "Church Stiles" and "Church Gates" not uncommon as village ale-house designations in some parts of England.

In our progress northward, we now traverse ground locally historic as the scene of a skirmish and bloodshed in the troubles of 1837. The events connected with this have been sufficiently described. The great conspicuous wayside inn, which here stood at the right of the road, usually called Montgomery's, was at the time of its destruction by the Government forces in 1837 in the occupation of a landlord, named Lingfoot. The house of Montgomery from whom the inn took its name, he having been a former occupant, was on a farm owned by himself, beautifully situated on rising ground to the left, subsequently the property and place of abode of Mr. James Lesslie. Mr. Montgomery had once a hotel in York named "The Bird in Hand" on Yonge street, a little to the north of Elliott's Sun Tavern.

Having reached this famous spot, a site where the modern history of Toronto may be said to begin, we can now leave Yonge Street and return in thought to a no less famous thoroughfare; that is, King Street:

The block on the south side of King street, between George and Frederick, is one of the most interesting sections of the city. Here were laid the foundations of Toronto's mercantile prosperity, and here also were the first beginnings of education in York. At the south-west corner of King and Frederick streets originally stood the store of D'Arcy Boulton, a large frame building, painted white. Mr. Boulton was barrister and merchant, and practiced law as well as kept shop. The firm afterwards became Boulton and Proudfoot. Probably it was about

1833 when the plan of numbering houses superseded the method of distinguishing them by signs which told their own story, such as a crowned boot, tea chest, axe, saw, fowling piece, plough, golden fleece, anvil, sledge-hammer or horseshoe. On the north-west corner of King and Frederick streets was the shop of Alexander Wood, in front of which the first sidewalk in Toronto was laid down. Mr. Wood's brother had been engaged in busi-ness in York both alone and in partnership with Mr. Allan, and at his death Alexander came here to settle up the estate and until after the war of 1812 he continued the business. He was a bachelor and lived above his store. He returned to Scotland where he died intestate and it was some time before the lawful heir to his property was established. Wood and Alexander streets run through land that once belonged to him and they are named after him.

Another note of interest is that the first brick house in Toronto was erected on the corner of King and Frederick Streets. From 1835 to 1850 King was *the* street of the city.

Yonge street, above Queen, did not amount to much as a business locality, and between Shuter and Yorkville there were gaps of land, many of which retained the forest trees of a century. Queen street was not even a street of small shops. King street was the hunting ground for all that was fashionable in dry goods, tempting in groceries or exquisite in jewellery. If you wanted anything in the clothing line, ample variety could be found in the shops of this street, and in fact anything from a needle to an anchor could be found in some of the numerous stores that graced the main street of the miniature metropolis.

To copy the door-to-door assembly of names that are given in the chapter cited, which was published in 1894, would only have a pot-pourri interest these sixty years later. We con-tinue with the memories of Mr. Alexander Jacques, "an old Torontonian".

Writing about the landmarks of his native place and espe-cially about King street east in 1834, he says:—

About that date my father, a baker, resided at the corner of King and Francis streets, opposite the St. Lawrence market. The building, a two storey frame one, was owned by Mr. Cawthra, sen. On the west or Petley corner was Schofield's hotel, with a sign of the old English coach-and-four. West of this the hotel gateway, for then it was a large market hotel, and the principal house of call for visitors from the north and west. In the next house was Mrs. Platt, a kindhearted old lady, the mother of the late Samuel Platt, as also John Platt; then some two frame structures, one later occupied by Paddy Burke, the auctioneer, with an old man, a real piece of Irish eccentricity who used to ring the auction bell. West was St. James' graveyard, and the Cathedral with its wooden spire. The half acre took possession of the whole block back to Adelaide and east to the property occupied by the Rev. Dean Grasett for many years. North up Francis street to the lane running west from Nelson was known as the Devil's Elbow, very filthy and no residences except at the south-west end, just up to the graveyard fence. Mrs. McLean kept a tavern, the sign of the Crown and Anchor, and in those days it was a resort for the men who wore her Majesty's uniform, and who made it their favourite house of call, and here indulged, without fear of hindrance, in that classic game of "Forty-fives." Opposite the Cathedral, on the southeast corner of Church and King streets, was a frame building known as the Checkered Store, painted like a checker-board. East of that came Joseph Rogers' fur and hat store. The old sign, the Indian with his gun and the fur pelts in his belt, is to-day in front of his son's store on the corner. It is a grand old relic and was the artistic work of either Paul Kane or Charles March. Mr. Rogers was a tall, dark complexioned man, black hair, and heavy eye-brows, with correct, firm features. From 1822 down to that date when our aborigines began to retire back into the depths of our forest, shrinking from the advance of our civilization, Uncle Joe was deservedly famous amongst the tribes that visited York, the great fur trading depot; and when the dusky sons of the forest had been bathed in the curse, Uncle Joe's generosity was often tested to feed and furnish shelter to the suffering ones. He was known as the great Waubaskonjuba, the straight pine.

From this east to Market Square there were but few buildings, none brick. Dr. Lang, as he was called, had an apothecary shop, and extracted teeth, old style, with the key. Down the west side of the Market Square resided, or rather carried on business, Mr. William Helliwell. Thomas McIlmurray had a clock and watch repairing shop. His sign was a golden lion, held to the one storey building by iron rods, and in the paw or forefoot a watch. Down at the south-east corner of Front street stood an old two storey frame building, on the upper front a verandah. For many years this was known as Billy Plain's.

And before we leave King Street it may be of interest to mention a view in the days of 1836 on the north—the official—side, as the south was the mercantile:

This landmark is taken about 1836, and represents the north side of King street, from the north-east corner of Yonge and King, to the north-east corner of King and Church streets, where stands St. James' Cathedral. The building to the left of the picture, at the corner of Toronto street, is the jail, which stood in off the King street line about sixty feet, but about forty feet from the line of Toronto street. The front of this building was exposed for the first time in seventy years—for it was built in 1826—when the Rice, Lewis building, on the corner of Toronto and King streets, was torn down to make way for the red brick structure now on that site. A portion of the front showing the windows of the building may yet be seen from the rear of Walton's barber shop, a few doors east of the corner. The scaffold upon which the patriots Lount and Matthews suffered, was erected in the centre of the ground in front of the building. The building in the rear centre, with a cupola, was the firehall on Church street. It stood directly south of old St. Andrew's church. The building to the right, similar in architecture to the

jail, was the Court House. There were apparently two entrances
to this building, one from Church street, and the other from
King street. The picture shows a King street entrance, but the
entrance since 1841 has been on Church street. The massive
building with the short tower was St. James' Cathedral, which
was burned in 1839. The original drawing of this picture was
made by a Mr. Young, a Toronto architect of considerable
repute.

Considerations of space forbid, for the present, any adequate
description of Queen Street, which—first as Dundas and then
as Lot Street—has always been the main highway out of
Toronto, east and west. It is the horizontal highway; Yonge
Street the vertical. The chapter that follows was written in
1888, a date that still found "muddy little York" possessed of
houses built during her first quarter century. It must be remembered that Teraulay Street in that earlier day did not exist
as at present. Turn to the Toronto *Directory* of 1846: here
we find "Teraulay street—second street west of Yonge street,
commences at Queen street and runs north". As an aid to
placing this vanished thoroughfare we have the following
note on Bay Street: "Second street west of Yonge street, on
south side of King street, commences at the bay shore and
runs north to *Queen street*." Will the reader who takes a
streetcar up Bay from somewhere south of Queen and who
keeps his balance as it swerves and sidles left, past the bulk
of the City Hall, consider that swerve as a curtsey offered
to dead-and-gone Teraulay Street: the little houses long since
removed to make way for our "magnificent pile of stone".
Bay Street then ended on the south side of Queen, and
Teraulay Street was the continuation north. Quite an important street; seven of its houses actually had numbers. The
Directory of 1846 has this to say about numbers:

GUIDE TO THE NUMBER OF THE HOUSES.—The
numbers are those put upon the houses in chalk, by Mr. George
Walton, in conformity with a plan adopted by the Corporation,

as follows: All those streets which run the full length of the City, and cross Yonge street, are divided into two, east and west; the numbers of both divisions begin at Yonge street, and strike off east and west; thus the store of Messrs. Ridout Bros., is No. 1 King street east; and that of Messrs. Sutherland, the opposite corner, is No. 1 King street west; the next houses each way, are Nos. 3 east and west, respectively—the odd numbers being on that side, and the even ones on the opposite; thus Betley & Brown's establishment is No. 2 King street east; and that of Messrs. Lynes & Brown, No. 2 King street west, and so on.

In all the streets running in the same direction as King, although not crossing Yonge street, the numbers begin at the end nearest Yonge street, and rise as they advance east or west.

In all the streets running east and west, parallel with the Bay, the odd numbers are on the north side, and the even ones on the south; and in all those running north and south, at right angles with the former, the odd numbers (beginning at the end at or nearest the Bay) are on the west side, and the even ones on the east.

By a plan of the Corporation, where vacant lots occur, a given space is allowed for a number, to prevent any disturbance of the order arising from the erection of new houses upon such lots. In some instances, this plan has not been strictly adhered to; indeed it was almost impossible for a person, without accurately measuring the ground, to place the numbers properly; but they are sufficiently correct for all the purposes of this work.

Mr. George Walton, by the way, was Toronto's coroner at that time.

We must now return to our muttons of 1888.

Along the north side of Queen street, between James and Teraulay streets, stretches a row of buildings, all with the exception of the two easternmost ones having an appearance of age. They are now, in this year of grace 1888, given over to boot and shoe men, barbers, and all the motley array of occupations which buildings that have seen their best days usually present. This is one side of the square on which the new court house will stand. With the exception of some on the James street side the other buildings on the block have been pulled down to make way for the new edifice. Beginning at the corner of Teraulay street the first building is a little low structure now occupied as a butcher shop. This building was put up about 1825 and at first formed two small cottages which some time afterwards were converted into shops. Behind the butcher shop are two small houses and sheds which were built by Joseph Bird, about forty years ago. Next to the butcher shop is the frame building now known as Lennox's hotel. It was built in 1827, by John Bird, and was occupied by him at first as a general store and residence. The house has been somewhat altered from its original appearance. When it was built the floor was considerably higher than the street and was reached by an ascent of four steps running up the side of a railed platform. The front projection was subsequently added by James Spence. In the rear is a brick addition put on by James Lennox, the present occupant, which a little red lamp, suspended over the Queen street entrance, declares to be Dufferin Hall. John Bird bought the land on which the house stands from James Macaulay in 1820. At that time there was a little cottage, painted green, standing on the site. Mr. Bird met a mysterious death in 1830, and it is supposed that he was murdered. Dying intestate, by the law of entail then in force, the property descended to Joseph Bird, his son. Joseph acted honourably, however, and of his own accord divided up the property among his sisters, keeping for himself the Queen street house, in which he opened a tavern. Upon Joseph Bird's death in 1859 his will was found to direct that the place should either be mortgaged or sold. Consequently the executors mortgaged it, but the rent was not sufficient to pay the interest, taxes and the expense of keeping it in repair. Then they wished to sell it, but could not on account of the word "or" in the clause "mortgaged or sold." Subsequently the building society which had advanced £1,600 on the property sold it at auction. It was bought by

"California" Metcalf, a man who, having failed here went to California at the time of the gold excitement, was successful, made money, came back to Toronto, paid his debts and invested in real estate. Some time afterwards the property was held for a brief space by a man named Robertson. It then came into the possession of William Charlton, who continued it as a tavern for many years up to about 1860. Charlton was the first assistant engineer of the fire brigade. A few years later, about the time of the Fenian raid, he was killed at a fire on Shuter street by a balcony falling on him. After his death Mrs. Charlton, his widow, managed the business two years, when she married John Elliott. She then transferred the property to James Spence, who in turn conveyed it to James Lennox, the present occupant. In a shed at the rear of the house, now torn down, a man by the name of Dawes once kept a rag shop. Next to the Lennox house on the east runs a passage, on the other side of which is a low wooden building of considerable age, occupied from the first, and still occupied, as a black-smith's shop. Long ago an American by the name of Treat carried on business there. He was succeeded by Rowell, Fitzgerald and the present occupant. The house to the east of the shop was built by Rowell, and used by him as a residence. John Boxall bought Rowell's house, and also built the one next to it. Behind these two houses used to be a little cottage, some time ago pulled down. The brick building, with the letters, "Globe Foundry," stretching across its front, is next. The land on which this stands was first owned by George Hutchison. His daughter, Mrs. Bennett, inherited the property which she sold to Edward Beckett. Originally there was a little cottage on the site with a porch which a Mrs. Manus rented, and where she kept a small hardware shop for many years. On Mr. Beckett's coming into possession, he built a foundry at the rear of the lot, and on the street the brick building where he sold the pots and kettles he made. Mrs. Beckett, who afterward became Mrs. McNeil, owned and lived in the house next to the foundry. The property at the corner of James street, originally belonged to a man named Blevins. The two corner buildings are of quite modern construction. There is a cottage on James street in the rear of the Queen street corner where a man by the name of Perkis lived. He was a sailor and boat builder, and once he built quite a large vessel in his back yard which was dragged down to the bay on rollers by oxen. Not far from this, standing back from the street, is a square rough-cast house where Miss Hussey once taught school. Years ago the rest of the square was a pasture field and there was an orchard in which the children delighted to get.

We think of an almost mature city in the year 1888; to reach "Old Toronto" we must divest her of at least forty years. Then we find that the Dundas Road has only one resident—a distiller—and that it starts at the toll-gate on Queen Street, goes north for a quarter-mile and then proceeds west.

In 1857, toll-gates abounded in every direction west, north and east of the city. As in England they are now things of the past; but, whether rightly or wrongly, they were the source of constant trouble, quarrels and annoyance while they did exist. The gates on Dundas street within ten miles of Toronto at the time referred to were: No. 1, at Brockton, on the north side of the street, about half way between Sheridan and Brock avenues; No. 2, always known as the "Blind toll-gate," on the north-east corner of the concession now known as Bloor street and Dundas street. This was a peculiar construction of two storeys, with a covered way extending across Dundas street. No. 3 gate was the one first mentioned in this article, and the fourth was the Mimico gate, some little distance to the west of St. George's church, Islington. Teams proceeding to Toronto from beyond the fourth gate paid toll at the fourth and the first, being free of the two intermediate ones; but those who came from places between the fourth and the third paid at the latter and also again at the first. The "blind" toll-gate never exacted a toll from teams proceeding direct along Dundas street, but was built for the purpose of catching those people who, coming from Toronto, drove along Dufferin street north to the concession, thence proceeding west to Dundas street, thus avoiding the Brockton gate. It often happened that a teamster going to the city would turn out of the way and proceed east along the concession so as to escape, or in the hope of escaping, Brockton toll. The keeper of the "blind" gate rarely missed noting the occurrence, and looked out for the return of this man. If he came by himself, he was all but certain to find the bar down and passage impossible. Then would follow a war of words, and "langwidge" flowed that would be extremely forcible even from a London cabby's point of view. Sometimes even blows were struck, which occasionally resulted in a meeting before the magistrates, with sometimes a conviction for assault. As a pretty general rule, though, the toll taker settled his own quarrels. Neither he nor his employers had much liking for Police Court proceedings. They knew that to a great extent they were Ishmaelites; every man's hand was against them. Precisely such scenes as have been described as happening at the "blind" gate took place over and over again at No. 3 gate with delinquents who tried to dodge the toll by going along St. Clair avenue.

The "blind" toll-gate disappeared when the city boundaries were extended in the northwest, as also did the Brockton gate, and in 1897 the old check gate at Lambton followed suit. Of them it may safely be said they were "unwept, unhonoured and unsung."

While on the subject we may note a street that is linked by its name to English history. This is Rebecca Street.

The reason it obtained this name was that the land it crosses was purchased by a contractor who supplied wood to the garrison. He disputed the right of the road trustees to exact toll from his teams at the gate on Queen street, near its junction with Dundas street. This dispute caused a great deal of ill-feeling between the contractor's men and the keepers of the gate, and constant quarrels ensued, and sometimes blows were interchanged. Eventually the plot of ground over which Rebecca street runs was purchased and a lane cut through which afforded access from Dundas to Queen street, avoiding the hated gate. Owing to these quarrels the lane got locally known as Rebecca street, after the Rebeccaites, who in South Wales in 1843 systematically destroyed toll-gates and bars. The reason they took the name of Rebeccaites was in allusion to the reference contained in Genesis, 24, verse 60.

The reader may be interested in a few other street names, how they came and from whence derived.

Nothing shows the loyalty of early York more clearly than the names which the founders of the town bestowed on the first streets laid out. The little quadrangular plot, from which has sprung Toronto, was crowded with the names and titles of the members of the royal family. Thus we have among the first rude roadways, designated as streets, King street, Duke street, Duchess street, Princess street, George street, Frederick street, and Caroline street. As the limits of the town were extended, the names of those prominent in its growth were applied to new thoroughfares, and these streets to-day are freighted with local associations in such names as Simcoe, Peter, John, Jordan and Scott. It is to be regretted that some of the ways suggestive of the early history of the town have been changed, and in fact through the annals of the place, up to the present time, an uncomfortable disposition to alter street names has been apparent. In most cases the changes have not been for the better, even in the point of view of euphony alone. With the gradual absorption of the suburbs changes of name in many of the village streets is necessary, for the sake of preventing duplication, but those of the older town might better be allowed to wear the names with which they were originally baptized.

Here are a few of the derivations for Toronto streets:

Admiral Road — Admiral Baldwin; Agnes street is called after the daughter of Chief Justice Sir James Macaulay, who owned property there; Albany Avenue — The name Albany, now quite common, was originally derived from one of the titles in 1664 of him who afterwards became King James the Second; Albert street was formerly known as Macaulay Lane, and now bears the name of Prince Albert, consort of the Queen; Baldwin street commemorates the name of Dr. William Warren Baldwin, who became possessed by the will of Miss Elizabeth Russell of a large tract of land in that portion of the city through which it runs; Berkeley street, which was formerly Parliament street, was named from a small town in Gloucestershire, England; Bin Scarth Road was named after W. B. Scarth, a land commissioner; Bishop street is named after Bishop John Strachan, of the Anglican church, first bishop of Toronto; Bond street is named after Sir Francis Bond Head; Booth Avenue is named after a coppersmith and ex-Alderman by that name; Borden street was named by the Denison family after one of their members; Broadview Avenue is the high-sounding, fanciful appellation given to what was once the Mill Road — the latter so called because it leads to the mills on the Upper Don; Carlaw Avenue is named after Mr. Carlaw, paymaster of the Grand Trunk railway; Carlton street, Gerrard street, Shuter street and Gould street, had their names from Montreal friends of Col. McGill, the first owner of this tract; Cawthra Avenue commemorates the Cawthra family, the Astors of Upper Canada; Chestnut street was originally Sayer street, and there was no call for the change, as it never had any association with chestnut trees; Christie street — Wm. Christie, biscuit baker; Crawford street is named after Thomas Crawford, a drover; Cumberland Road and Cumberland street are named after the birth-place across the sea of the late James Wallace, one of the first councillors of Yorkville; Davenport Road and Davenport Place are memorials of Davenport House, the residence of Colonel Wells, formerly of the 43rd regiment; Dean street perpetuates the name of a schoolmaster, father-in-law of one of the Gooderham family; Delaware Avenue preserves the name of the West family, Lord De la Ware. In the United States, the State, river, bay and tribe of Indians received their name from

Thomas West, Lord De la Ware, who died on his vessel in the bay in 1610. Dundas street has its name from the Right Hon. Henry Dundas, Secretary of State for the Colonies in 1794. Dundas was the name originally given to Queen street in 1794 by Governor Simcoe, but the name has been transferred from that thoroughfare to the modern Dundas street — a thing of quite common occurrence in the annals of York and Toronto. Hayden street is named after Mr. Hayden, a milkman; Hazelton Avenue was named by George White, a land-holder of this section, in honour of his wife, née Miss Hazelton; Leader Lane is so called, because the newpaper *Leader* was formerly published on it; Lindsey Avenue is named after Charles Lindsey, City Registrar, lawyer, newspaper man and author; Louisa street and Louisa Terrace are named after a lady in the Macaulay family; McCaul street is named after Dr. McCaul, a Professor in the University; Markham street and Markham Place are named after Captain Markham, of the 32nd regiment; Melinda street preserves the Christian name of the wife of Jordan Post, the first clock maker in town; Morse street is called after George D. Morse, a cattle dealer, who was drowned in the Don; Phoenix Block was originally the "iron block," one of the first iron blocks in Toronto. It was burned down, rebuilt, and christened Phoenix Block. Queen street was originally laid out by Governor Simcoe, as a portion of a great military road, to traverse the province from west to east. He named it Dundas street. It was afterwards called Lot street, from the fact that it was the southern boundary of the tier of park lots which stretched along it for two miles. Later it was changed to Queen street, in honour of Queen Victoria. Roncesvalles Avenue is a reminder of the valley in Navarre, rendered famous as the scene of the defeat of the army of Charlemagne in 778, by a force of Arabs, Navarrese and French Gascons; Rosedale Road derives its name from Rosedale, the residence of Sheriff W. B. Jarvis, who, with Mr. Bloor, projected and laid out the village of Yorkville, which narrowly escaped being called Bloorville: Rosedale and Cumberland were also suggested, but Yorkville was finally decided upon. Spadina Avenue, Spadina Avenue Place, and Spadina Crescent have their names from Spadina House, the residence of Dr. W. W. Baldwin, who laid out the street: Spadina is an Indian word, meaning an elevation of land. Temperance street was so named by Jesse Ketchum, a strong advocate of temperance principles, by whom it was laid out; Vermont Avenue was named rather inappropriately after the first State received into the American Union after the adoption of the Federal Constitution, for there is nothing of green about it, nor anything suggestive of a mountain; Virgin Lane — Sir Thos. Coatesworth called it after old Mr. Virgin, who lived there.

Finally, the street now called Sherbourne has no right to its "u". It was named after the little town of Sherborne in Dorset, the old home of the Canadian Ridouts; but transatlantic custom that takes the letter from "honour" and "favour" has here inadequately returned it.

There are other streets, other houses in which family life had its way for a few years before the children took up their own lives, and the parents moved and "it was torn down". There are stories of mercantile enterprise, the beginnings of great stores; but in such a continuous history no terminus can be final and the gentle journalism of John Ross Robertson ends, as it began, with promise.

IV. THE CHURCHES

Of the 4,080 pages that are comprised in the six volumes of the *Landmarks*, almost a thousand (or about one-fourth) are concerned with the Churches of Toronto. There are at least two hundred chapters, short and long; the shortest less than a page, the longest, in Volume Three, dealing with St. James' Cathedral — of two hundred and fifty pages. The whole of Volume Four is devoted to this "important feature in civic life", and contains one hundred and ninety-one chapters, each recording the life-history of a church. The first chapter gives some general particulars.

In the following pages the Anglican, Roman Catholic, Presbyterian, Methodist, Baptist and Congregationalist churches are arranged in groups. The Salvation Army, though having several places of meeting is dealt with in one chapter in which each place of worship is separately noticed. Chapters are also devoted to the Young Men's, also to the Young Women's, Christian Associations. Every place of worship whether it is Christian or Jewish, in or near Toronto is described in this book, every effort having been made to make it as complete as possible. As far as practicable the churches in the various groups have been arranged in chronological order, and in no single case have the names of lay members and helpers who have assisted either in the formation of the congregations or in erecting the edifice, been omitted. That, of course, means where it has been possible to obtain the names.

Another thing to be mentioned is this, that because the first Presbyterian church described, namely, St. Andrew's, was built in 1834, it must not be presumed there were no Presbyterians in York up to that time. There were many families and in-

dividual members among the very small population of less than 10,000 people. But they were in a minority, and assembled for worship in private houses or perhaps a hired room. The great majority of the residents in York in 1830 were Anglicans, Roman Catholics and Methodists, though among them all they did not provide church accommodation for more than thirty-three per cent of the population, if they even accomplished that. Now, on the other hand, in Toronto Township, Scarboro and Vaughan, there were flourishing Presbyterian churches and congregations, but neither Anglican nor Methodist ministers or churches. These latter were in as great a minority in the country districts as the Presbyterians were in York.

Forty Anglican churches are described; then come thirty Presbyterian, followed by the Roman Catholics with ten churches, and the Methodists with thirty-eight. Baptists have twenty-three but the Congregationalists only eight (or nine if we count "Bethany — an undenominational church on Congregational lines"). With the Table of Contents are vigorous notes: "The first free and open church", "The first frame church", "A West End Parish with a pleasing record", "An energetic Rector and a very large congregation".

After the Congregationalists comes the Society of Friends, one chapter; and then the remainder crowd in. Christian Scientists, Unitarians, the Salvation Army, the Latter Day Saints. These are "Popularly known as the Mormon Congregation". A little later we come to the Jews, to the African Methodists (the note says: "Many strange vicissitudes among the various bodies"), the Greek Catholics and the Deaf and Dumb Congregation. Then, " 'tis impossible to escape it," St. James' Church gets in again, although the editor admits that its history had been given fully in the first, second and third volumes of the *Landmarks*. On pages 577 to 584, we are introduced to the Collegiate and Conventual Chapels, from St. Joseph's Convent to Bishop Strachan School; and the concluding chapter is on "Churches of the past — Where Early Residents of the City once worshipped". Almost every church has its illustration, many have more than one: three hundred pictures altogether.

Volume four of the *Landmarks* was published in 1904, but most of the sketches and much of the information had been given to the Toronto *Telegram* in 1887; so we have in these reprints of "up to the minute" reporting, a series of pictures, not of olden-time churches but of last Sunday's sermon. The style of the preacher, his voice, his mannerisms, his most striking phrases; the attentiveness (or otherwise) of the congregation, the singing, the organist, all come under review. St. James' does not escape.

After a preliminary service of three-quarters of an hour, Rev. P. H. DuMoulin ascended the pulpit, to the right of the chancel, and delivered a sermon of 25 minutes length. He is a gentleman a little past middle life, with stately bearing, a fine presence and an exceedingly rich voice, and in his earlier life undoubtedly possessed the possibilities of oratory. While his sermon on this occasion was not distinguished by any great originality of thought yet it was couched in well-chosen language and brought within the easy comprehension of the 450 listeners. His style of delivery becomes more natural as he loses thought of the surroundings and it is attended with considerable animation and some expressive gesticulation; but the monotone predominates and has a tendency to produce a soothing effect upon the hearer. And this, with the distressingly oppressive heat, at least in the gallery, induced a popular condition of somnolency. Many were seen asleep and others resorted to all those little tricks which are used to convey the impression of wakefulness while the prima facie evidence convicts them of the contrary condition.

Still, there was good sense in the sermon, as the three extracts here given will show.

(1) "Try your condition by your dominant passion. Are you still its obedient and most miserable slave? Is it as powerful now as when you began your Christian ways? These are ques-

tions of which every Christian can take stock before his God to-night."

(2) "Try yourselves by the matter of service. There are 15 organizations for work in this church; in which do you work? If you walk about the streets and lanes around this cathedral church and never put forth a finger to help and lift up from sin and degradation, and make the poor your brothers and sisters, you haven't heard the voice of Jesus Christ, and your life is not one of service and devotion to your Master. If you can't *do* anything *give* something."

(3) "There is so much more of conscience than consistency in us that we pass sentence and inflict just punishment on ourselves."

We may note in addition that "a great many young men were present and seemed interested in the ritual; a few came in half an hour late: the gallery contained many little children who were soothed to sleep by the monotone running from the chancel down the nave. The singers numbered 25 and were led by a choirmaster buried behind the clock and vigorously beating time with the only part of him visible, viz. a kid-gloved hand waving above his head." The earlier music in the Cathedral was sometimes open to criticism. "The first clerk was Mr. Hetherington. His habit was, after giving out a psalm, to play the air on a bassoon and then to accompany, with fantasias on the same instrument, such vocalists as felt inclined to take part in the singing. A choir from time to time had been formed. Once two rival choirs were heard on trial in the church, one of them strong in instrumental resources, having the aid of a bass viol, clarionet, and bassoon; the other more dependent on its vocal excellences. The instrumental choir triumphantly prevailed, and in 1819 an allowance of £20 was made to Mr. Hetherington for singing and giving instruction in church music. But all expedients for doing what was in reality the work of the congregation itself were unreliable, and the clerk or choirmaster often found himself a solitary performer. Mr. Hetherington's successor was Mr. John Fenton, a rather small, shrewd-featured person, not deficient in self-esteem. Not infrequently Mr. Fenton, after giving out the portion of Tate and Brady, which it pleased him to select, would execute the whole of it as a solo to some accustomed air, with graceful variations of his own. All this would be done with great coolness and apparent self-satisfaction. While the discourse was going on in the pulpit above him it was his way often to lean himself resignedly back in a corner of his pew and throw a white cambric handkerchief over his head and face. Mr. Fenton's employment as official mouthpiece of the English church did not stand in the way of his making himself useful as a class leader among the Wesleyan Methodists." Charles Dickens might have written that.

To go through the volume page by page is to become aware that many of the churches noted as ministering to the full tide of the city's life are now in backwaters. Even in 1904 this could be written:

More than half a century has gone by since it arose, in 1843, a magnificent piece of architecture that was the pride of faithful churchmen. Within its walls were wont to meet the ancestors of those whose industry and enterprise in these later days have given Toronto an enviable position amid the beautiful cities of the world's occident. Upon the musty records in its archives are inscribed names that are honoured in civic history for probity and integrity, and fondly cherished in the affection. But now the time-honoured walls, upon which the storms of nearly five decades have beaten, are worn with age and dingy with the dust and dirt of many years, and Trinity stands like some weather-beaten mausoleum burying within itself the greatness and glory of the past. All over this city are scattered thousands of people whose feet have crossed its threshold and whose heads have bowed in adoration before the God to whom its altar was dedicated so long ago. And in that other quiet city of the dead forever rest many who, in the time-honoured past, united their voices in the celebration of its beautiful ritual, and doubtless found therein that comfort and guidance that smoothed their pathway to the grave.

One parish after another has been taken from its territory; one family after another has left its pews to find a new church-home more convenient; a long procession has gone from its doors never to return, but even with all this draught upon its strength, its energy, though impaired, is unabated. The families that had worshipped in the old church were forming part of the new; in the north or the west of the city, in Davisville, in Scarboro. "Non omnis moriar" says the reporter. But for the most part the tale is of profit and not of loss.

To enquire what manner of man was this Sunday critic may be to enquire too curiously. He was (or *they were,* there is no knowing) essentially religious, in the sense in which St. Paul applied the term to the men of Athens. In the course of perambulations to a hundred and ninety churches he was able to make comparisons and to arrive at conclusions: not alone upon the individual church but also upon the work of the church in Toronto generally. And, to begin with, we of the mid-twentieth century are obliged to examine a 65-year-old eulogy of "Toronto, City of Churches", "Toronto the Good".

There is no city on the American continent of the size of Toronto that is to be compared with it in the number and magnificence of its churches. Their architectural beauty of construction, their elegance of furniture and decoration, and the convenience of all their appointments are justly not only matters of astonishment to the foreign visitors but matters of admiration and wonder. Of course we have simple, plain and unpretending churches and meagre mission chapels where poorly paid ministers officiate, but these exist everywhere; not every place, however, can boast of such beautiful churches and so many of them as this fair city whose heaven-reaching spires speak of its moral character to the traveller coming from over the green hills of the north and the blue waters of the lake on the south.

A little later, whether on paper or in time, it must have seemed to the reporter that some consideration of the church-going habit would be convenient. So we are offered a pointed paragraph with a sturdy addendum of fact.

It is just to say that no other city on the American continent presents such a spectacle as is seen every Sunday evening on the streets of Toronto. Thousands of people walk the avenues and thoroughfares on their way to church. It is the real "live" hour of the day. The stern discountenance of any and every form of recreation is sometimes said to be the cause of so many people going to church. They must go somewhere, it is said, to break up the dreadful monotony and lifelessness of the day, and so when evening comes they are glad to go to church—not so much for purposes of worship as for social relief from the oppressiveness of the day.

"But for all this, the large majority of people go to church to be benefitted; and whatever may take place on the street the conduct in church is without reproach. As is usual, an enormous crowd was there, at least 1,400 people, and yet the attention throughout was of the most respectful kind and the decorum reverential, and that is saying very much when it is remembered that nine-tenths of the audience were composed of young people." This is applied to a Methodist church, which "seats 1500 and is full at every service; so full sometimes that no more can be admitted". But then we learn — "very much of the good success of this church is due to the energy and industry of a *former* Pastor". Other agencies assist, good music and a friendly welcome — but, essentially, the success that is indicated by full pews and a brimming treasury, is always one man's work.

To continue with our Reporter; in general he settled himself and his note book somewhere unnoticeable — in a back seat or in a gallery. Let us try an Anglican church.

'I should like very much to have the privilege of sitting in the gallery in order to get a good view of the choristers,' said the writer to the black-robed beadle of Holy Trinity.

'Just wait a minute,' said that busy functionary, as he turned away to look after a stove. 'Now, step this way,' he resumed, opening a narrow door at the front of one of the turrets. 'Just keep right on till you come to a green door and push it open,' was the parting instruction as the little door was closed behind him, and the writer found himself in total darkness. With one hand groping along the damp circular wall and the other outstretched to ward off any unseen danger, the narrow winding stairway was followed by faith, not by sight, until the green door was reached; after an almost despairing effort to find the latch, an effort not conducive to the cultivation of a reverential temper, the door at last flew open with a bang and threatened to bring the eyes of the whole congregation gallery-wards. After enough of the accumulated dust of months had been cleared away from the unused seat a fine view of the nave and chancel, brilliantly lighted, was deemed a reward for the perilous ascent.

Far away the processional chant was faintly heard, like the distant murmur of some hidden waterfall; its soft, gentle music grew stronger and louder until the vestry door was opened and the surpliced choristers slowly and reverently entered.

Here the emphasis is on music; a later "perambulation" found a Presbyterian church where the sermon was a predominant interest.

The congregation was composed very largely of young people with an equal proportion as to sex, and they were very reverent and decorous in conduct. They were of what is called the "middle class," not very rich and not very poor, at least so far as outward indications are a standard. In a beautiful church like that one hardly expects to find poor people whose clothes would wound their self-respect in contrast with the almost luxurious furnishings of the church.

Perhaps it was hotter in the gallery than elsewhere, but the atmosphere up there was very uncomfortable; one young lady was so much overcome as to be obliged to get out into the fresh air; others opened their wraps and expressed themselves

by weary longdrawn "whews"; a number enjoyed a little nap
during the sermon; the far-away voice of the speaker and the

ST. ANDREW'S CHURCH

burdensome heat were very favourable to this indulgence; one
young lady, snugly ensconced in the corner of the nook opposite
the reporter, laid her head against the cushioned wall and
her feet upon an ottoman, so that she was rapidly acquiring

the horizontal position; wearied with the heat, her eyes gradually closed with a corresponding gradual opening of her mouth until she suddenly recovered herself, and the mouth went shut with a click, and the eyes came open with a not very friendly glance at the amused spectators; but she didn't fall asleep again. No matter how serious the subject of the preacher's sermon, if the physical comfort of the hearer is not assured, all pictures of the judgment after death fade into insignificance compared with the discomfort of a badly-ventilated church.

The next gallery visited was Roman Catholic, and the Protestant observer was evidently impressed.

No difference was made on the score of dress or appearance; a very richly dressed lady and a poor old woman with faded calico dress and plain shawl occupied the same pew; the rough garb of the labouring man did not debar him from a good seat; a cluster of scantily clad little children was carefully looked after, and there was that cosmopolitan character about the congregation that seemed to fulfil the prayer of Him before whose cross they all bowed: — "I pray that they may all be one."

Seated in a quiet corner of the gallery a picture like this was spread out before the reporter. It was during that part of the service called "The Elevation of the Host." The vast congregation was kneeling; silence was supreme, the sweet tones of the organ were hushed; the voices of the singers were quiet; no sonorous chant threaded its way along the vaulted roof to enkindle the musical antiphony; within the sanctuary the venerable prelate bowed low over the kneeling desk; the attendants knelt low on the floor by his side; with clasped hands and bent heads the white-robed sanctuary boys reverently knelt before the sublime and mysterious Presence; not only quiet reigned supreme, but all motion of life seemed suspended save the slow swinging movement of the censer throwing its fragrance out over the sanctuary, and the noiseless uplifting of the Sacred Host clasped by the veiled hands of the priest.

A parallel expression of reverence was noticed later in an Anglican church: —

And a most remarkable fact in connection with the service was the silent adoration on the part of the people. In fact, the order was so good and the attention so intensely concentrated that the moments of silence were almost painful in their nature. And it is always so in this church. The average attendance is five hundred, and yet there is never the slightest infraction of good order or of that devout spirit that should characterize Christian worship. And this is more remarkable when the locality and the consequent character of its audiences are considered.

Of this necessity for reverent behaviour the reporter speaks again and again. It must be said that few congregations meet with criticism in the matter. Here are opposing passages, both Presbyterian: —

(1) So far as external indications go it was an audience composed of people in the middle walks of life, not very rich and not very poor; a special feature of the congregation was the large number of young people present; doubtless many were there from force of habit alone, and from some exhibitions a few, at least, were there owing to that peculiar attraction of the opposite sexes which no religion can sufficiently bring within reverential limits. The behaviour of the young folks was very good, if not worshipful in every case, except on the part of some unfledged young men in the gallery.

(2) Going up the winding stairway and through the crimson portiere hung at the entrance, a cosy seat was shown the visitor amid a company of young men, evidently students. The first natural impulse was to look for the young ladies who were supposed to be the magnets of attraction; in no other way could the unusually large attendance of young men be accounted for. But there were comparatively few young ladies there; whether because of the very bad walking or because the preacher is intensely intellectual, has not been revealed. No explanation of

this influx of students was afforded until the sermon was begun, and then it was clear. The undivided attention of these young men and the eagerness with which they followed the masterly discourse showed that they came to be instructed, and for no other purpose.

NOTE: The minister in the second instance was "a cogent reasoner, a profound thinker and a most original preacher"; and if there is thought, originality, or honesty in the sermon the reviewer does his best for it. One minister

drew a forcible picture of a visit to a doomed murderer and described his death upon the gallows. And then he launched boldly out in support of the effete doctrine of the eternal loss of the soul in hell. And it was very refreshing to hear a minister with that courage of his convictions which compelled him to bravely maintain such a loss; not that it is a refreshing thing to contemplate, but that it is creditable for a minister who is committed to the belief of an everlasting hell to openly maintain it. But, despite the awful horror of the presentation, the congregation did not seem to realize the truth of it and accepted the dictum placidly as if not caring anything about it.

One rather wonders what he expected them to do. For this was in 1886, and the old Methodist habit of openly showing conviction of sin by groanings and prostrations had long been lost in Toronto. In 1818 people were more primitive, more natural, less inhibited. Here is described the building in which they worshipped.

In the summer of this year was erected the little church shown in the illustration.[1] It was the first place of public worship of the Wesleyan Methodists in York. The chapel was a little low commonplace-looking frame structure, originally forty feet square, but afterward enlarged to forty by sixty feet. Its builder was a Mr. Petch. It stood a few feet back from what is now the corner of King and Jordan streets, but at the time of its erection Jordan

[1] Not reproduced.

street had no existence. It was on the south side of King street and stood north and south. On the site of the chapel was afterward built Hay's furniture establishment. The little chapel had a solitary double doorway opening toward King street. On each side of the entrance was a window, which, as compared with the size of the building was of considerable dimensions. Three windows of similar size lighted the interior from each side. The interior was fitted up with a high square box-like pulpit at the end. Rude wooden benches were ranged along each side, leaving a narrow passage down the middle from the door to the pulpit. The entire cost of the building was about $250, and it is said that the congregation were three years in raising this amount.

On the western side of the chapel, and at its rear, was an orchard extending southward to Wellington Street, beyond which trees and shrubs stretched down to the water's edge across the road leading to the Garrison. The chapel continued to be used as a place of worship for fifteen years. In 1833 it was converted for a time into the Theatre Royal. As Ophelia said:

"We know what we are but we know not what we may be."

The next Methodist chapel to enter Toronto was built by the Primitive Methodists in 1832. This was a substantial and respectable building of red brick, and would hold comfortably about six hundred people.

Early in the year 1829, Mr. William Lawson, a Primitive Methodist local preacher, settled in the old town of York, and preached with great regularity in the market square. He then formed a society, and wrote to the Primitive Methodist Conference in England for a missionary. One was sent out who arrived in 1830, and took the society thus formed into the connection of the said Conference.

The church was a popular meeting place in the early days,

and was known among the young people as the "match factory," from the fact that a great many young men and women who attended the church afterwards entered into the holy bonds of matrimony. In 1850 the church was torn down.

A year earlier than the Methodists, in 1831, the Presbyterians of York had organized what was afterwards famed as "Old St. Andrews".

The Hon. William Morris, of Perth, was a member of the Legislative Assembly of 1830, and connected with the Church of Scotland. One Sunday morning while on his way to the Episcopal church he passed the ruins of the former Parliament House, and the sight suggested to him the possibility of securing the ruined building and converting it into a place of worship in connection with his favourite denomination. Perhaps the contemplation of these ruins detained him; at all events he was late at church, and just as he entered, the Episcopalian clerk was reading the 132nd Psalm: —

"I will not go into my house, nor to my bed ascend;
 No soft repose shall close my eyes, nor sleep my eyelids bend,
 Till for the Lord's design'd abode I mark the destin'd
                                         ground,
 Till I a decent place of rest for Jacob's God have found."

The coincidence so impressed him that the impression became an inspiration; the next day he called a meeting of his associates who were of like faith, an organization was formed, subscriptions received, and the list bears the names of some of the most prominent men of that time, among them the men of the 71st and 79th Highland regiments then stationed at York.

Thus the accidental reading of those particular lines on that particular Sunday morning just as a certain man who happened to be late was entering an Episcopalian church, originated the Presbyterian church in Toronto.

The first Anglican church was built in 1803, on the site where St. James' now stands. It was a little wooden structure, just a meeting-house, with dark pine woods on three sides, a cleared space in front, except for the stumps, and beyond that the mud of King street. In the year 1797 President Peter Russell had granted one lot, six acres in extent, bounded by New (now Jarvis), King, Church (which did not then exist) and Adelaide Streets, to be set apart as a church plot. The south-east corner of this plot was marked "for the parson". On the 8th of January, 1803, "a meeting of subscribers to a fund for erecting a church in the town of York was holden at the Government Buildings with the Hon. Chief Justice Elmsley in the chair." At first the idea was to build with stone, and the committee advertised for "boards and scantling, stones and lime". But a consideration of the estimated cost and of the money in hand led to revision; and the primitive church was built of pine; the soldiers of the garrison, by order of Colonel Sheaffe, raising the frame. The Reverend Doctor George O'Kill Stuart was the first incumbent and the first service was held early in 1807. The pews were offered for sale in March of that year, and the cost for heating the building, with some other charges, was £1/7/6, Halifax currency.

It might be supposed that the garrison would frequent a church in whose erection soldiers had taken such a part; but the Fort was far from St. James's and a petition against unnecessary marching went to the Government. A grant of two acres of land was made to the Church of England; and there, on the corner of Stewart street at the back of Portland street, a church and a burying ground for soldiers came into being.

At the corner, protected by two posts, may yet be seen the stone, with a broad arrow engraved upon it, to show that that is Government land. This is the Church of St. John the Evangelist. It was the military church until 1870. The soldiers worshipped there, and now seats are assigned to the officers and soldiers of No. 2 Co., R.R.C.I. There are about 400 graves in Victoria Square, some of them the resting place of men very prominent in the early history of Canada. And so sacred are these graves in the memory of some that the descendants of these long-buried soldiers bring their children to St. John's church for baptism, and many a marriage is consecrated there because of the veneration felt for the dead heroes lying outside.

That church is now torn down, and another stands on the site; the descendants of its former congregations have moved away; fire, age, and changing environment have brought about the destruction of all the early wooden churches of the city. But the volume of *Landmarks* that records their decline and fall brings also sharply into focus something for which they stood, something of what they did. One church, opened for service the Sunday after Easter, 1882, faced a preliminary debt of $27,100.

Salaries and maintenance cost money, the people were few and poor; yet in October of 1890 the church and lot were free from debt. The congregation has not exceeded 500 regular attendants at any time. It has never had but one member (and that only for a short time) who has not had to earn an income. It has never had more than five members at any time who have not had to practice economy to live, and yet these results have been attained. Shall we not thank God for His grace given, and take courage?

Continually one reads in the accounts of church work, the words, "The little building was soon found to be too small." Emphasis is always laid upon Free Pews and a welcome, and the following account of an Easter morning service in 1886 with an immense crowd "overflowing out into the porches" gives additional force to the recurrent picture of Christian observances making glad a civilized people: —

No distinction was observable on account of dress, as has been noticed by the reporter in certain other churches, but everyone was cordially welcomed to a seat until no more seats were available. Evidently the purposes of the originators of the free pew system have been well carried out here, because a congregation of various classes of people fills the church at every service, so that extra chairs are constantly in demand; in this respect the name of the church is well taken.

In this connection an incident occurred that, to those who saw it, was novel and interesting. Two little girls strayed up the centre aisle and found seats on the steps of the chancel, where they presented a picture that was very touching in its simplicity. They were evidently sisters, and of very affectionate natures, clinging to one another during the entire service; they were commonly dressed and wore old winter skull-caps, but they had refined features, beautiful blue eyes and sweet faces. During prayer they buried their faces in their hands, and during singing the elder stood. with her arm about the shoulders of her little sister, while the contrast of their humble appearance with the beauty of the decorations and the rich dresses of other children near them made them more conspicuous . . . The naïveté of childhood was well illustrated when the elder sister, not knowing what to do with a book she held in her hand, deliberately went up to Mr. Baldwin and told him all about it. Fortunately at that moment the choir was singing, so he very kindly leaned down to her, listened to what she had to say, smiled pleasantly into her face and told her what to do. Many a minister would have had his clerical dignity terribly shocked by this unusual break upon the solemnity of a service, but Mr. Baldwin had the grace and coolness to grasp the situation at once and dispose of it at once. The little sisters were very devout, and when they leaned their faces together and held their hands clasped, the old caps and plain dresses and well-worn winter coats were entirely forgotten in the sweetness of the picture they unconsciously made. When the officers passed by with the silver plates ladened with Easter offerings these two little children stood up and each dropped a penny upon the plate — than which no gift was more acceptable to the Giver of every gift.

Two more accounts (one for re-inforcement of what is written above, and one — it may be — for anti-climax) will serve to end this chapter.

We are again in 1886 and are going with the reporter to hear a popular preacher, Dr. Joseph Wild, of the Bond Street Congregational church.

As a preacher he occupies a position not only in the city, but throughout Canada, that is unique. His reputation as an original thinker, a fearless and outspoken advocate of his thought, and an eloquent preacher, has probably become more extended than that of any other preacher in the dominion. It may safely be said that no other preacher than he could for six years attract the audiences that have crowded to hear him.

The average attendance at his morning service is 1,200. Frequently as many as 500 people are turned away, being unable to obtain admission. In order to secure their seats the members and pew-holders are admitted at a side entrance by card, the front doors being closed until within five minutes of the hour for services; in the meantime the crowd increases about the side-walks until sometimes it extends half-way across the street; an officer is always on hand to keep a passage-way open, and he does it with no little difficulty. When the doors are open there is a wild, mad rush for entrance; men, women and children scramble and hurry and stumble, and are carried along by the tremendous pressure from behind until not even standing room is available, and hundreds are disappointedly turned away. On a Sunday evening when the subject was "Britain and the Coming War," the pressure was so great that the doorkeepers at the side entrance on Wilton avenue were actually borne down and obliged to admit the surging mass of people, leaving many pew-owners on the street, and even then about 800 people were outside when the service began. At one time when Dr. Wild was delivering a series of sermons in reply to Archbishop Lynch on "The True Church," the pressure for admittance became simply intolerable and he was compelled to discontinue preaching on that subject in order to keep people away. Comparatively little room is left after the pew-owners are seated, because all sittings in the body of the church and about one-half of those in the gallery are rented. The auditorium seats 1,575 with draw seats, chairs and camp stools for 600 more and standing room for 200. Every available foot of space is utilized, so that even the few steps leading to the pulpit and choir platform are sometimes occupied, while the chancel dais affords a convenient resort for some who are content to face the immense audience while listening to the speaker behind them.

By courtesy of the officials a reporter was admitted at the side entrance on a Sunday evening in the early spring of 1886, and politely shown to a front seat in the gallery. Within their little room these officers were overwhelmed with applications for sittings, while the door keeper was energetically and rapidly inspecting the cards of admission as the stream of people wended their way into the beautiful room, until it seemed full even before the main doors were opened, and then what a rush! There was first a low, far-away murmur, growing louder and clearer as the crowd found its way up the staircase until the inner doors were reached and an entrance more rapid than decorous was made, followed by a genuine scramble for seats, some in their excitement and haste actually stepping over the tops of the back pews. And the women were just as bad as the men; with a sort of a wild-eyed go-aheadativeness that forbade all interference, with hats and wraps awry, with an air of nervous excitement long suppressed, and fostered by the tiresome wait on the sidewalk, a few, at least, of the sex called "gentler" showed themselves capable of a most courageous onset where the ultimate goal was a seat. Below, the incoming flood was steadier but equally full of business; down the eight aisles it poured until every pew was full, every draw seat occupied. Then chairs and camp stools were made to do duty until at a fair estimate 2,300 people waited for the coming of the minister.

Are we better or worse that such scenes no longer take place at a Sunday evening service in Toronto? The sermon was on the speaker's pet theme of British Israel and included the prophecy that in fifty years Palestine would be prosperous and international. "The Jews will go there as a whole people; in a few years (from 1886) they will be subject to a severe persecution and then be glad to find a home of rest and citizenship in the home of their forefathers." Applause and laughter punctuated the address, which was treated rather as a lecture than as a sermon. The absence of reverence was marked; and this matter of reverence is the subject of the last account; a visit to "a small, rough-coated frame building, topped by an old-fashioned little belfry with green blinds." The church only seated two hundred people, and one gathers that fewer were there.

In visiting churches of every variety of belief, while gathering material for this series, the writer has been treated with uniform courtesy. But in no church was he shown such friendliness and heartiness of greeting as in this little frame church. And it was a very reverent and attentive congregation; not a single whisper, even, disturbed the solemnity of the service; there are grander and wealthier and more popular churches in this city, but none to exceed this humble little society in reverential decorum.

Five pages are given to the tenets of the sect, that of the Swedenborgians. Dr. Joseph Wild had little more and it is not difficult to tell which creed the writer of these chapters prefers.

V. REBELLION, 1837

Perhaps there is no single incident in its history that has meant so much to the City of Toronto as Mackenzie's Rebellion. He had represented her in honour as her first Mayor; he had been cast out in dishonour. He had returned from exile and won his place again in the Legislature; and there were many who felt that he should never have been expelled. The feeling, for and against, still persists. A lady invited to be present when the Mackenzie Homestead on Bond Street was dedicated to the public in 1951, refused to attend "the opening of your Rebel House". Her great-grandfather, in 1837, was a member of the Family Compact. "Reason good enough!" And, on the other side of the fence, many a man, in the same house, during the last two years, has offered reverence to the little Scot as a saint and a martyr; even though in certain cases they confused him with his grandson. But that is another proof of the way in which the action lives, compared to much later events. The Riel Rebellion of 1885 is Canadian history and belongs to the past; Mackenzie's Rebellion in 1837 is Toronto's property, and a part of the present.

In the life of a community that is old enough to stand on its feet and to think of itself as corporate, any event that threatens to sever family ties cuts deep. Any event, among a people predominantly loyal, that can justify a charge of disloyalty, leaves a scar like a burn. But many a man, after John Montgomery's Tavern was ashes, considered what Mackenzie did in the light of what needed doing, and murmured to himself " 'Twas the right thing, done in the wrong way."

The *Landmarks of Toronto* gives both sides, and, on the whole, the treatment of the rebels is sympathetic and the

judgment on their action gentle. It is pleasant to rescue from
near-oblivion the action of the crew of No. 3 Engine, Toronto
Fire Brigade; no less pleasant to record the refusal of "a
staunch Loyalist" to join in the search for Lount — and to
note that some men would have nothing to do with erecting
his instrument of death, the gallows.

The extracts we print are as follows:

(1) How Dick Frizzell alarmed the City
(2) How Thomas Anderson joined the rebels
(3) The British American Fire Brigade goes into action
(4) The fight at Poplar Plains
(5) The York Street home of William Lyon Mackenzie
(6) Lount and Matthews
(7) The return from exile.

(1) Sutton Richard Frizzell, the subject of this sketch, was
the eldest son of Mr. Sutton Frizzell, of Thornhill, who had
come to Toronto, then Little York, in the old 100th Regiment
during the autumn of 1808, or spring of 1809. It was with
the greatest difficulty that the Commandant could procure
supplies, and to relieve this Sutton Frizzell contracted to furnish
the garrison with beef. He retained this contract for two years
and a half, when orders were received that the 100th Regiment,
stationed at Little York, should be removed to Kingston, Jamaica.
Shortly after the notice of removal was received at York, Frizzell
left the army. About this time such injuries were sustained by
him in a fall from a horse as ultimately led to the partial loss
of his reason.

In May, 1812, it became certain that there would be war
with the United States. Some of the leading citizens of
Little York petitioned the Colonel of the 100th Regiment
stationed in the town to appoint a person competent to teach
men their drill to instruct those young men who were desirous
of obtaining commissions as officers of the Militia. Frizzell
was the man recommended, and his appointment was confirmed.
A military school was then started. Among others who learned
their exercise from him were John Macdonell, who fell with

Gen. Brock at Queenston, and the late Chief Justice Robinson. Later Frizzell disposed of his property in Toronto and took up his residence at Thornhill, ten miles out on Yonge street. Here his son, Sutton Richard, or Dick as he was familiarly called, attended school until 1833 when he entered the employ of a distiller and brewer named Morgan, afterwards well-known throughout America in connection with the anti-Masonic excitement. While in the distillery young Richard contracted a fondness for liquor, which brought him into rough company. He was a fearless youth, possessed of extraordinary physical strength. Political excitement in those days ran high. Meetings were not the most orderly and were being held in all parts of the district. Dick was an attendant at these meetings, ready at any time to fight for himself, his friends or for the British Government.

In the spring of 1837 some of those reformers who advocated armed resistance to the Government led many to believe that rebellion was meditated. The general opinion, however, was that no outbreak would take place as most persons thought that no preparations could be made for such a move. But Frizzell was of a different opinion. He believed that many on Mackenzie's side would rebel and that some of their leading spirits would risk their all, even their lives, to enforce what they believed to be their rights. By the time the autumn of 1837 had come round the excitement had become intense. Largely attended meetings were held by both parties at different places. A place of rendezvous was Finch's Hotel, ten miles from the city on Yonge street. Tories and Reformers had called a meeting, at this place, for October 18th. The day arrived and, as both meetings had been called for the same hour some change was necessary. Not desirous of a collision the Reformers adjourned to the house of David Gibson, the gentleman then representing West York in the Parliament of Upper Canada. That morning a Nova Scotian named Stephen Harvey had come down Yonge street from beyond Thornhill bearing a white flag, on which were inscribed in large black letters the words, "Liberty or Death." Arriving at Gibson's, Harvey planted the flag firmly in the ground, between the house and the street. Frizzell had agreed to be present at the meeting at Finch's, but two days before he had gone into Toronto, and it was not until noon of the 18th that he recollected his promise. He at once found a man that would take him to Finch's, and they immediately drove out Yonge street. They had to pass Gibson's. When they approached the place the flag was seen floating in the wind. The horses were stopped and Frizzell, turning to his friend, who was a loyalist from Richmond Hill, said: "I am going to take that flag, and if the crowd should catch me I have a job on hand." With this he started for it. Harvey knew Frizzell, and seeing his object, also made for the flag. Before it was entirely clear of the ground Harvey seized the lower end of the staff and, being a heavier man but less active, a fierce struggle ensued. He shouted for assistance which promptly came, but not before Dick Frizzell had escaped with the flag, leaving only the bare staff in the hands of his adversary. The two having made good their escape made in all haste for the hotel. They arrived just as the chairman, the late Col. Boyd (father of Chancellor Boyd), was bringing the meeting to a close. Frizzell and his friends were greatly elated over the capture of the first rebel flag, while Harvey and his friends were correspondingly depressed. The ensign was torn into shreds and fastened as decorations to the tails of horses. Even the chairman's horse was so decked. Political affairs continued to be exciting. In some places the rebels had purchased arms and begun to drill. On the 4th of December, Dick Frizzell was at his home, depressed mentally and physically, the results of a recent "outing". About 9 o'clock in the evening he arose and demanded his clothes, which he could not find, for his mother had hidden them away thinking thereby to keep her son within doors. This however had no effect, and after searching about for some time and finding an old pair of pants, old coat, old boots and a straw hat he went out into the dark and the cold. He remained away but a short time. He again demanded his clothing saying it was necessary for him to go to Toronto as a large body of armed men were going down Yonge street at that moment whom he positively knew were men bent on taking the city. Dick

asked his younger brother Nelson to accompany him but he
refused. The family thought from the apparently wild talk
that he was off his head. They could not believe that he had
seen any one, for there was not a soul moving on the street,
nor were any sounds to be heard. Finding that he could get
neither clothes nor his brother's consent to go with him, Frizzell
left the house. Nelson followed him afterwards, but seeing him go
north along the street instead of toward the city concluded that
he was on his way to the tavern. Frizzell, however, did not
go to the tavern, but to Thorne & Parson's store that he might
procure a horse. On going into the office and making known
to Mr. Thorne what was wanted, the latter enquired of Richard
Murphy, a young Irishman in his employ, if there was a horse
in the stable fit to go to Toronto. Murphy replied that there
was not, "nor," continued he, "will any horse leave this stable
this night." Dick said, "I suppose, Mr. Thorne, you can let
me have a horse without Murphy's consent. You know the
rebels have gone down street, armed, and intend to take the
city if they can." Mr. Thorne said he knew this, and said also
that he had only just found out that over half the men in his
employ were rebels and had threatened revenge if any active
measures were taken against them. "We have a great deal of
property exposed: I dare not let you have a horse." Though a
horse could not be got Frizzell was resolved to reach the city
if his life were spared. As he was leaving the store Mr. Thorne
whispered to him "Go for God's sake, but be cautious." Mr.
Thorne had taken Frizzell into his private office, when the later
talk took place. Murphy immediately followed him out and soon
overtook him on the road. Every means were used to provoke
a quarrel. Murphy said he could thrash Frizzell or any other
Tory on the street. Frizzell took all this coolly. He saw the idea
was to prevent his reaching Toronto. Finally he thrust his hand
in his pocket and said in a stern voice to Murphy, "The man
that stops me to-night will come out missing." This ended the
interview, and Murphy left him alone to pursue his way. He
had proceeded about a mile when the sound of an approaching
horse was heard. As it came closer the rider, who proved to

be Frizzell's neighbor, Duncan Weir, a resolute Scot, active and intelligent, with all a Scot's love of freedom, drew his horse up to a walk. He was armed with a sword and a pair of pistols. Suddenly Weir stopped, saying at the same time, "I don't know but that I had better arrest you." The retort he received was short and pointed. "I know damn well you won't."

It was sufficient. Weir rode at first slowly, but he soon urged his horse into a gallop and disappeared in the darkness. Dick walked rapidly, occasionally overtaking small squads of rebels with whom he had some conversation. Once he stopped at the house of a Loyalist for the purpose of having some parties living a distance east of Yonge street notified of the movements of the rebels. The person whom Dick called upon was Alexander Montgomery, and the persons he wished notified were David and William Yeomans of Scarborough and two other persons in that vicinity. As he came near to Eglinton a number of men were seen in the street opposite Montgomery's hotel. He thought that his friend Weir had not made him his prisoner in the road intending to do so when he came down the street; so to avoid any more detention and all chance of arrest Dick entered the field to the west and then struck south till he came to the flats or what was generally called then "No. 1." Thence he returned again to the street and entered the city without further molestation. He went directly to the City Hall. A policeman was stationed at the door and forbade admittance. The officer told him the Governor was within and he was given orders to admit no one without permission. "Tell them," he said to the officer, "the rebels are coming down Yonge street; and that there is a person at the door who can give them information which it is necessary they should possess." This being announced, admission was at once granted. Though Mr. George Munro, an alderman of the city who was present, and Richard Frizzell had spent their younger days together, so many changes during their ten or twelve years' separation had caused Mr. Munro to forget Richard. "You come from Yonge Street? This is the Governor Sir Francis Head. You will state what information you have to impart to him," was his introduction to the Governor.

A short conversation took place between the Governor, the Mayor and Mr. Munro which evidently was concerning the identity of the informant. Both Mr. Munro and Chief Justice Robinson stated they had formerly known a person of his name, but could not certify that Richard was the same. After the information relative to the rebels had been given Frizzell prepared to leave. He said to Mr. Munro that he was going to Harley's Hotel. The alderman volunteered to go with him. The two went away and while at the hotel drank together. All the time, however, Mr. Munro seemed to be watching Frizzell so closely that Dick became angry and demanded an immediate explanation of his conduct. Mr. Munro explained. He said, "the fact of the matter is the Governor has made up his mind that you have come with a statement that is not true, for the purpose of alarming the Loyalists. He suspects you have been sent by the rebels or by some persons who are aware that the Governor and Council and members of the corporation are assembled in the hall to provide some plan of defence should the rebels here who are in sympathy with the insurgents in Lower Canada attack the city." Dick was astonished beyond expression. He could not speak. Mr. Munro continued. "Frizzell, if you have been doing any such thing as the Governor suspects you will be in a bad box. Alderman Powell has ridden up the street to see if what you say be true or not." Dick wished to return immediately to the hall, and on the way he told Mr. Munro that "if Sir Francis Head had his own way the rebels will have the city without fighting." Shortly after they entered the City Hall Mr. Powell entered also. He reported that he had been met near Gallows Hill by Mackenzie and another person and was placed under arrest by them. Mackenzie and Powell had ridden side by side for a long way following a stranger who was rather above the average in point of size and was thoroughly armed. Powell drew a pistol and fired at him whereupon Mackenzie rode away, making his escape in safety although he too was shot at.

Every man was alarmed at the sudden turn affairs had taken. Sir Francis Head to whom all looked for advice bowed

his head in his hands leaning his arms upon the table at
which he sat. Christopher A. Hagerman, the Attorney General
who was present, was asked what was to be done as evidently
some action must be taken at once. The proper person, he said,
for directing such action was present and something must be
done. The Governor's reply was: "We can do nothing. Why,
what can we do? There is not a soldier in Upper Canada. I
wrote Sir John Colborne to take every man there was here if
they were required, and they were taken to Lower Canada."
Excepting Hagerman, who from the first was resolute, there
did not appear to be a person present who was decided. So
when the Governor asked who there was to do the fighting, Mr.
Hagerman replied, "I, and there are others that will. We have
made no exertion to get any one, but before it shall be said
that we gave up the city without striking one blow I will take
a musket and go out alone and die like a man." He advised
men to be sworn in and properly equipped as there were plenty
of arms in the City Hall. A short form of oath was drawn up,
but it was not until Frizzell and some five or six others had
been sworn that the Chief Justice said to Mr. Hagerman
he did not think it necessary to swear those who came forward
voluntarily and offered their services. They should be given
arms. So no more were put under oath. The Chief Justice
began to question Dick. When he learned that this man's
father had been his military tutor in 1812, the Chief said that
now that his memory was refreshed he recollected the name very
well.

People continued to come and go to the City Hall throughout
the night. By 3 a.m. guards were stationed at different places
throughout the city. Dick Frizzell was a sentry on duty at the
south entrance of College Avenue until late in the morning of
the 5th. The citizens were so alarmed that work and business
were entirely suspended. Tuesday, the 5th, was an uneasy day
for both parties, for each was expecting to be reinforced by
their supporters. It was not until Wednesday that Sir Allan
McNab arrived by steamer from Hamilton, bringing about 60
men. Preparations were at once begun for an attack on Mac-

kenzie's position. Thursday morning Sir Allan moved up College Avenue with the main body of the loyal force. The second brigade marched up Yonge street, but it failed to reach Eglinton until after Sir Allan had attacked the rebels. When they were passing No. 1, firing was heard to the west. The men went up the hill to Montgomery's Hotel on the double quick. Dick Frizzell was among the very first to reach the top of the hill, where he saw two shots fired from behind some bushes and stumps on the west side of the highway. A horse came galloping from the fields in this direction. As it was passing the bushes a man rushed out and caught the horse and immediately mounted. Some of those around opened fire on the man, but as soon as Dick signalled to them that he knew him, it ceased. It was too late, however. Wideman (for that was the man's name) fell from his horse. While standing around the body the cry of fire was raised. Smoke was seen issuing from Montgomery's Hotel. Some were for letting it burn, others for putting it out, until Judge Jones came up. "Let it burn, boys," said he, and soon it was reduced to ashes. With a few others, Dick continued his way slowly up street until they reached the "Golden Lion" hotel, where they had dinner.

Evening was drawing on when a man came in and said a building was burning in the direction of Gibson's. Dick started out, but before Gibson's was reached the place was nearly consumed. Many of those around were well known to him, and he reproached them for destroying property in such a fashion. His intention was to go up Yonge street, but many of his friends insisted on his returning to the city, which he finally did. On the way down from Gibson's residence to Yonge street, the premises of Mr. Poole were found to be on fire. (Poole's house was the first house north of the Methodist Episcopal church at Willowdale). Dick Frizzell himself removed and extinguished the brands, which had not commenced to burn fiercely. This annoyed some of the spectators, and had it not been well-known that he was a staunch Loyalist no doubt he would have received harsh treatment. The night was spent in the city. Next morning all persons over whom the slightest suspicion rested were to be arrested. W. B. Jarvis, Sheriff of York, employed Frizzell who, thus authorized, made many arrests in the Township of Vaughan, Markham and York. The jail was soon filled. Many persons were incarcerated who wished to send for friends who would bail them out.

While this was being discussed by the authorities the sheriff noticed that Dick knew nearly every man whose name was mentioned. The fact was none of the old inhabitants were unknown to him. The sheriff asked if he knew Sam Lount. "Sam Lount? Yes, ever since I have been a boy." "Then you are just the man I want," said the sheriff. "I want a man to hunt him up." Dick emphatically refused to do this, saying by way of excuse that he had now more to do than he could possibly attend to in three weeks. Mr. Jarvis pointed out to him that Lount commanded the rebels; that they had those with them who could give evidence that it was by his order Col. Moodie was shot and that therefore he must be taken. Still Dick was persistent in his refusal to make the arrest. He had known Lount for a long time, and they had always been on the most friendly terms. Once they had fished, hunted, slept together, and partaken of one another's hospitality for days on the shores of Lake Simcoe. Although the sheriff was apparently dissatisfied, he did not press the matter further.

In the spring of 1838 Richard Frizzell joined and became a sergeant in the 3rd Battalion, which, when it was first organized, was under the command of Col. Kenneth Cameron, of Thorah, formerly a major in the 79th or Cameron Highlanders. Later he married and settled down, and in September 1876 he died in his 59th year.

The other side of the story is told by Thomas Anderson and Thomas Sheppard, rebels. First Mr. Anderson: —

(2) "My father was a Tory, but I was a pretty lively young man, and used to run with the Reformers who took up with Mackenzie as soon as he came to the city. My brother John and I sided with him and attended at the printing office when Dr.

Rolph and all the Reformers of the city met. Any one who wanted to see the country happy had to be a Reformer in those days. Why, you couldn't collect a cent of debt from any of the Family Compact crowd if they didn't want to pay you. You could sue and get judgment all right, but you had to pay your own costs, for no matter how good the man was, if he belonged to any of the Family Compact houses the judgment would come back from the sheriff's officer marked *nulla bona.* All along we expected to straighten things out at the polls until Sir Francis and his crowd swamped us at the election in the summer of 1837. Why, his men distributed tickets giving titles to farms on the lake shore road and the bush that no one ever knew were farms. There were no such farms, but with these tickets in their hands the hired men would go to the polls and swear that they got four dollars a year out of farms that they did not own nor no one else ever did own. But these ticket holders swore enough votes through to beat us Reformers who had property in the country, and after that we saw that there was nothing before us but a fight. We met oftener in Mackenzie's office. Lount, Matthews and other Reformers used to come in, and we were all arming for the rebellion. The rebels were to meet over my store on the Monday before the fight at Montgomery's, but there was a girl [1] hanged in front of the jail on Toronto street that day and there was such a crowd in town that the arrangement fell through. I knew that the rebels were out at Montgomery's for I think my brother John, who kept a dry goods store on Yonge street, went out to join on Monday night. But bright and early Tuesday morning I started. I left my wife, as she remembers, at our place and took my double-barrelled gun and walked along up Yonge street. Up near Jonathan Scott's corner, McGill street, I met Sheriff Jarvis coming down. "Good morning, Anderson," said the sheriff, looking closely at the gun I was carrying. "Good morning, sheriff," I answered; "it's a nice day!" I passed on. He did not try to arrest me, although he knew where I was going. I had a gun. He had no arms, and I would have fought, I think,

[1] Julia Murdoch. For actual date see p.172.

before I could have been kept from going out to join the rebels.
When I got out to Montgomery's two or three hundred rebels
were there. This was on Tuesday, and all that day the reformers
from the township were coming in. Some rode in, some marched
and a good many of the farmers were driven in by their young
sons, who took the waggons back again.

That night we marched down as far as McGill street and
then fell back when we could have chased Sheriff Jarvis'
men right into the city. Things would have been different
if we had had a leader. Poor Mackenzie meant well, and was
brave enough, but he was no soldier. If old Colonel Van
Egmond had been there that night all the English in Toronto —
and there were not many just then — could not have kept
the city from us. But he wasn't there, and we missed our
chance. After we got back to Montgomery's I was on guard
part of the night. Wednesday morning we marched down
to Bloor street, and after we got back Mackenzie and Lount
went off with eighty or a hundred men. They were away
stopping the Hamilton stage, and in the evening they brought the
mail bags which they took to the tavern, where Mackenzie
opened them. I was not very well acquainted with Lount or
Matthews. Lount was a member of parliament and they were
colonels while I was a young private. But they were both fine
men. Lount was an axemaker up near Holland Landing. An
axe was a big thing in the bush in those days, and if a man
had not money Lount used to make him an axe and trust him
for the pay. In that way he started many a poor fellow. He
made axes for the Indians up there, and some of them came
down to Toronto to see if they could not save him, but of course
it was all no use, poor fellows. After I left Montgomery's I saw
them no more in life or death until years later when David
Gibson and I dug up their bodies from the old Potter's field,
near Bloor street. When they were first buried it was ticklish
times for Reformers. David stepped quietly into the field and
dropped a marble in Lount's grave, so that it might be told
from Matthews'. William Lyon Mackenzie came up just as we
were lifting the bodies into the waggon, and the three of us rode

in the waggon to the Necropolis, where we buried these
murdered men, for I call it murder, in one grave.

A more detailed account is that of Thomas Sheppard:—
The Sheppards in the old days were known all over the country
as Reformers and my brother Mike and I busied ourselves
election time working for Mackenzie. M. thought we could
break the Family Compact by sending the right sort of men to
parliament, but the last election before the rebellion they
drowned us with crooked votes. After that Mackenzie used to tell
us we would have to shoulder muskets to get our rights. The
leaders met quite often in Toronto that summer after the election,
and in the early fall the word was passed for us to commence
drilling.

Mike and I then lived at the mill back of Lansing, up
Yonge street. We would take our muskets and join the other
Reformers who were drilled by an old soldier who worked
I think in Mackenzie's printing office. We drilled at Uncle
Jake Fisher's farm in Vaughan. Mackenzie used to ride out
from the city and watch the old soldier put the farmers through
their facings [as we should now say, through their paces]. All
the men from our neighbourhood carried muskets, but Mackenzie
had only a brace of pocket pistols. Altogether we must have
drilled at Uncle Jake's four or five times before we were called
out. I knew the day set for the muster at Montgomery's. The
Monday night before the fight I was sitting by the fire at
mother's getting ready to join the rebels on Tuesday when we
heard a knock at the door. My mother hurried across the
floor to open it and there stood Samuel Lount with fifty
Reformers from up Lloydtown way. They had marched thirty
miles down from the street and were tired and cold and
hungry. Poor mother couldn't do enough for them when she
saw who they were. They crowded around the fire, and after
getting all they could eat Lount ordered them to fall in and
away they marched down to Montgomery's. Next day I said
good-bye to my wife and the folks at home and went down
to join the boys. There were seven or eight hundred of them

at the tavern, I suppose; fine fellows, too, men who had
families and farms to fight for. Some farmers drove in from
up country, with their boys. They were brave enough, and
if they'd all had muskets they would have beaten the Tories
I believe. Lount and other blacksmiths who were reformers
made a lot of pikes, but these were no weapons for real fighting.

But that Tuesday night we made a start. Mackenzie ordered
us to march down Yonge street, and away we went. He led us.
I was in the front rank, along with Thomas Anderson and his
brother John. We stepped gently along until we were coming
out of the woods at Jonathan Scott's corners. All at once
some Tories who were in the brick house then with Sheriff
Jarvis, fired on us; don't know but they fired another volley
before they ran. They took the back track quick enough, and
if our fellows had only been steady we would have taken the
city that night. I don't know what started our men running,
but most of them made off up Yonge street as fast as the
other fellows did down to the town. For a while some of us
at the front stood our ground, and I was firing away among the
last of them. But after three or four minutes of this work,
I said to myself, "Here, a handful of us can't go down and
capture Toronto," so we took after the rebels who were making
for Montgomery's again. Next day Sir Francis sent out Baldwin
and Rolph with a flag of truce, but nothing came of it. Early
Thursday morning, the day of the fight at Montgomery's, Col.
Peter Matthews took a couple of hundred of the best shots and
started away to attack the Tories who were guarding the Don
bridge. John Anderson, my brother Mike and I were with
Matthews' men. It was while we were away that the Tories
came up to the farm. If we had been there with our muskets
things might have been different but when all the men who had
good weapons were away with Matthews the men under Lount
had no chance to stand against the muskets and cannon brought
against them. Matthews led us around the Don bridge, when
we came on the Tories. We fired a volley and they scattered
and didn't wait for more. Then he marched us four miles down
the Kingston road to a tavern, where we had supper at Her

Majesty's expense. The man gave us what we wanted and charged it to the Government, I suppose. By this time we had heard about the ending of the fight at Montgomery's and knew that all was over with the rebellion. I stayed guard at the tavern while the others were in at their supper and in an hour my turn came. Then I had a chance to speak to Matthews.

"Let's make for the Rouge," said I to him. "We can seize a stone-hooker there and get clear across the lake to the States." He didn't like the idea and lost his life by thinking we had a better chance to get off by straggling in couples than by making a break all together for the Rouge. We stayed in at the tavern that Thursday night, and Friday morning we said good-bye to each other and took the track through the wood. John Anderson, Mike and I kept together. That night we slept at the house of a friend east of Yonge street. Saturday noon we put into John Milne's house. We had driven there. It was at this house that poor Matthews was captured. He and some more rebels tried to dodge in at the back door. But a neighbour named Johnston spied them and sent his little girl over on an errand to see who was in the house. The girl went back and told that there were strangers at Milne's: Johnston, whose sons used to live in Yorkville, quickly raised a crowd of armed Tories, surrounded the house and fired in at the windows until Matthews gave himself up. Johnston took him down to Toronto and got his blood money. Sunday afternoon we were overtaken. We went into Silverthorne's, out near the Humber, for dinner. This Silverthorne was a Reformer, although the rest of his folks were Tories. While we were eating our dinner Mr. Silverthorne ran in from the door and told us that some men on horseback were coming up to the house. We started up from the table and footed it away through the woods. Just as we were nearing the river we heard a horseman behind us. It was a Tory neighbour of the Silverthorne's. He told us that we had not a ghost of a chance to get away, and that the governor would pardon us if we gave ourselves up. We took the chances and went off with him. He drove us into Toronto and we were lodged in the old parliament buildings.

We were members of Parliament until near Christmas, and
then they carted us off to the jail. We were put into a cell in
the south-west corner. Looking out from my window one day
I looked my last on poor Samuel Lount. They were bringing
him into the gaol that he never left until they led him out to
the gallows. He was strongly guarded, loaded down with
shackles, and looked a heart-broken man. We were never
brought to trial at all. They did better for John Anderson
and old John Montgomery. They gave them what they called a
trial and sentenced them both to the gallows. John Anderson
took his sentence quietly, but they say that old John Montgomery turned on the chief justice and the lawyers who were
against him and said: — "You think you can send me to the
gallows, but I tell you that when you're all frizzling with the
devil, I'll be keeping tavern on Yonge street." And sure enough
he came back and kept tavern at the old spot. We were all
kept in the jail on Toronto street until June the 8th, when
they packed us off to Kingston on the steamboat. John Montgomery and John Anderson were pardoned and they were in
the crowd that marched in chains down to the Yonge street
wharf. We thought it was Van Dieman's land sure. The
mothers and wives of the rebels crowded around to see the
last of us as they thought. I tell you it was a hard parting
with the old folks, who stood there on the wharf looking after
the steamer until we were out of sight. At Kingston we were
marched to Fort Henry, where we were supposed to stay until
Her Majesty was ready to give us a free passage to Van
Dieman's land.

There were with us John Anderson, John Montgomery, Wilson
Reed, of Sharon, Mr. Kennedy, Thomas Tracy, John Stewart,
Leonard Watson, John G. Parker of Hamilton, Mr. Stockdale,
Gilbert Morden, Mr. Brophy, Mr. Marr, my brother Mike
and I. We were not well settled before the colonel in charge
of the fort eyed us all over. "Now, prisoners," said he, "I'll
not allow you even to drive a nail in the wall or deface this
room in any way." I couldn't help thinking how well we minded
him when we dug our way out through the wall. We were not

long in prison before we commenced to think about getting out. One day we were talking of it, and Gilbert Morden asked who would try to loosen the stones. I will, I said, and with a little hard work managed to loosen a stone six inches square. We put it back in its place and told the bailiff that we wanted lime to sweeten the air of the cell. He brought in the lime, and we made the mortar that plastered up the crack so that he couldn't see it. Then we heard that Lord Durham was coming through, and we drew up a petition asking him to set us free. A few days before the 29th of July he walked through our cell and told us that he had forwarded our petition. That didn't satisfy us much, and when we heard that we were going to be shipped to Van Dieman's land pretty soon we thought we were not likely to get much good out of his Lordship's forwarding our petition.

We met that Sunday morning and decided to bolt. Some of us worked on all day trying to make the hole in the wall bigger. I was in that crowd, and the others tore Her Majesty's bedding into strips for rope ladders. At midnight we were all ready. Each man had a number and waited his turn to crawl through the hole in the wall. John G. Parker was the first to go. Then one after another we made our way to the yard. It was as bright as noonday outside. Parker looked up at the sky and whispered — "I wonder is it going to rain." "Not a drop," I answered and just at that moment a burst of thunder startled us. Five minutes after it was as dark as pitch and the rain was coming down in sheets. But for that we would never have passed the sentry who was on the wall. Old John Montgomery slipped into the pit in front of the cannons. Parker who was with him kept right on but John Anderson, Mike and I lifted him out. He couldn't walk, but was just able to limp along. John was a heavy weight, and we had an awful time in helping him to scramble over the wall. But at last we landed him on the other side and steered our way along to the woods. Then we waited for sunrise. When it was daylight the provisions we brought with us from the fort were divided. After breakfast we began to get ready to make our tracks, each man for himself. It was hard work for the poor rebels who had been together for so many weeks to say good-bye. Just as we were going one of the men spoke up for having a short prayer meeting, and down in the wet grass we all knelt while Parker, Watson, and Brophy prayed that the Lord would lead us safe across the St. Lawrence.

Then we said good-bye to each other and arranged to meet at Watertown. Poor John Montgomery cried like a child as we said good-bye to him. "It's all right boys," said he, "you'll get safe off, but I, with this lame leg, I'll never see the States; they'll catch me sure." But John was one of the first to get across. Every man but Parker and Watson dodged the Tories. We then wandered through the woods, travelling in the darkness and sleeping in the light for eight days. We had nothing to eat but a couple of pounds of salt pork and the beans and potatoes we could steal from the farmers all this time. One dark night we struck out from the woods near Brockville and borrowed a boat and rowed across the river. The people there used us grandly when they found that we were rebels. They boarded us free and drove us to Watertown, where we met all the boys from Fort Henry except Parker and Watson who were captured. Together we all went to Lewiston, where we had a good time. Mother and my wife crossed over to see us, and it was then I first saw my child, born while I was in prison. After the folks left for home most of us went westward. Mike and I chopped cordwood for three years until two good Tories, old Gen. Thorne and Joel Harrison took round a petition for the Sheppard boys and we were pardoned. Thomas Anderson escaped from Toronto a few days after the fight at Montgomery's farm, and made his way to Alabama, where he lived for a couple of years, when he returned.

It can be seen that the insurgents thought their chance of taking Toronto was good; but it is equally evident that, from the time when the first alarm was given, a number of men were enlisted in defence. Among these were the men of the Fire Brigade. Let us quote from their Minute-book: —

(3) On December 4th, 1837, the regular monthly meeting night, the company met at the usual hour. It was resolved that

THE BLOCK HOUSE, SHERBOURNE STREET, 1849

the name of George Nicholls be expunged for non-attendance. The following new members were proposed, and, rule 12 being suspended, were immediately initiated: Henry Stewart, proposed by John Dixon, seconded by James Ferguson, John Campbell, proposed by Thomas Mills, seconded by Robert Barnes.

On December 5th, 1837, about one a.m., the city was alarmed by the ringing of the fire bell; but on enquiry the alarm was found to proceed not from any fire, but from a report that a number of persons, said to be associated with Mackenzie (noted character for disaffection and opposition to Government), were in the vicinity and approaching the city, for the purpose of burning and pillaging it and overturning the Government. Some of the company believing and some disbelieving the report, some immediately repaired to the City Hall and took up arms, and some repaired to their respective homes. On the return of day, the report being fully confirmed, a number of the members volunteered into various militia for active duty, but the day passed without anything decisive being done, the rebels threatening to attack the city, and the citizens, who were loyal, preparing for their receiving a warm welcome. This day Dr. Holmes' house was burnt by the rebels, and one of their men shot by a reconnoitering party under W. B. Jarvis.

The entry of Wednesday, December 6, 1837, says: "This day Dr. Morrison was arrested, and the volunteers from the Gore and Niagara districts began to arrive."

Thursday, December 7, 1837. This morning the secretary addressed circulars to every member of the company to meet at the engine house at ten o'clock a.m. All not on active duty repaired to the spot, when it was moved by Alexander Hamilton, seconded by Joseph Wilson and resolved that the time is come when we feel it to be our duty to take arms as an independent volunteer company, to resist the attempt of traitors and rebels to invade our rights and disturb our peace, and that a deputation do immediately wait upon his Honour the Mayor to offer our services in any way he may think proper, and receive his orders.

It was moved by Richard Woodsworth, seconded by Joseph Wilson, and resolved that the captain, secretary and treasurer be the deputation to wait upon the Mayor. Accordingly the Mayor was waited on instantly, when he informed the deputation that he felt gratified and obliged by the voluntary offer of service by the British American Fire Company. He requested, as the safety and defence of the city was by his Excellency the Governor committed to him, that the British American Fire Company would not leave the city, but repair forthwith with their arms and engine, cistern, etc., to the market square and there await his further orders. The deputation returned to the engine house, delivered the orders of the Mayor to the company which were immediately complied with, and with the greatest alacrity by the company, with the exception of Robert Stewart and John Bugg to supply whose place and fill up deficiencies were proposed and elected John Phillips, proposed by Mr. Woodsworth seconded by John Adamson; George Simpson, Alexander Simpson, and others; Mr. Alexander Simpson being rather old requested leave to resign and substitute in his place his son Robert Simpson. His request was acceded to most cheerfully by the company. The company continued some time on the square exercising, when the report was brought that the rebels to the number of 700 or 800 were entering the city by the Don bridge, and our company ordered to be in readiness to give them a warm reception. Immediately after, the Mayor ordered the company out with the machine, as the rebels had commenced firing the city in the neighbourhood of the Don bridge.

With great spirit the members of the company started for the scene of action, most of them with muskets in their hands and the drag rope in the other, but ere their arrival at the building on fire the enemy had disappeared, not even waiting to see us, much less to fight, the heavy rumbling of the engine and cistern having frightened them into the belief that the cannon was on the track. On our arrival at the bridge our gallant captain ordered the engine into operation, but upon reconnoitering it was found the buildings were beyond salvation, with the exception of the toll house. The bridge we saved by pulling up some of the planks and pouring water from buckets upon the burning timbers. After the fire was extinguished the company again made its way to the station in the Market Square about 9 in the evening. The committee of the news room granted to us the use of it for a guard room for the night, where we took up our station, the engine being in the vestibule of the market under sentry of our own. An alarm was given in the evening, which was attended to by the company in their usual spirited style, but found to be only a chimney. At midnight the Mayor came in and informed us that he had just received intelligence that about sixty-one of the rebels were but a short distance below the Don bridge and that he wanted volunteers to go with him and attack and secure them. Immediately Thomas Storm, John Collins and Alexander Hamilton volunteered to follow wherever he would lead. To those he added fourteen more with himself and the high bailiff on horseback, and with these he proceeded down the Kingston road to the lower toll gate, or the fourth mile tree, when seeing or hearing nobody the Mayor ordered us to return, thanking us most handsomely for the firmness and resolution in following him so far from the city at midnight. About three o'clock we arrived at the guard room again and were welcomed by our comrades. After daylight, the rebels being dispersed and routed in all directions, the company took the machine again to the engine house, but as a precautionary measure, well aware that many incendiary traitors were still in the city, though as yet unknown, it was unanimously resolved that the members of this fire company consider it expedient, under existing circumstances, to hold themselves in active duty as volunteers or firemen night or day.

On the 8th it was moved by Joseph Dixon, seconded by Mr. Miller, and resolved that Robert Stewart and John Bugg be expelled from the company for refusing to take arms as military volunteers in times of imminent danger. During this, as well as the following night, the company kept up a guard of from twelve to twenty men, a party of which were constantly patrolling the streets to prevent fires and arrest suspicious persons. On Saturday, 9th December, 1837, the company was still on the alert, and the patrol still kept up, as also on Sunday, the 10th.

On Monday, January 1, 1838, the regular monthly meeting took place at the engine house. It was enquired into the cause of Henry Cowan's being confined in jail, and found to be on a charge of high treason; but upon his producing a certificate from R. S. Jamieson, Vice Chancellor of the province, and one of the commissioners appointed to enquire into the charges of treason, he was allowed to remain a member of the company. The company still continued to act as night watch and patrol in conjunction with a number of respectable citizens under Clark Gamble, Esq., the company taking the duty of two nights out of five.

(4) Mr. James S. Howard, once Postmaster, lived on the Poplar Plains in a house called Olive Grove. During the rebellion this house was the scene of the following incident: —

It was on Monday morning the 5th of December, 1837, when rumours of the disturbance that had broken out in Lower Canada were causing great excitement throughout the home district, that the late James S. Howard's servant, a man named Boulton, went into his master's room and asked if Mr. Howard had heard shots fired during the night. He replied that he had not, and told his man to go down to the street and find out what was the matter. Boulton returned shortly with the news that a man named Anderson had been shot at the foot of the hill, and his body was now lying in a house near by. Shortly afterwards came the startling report of the death of poor Colonel Moody, which was a great shock to Mrs. Howard who knew him well and was herself a native of Frederickton where the Colonel's regiment, the old Hundred and

Fourth, had been raised during the war of 1812. Mr. Howard immediately ordered his carriage and started for the city from whence he did not return for ten days. About nine o'clock a man named Pool, who had held the rank of captain in the rebel army, called at Mr. Howard's house and asked if Anderson's body was there. Being told where it was said to be he turned and went away. Immediately afterwards the first detachment of the rebel army came in sight, consisting of some fifteen or twenty men, who drew up on the lawn in front of the house. Presently at the word of command they wheeled around and went in search of the dead rebel. Next came three or four men, loyalists, hurrying down the road who said that there were five hundred rebels behind them. Then was heard the report of fire arms and anon more armed men showed themselves along the brow of Gallows Hill and took up ground near the present residence of Mr. Hooper.

About eleven o'clock another detachment appeared, headed by a man on a small white horse, almost a pony, who proved to be Commander-in-Chief Mackenzie himself. He wore a greatcoat buttoned up to the chin and presented the appearance of being stuffed. In talking among themselves they intimated that he had on a great many coats as if to make himself bullet proof. To enable the man on the white pony to enter the lawn, his men wrenched off the fence boards; he entered the house without knocking, took possession of the sitting room where Mrs. and Miss Howard and her brother were sitting, and ordered dinner to be got ready for fifty men. Utterly astonished at such a demand Mrs. Howard said she could do nothing of the kind. After abusing Mr. Howard for some time, who had incurred his dislike by refusing him special privileges at the post office, Mackenzie said Howard had held his office long enough, and that it was time somebody else had it. Mrs. Howard at length referred him to the servant in the kitchen, which hint he took and went to see about dinner himself. There happened to be a large iron sugar kettle in which was boiling a sheep killed by dogs shortly before. This they emptied and refilled with beef from a barrel in the cellar. A baking of bread just made was also confiscated and cut up by a tall thin man named Eckhart from Markham. While these preparations were going on other men were busy in the tool house mending their arms which consisted of all sorts of weapons from chisels and gouges fixed on poles, to hatchets, knives, and guns of all descriptions.

About two o'clock there was a regular stampede and the family was left quite alone, much to their relief, with the exception of a young Highland Scotchman mounting guard. He must have been a recent arrival from the old country, as he wore the blue jacket and trousers of the seafaring men of the western islands. Mrs. Howard seeing that all the rest had left, went out to speak to him saying that she regretted to see so fine a young Scotchman rebel against his Queen. His answer was, "Country first, Queen next." He told her it was the flag of truce which had called his comrades away. About half past three they all returned headed by the Commander-in-Chief, who demanded of Mrs. Howard whether the dinner he had ordered was ready. She said it was just as he had left it. Irritated at her coolness he got very angry, shook his horse whip, pulled her from her chair to the window, bidding her look out and be thankful that her own house was not in the same state. He pointed to Dr. Horne's house at Blue Hill on the east side of the road, which during his [i.e., Dr. Horne's] absence he had set on fire, much to the disappointment of his men, whom though very hungry he would not allow to touch anything but burnt it all up. There was considerable grumbling among the men about it. Poor Lount, who was with them, told Mrs. Howard not to mind Mackenzie, but to give them all they wanted and they would not harm her. They got through their dinner about dusk and returned to the lawn where they had some barrels of whisky. They kept up a regular or rather irregular firing all night. The family were much alarmed, having only one servant woman with them: the man Boulton had escaped for fear of being taken prisoner by the rebels. There the men remained until Wednesday, when they returned to Montgomery's tavern a mile or so up the road, where is now the village of Eglinton.

About eleven o'clock in the morning, the loyalist force marched out to attack the rebels who were posted at the Paul Pry Inn on the east side of the road, with their main body at Montgomery's, some distance further north. It was a very fine sunny day, and the loyalists made a formidable appearance as the sun shone on their bright musket barrels and bayonets. The first shot fired was from the artillery under the command of Captain Craig; it went through the Paul Pry under the eaves and out through the roof. The rebels took to the woods on each side of the road, which at that time went much nearer than at present. Thomas Bell, who had charge of a company of [loyalist] volunteers, said that on the morning of the battle a stranger had asked leave to accompany him. The man wore a long beard and was rumoured to have been one of Napoleon's officers. Mr. Bell saw him take aim at one of the retreating rebels who was crouching behind a stump firing at the loyalists. Nothing could be seen but the top of his head. The stranger fired with fatal effect. The dead man turned out to be a farmer of the name of Wedman from Whitechurch. Montgomery's tavern, a large building on the hill side of the road, was next attacked and quickly evacuated by the flying rebels, who got into the woods and dispersed. It was then that Mackenzie made his escape. The tavern having been the rebel headquarters and the place from which Col. Moody was shot, was set on fire and burned down. The house of Gibson, another rebel rendez-vous about eight miles up the road, was also burned.

With that small effort the rebellion in Upper Canada was crushed. A few days after some fifty or sixty rebel prisoners from about Sharon and Lloydtown were marched down to the city roped together two and two in a long string, and shortly afterwards a volunteer corps commanded by Colonels Hill and Dewson, raised among the log cabin settlers in the county of Simcoe, came down in sleighs to the city where they did duty all winter. While retreating eastward a party of the rebels attempted to burn the Don bridge, and would have succeeded but for the determined efforts of a Mrs. Ross, who put out the fire at the expense of a bullet in her knee, which was extracted by Dr. Widmer.

The repeated narrative of the attack on the Tavern serves to draw attention to the well-known difficulty of establishing truth "out of the mouth of two or three witnesses". Both Dick Frizzell and Thomas Bell narrate the death of Wedman (or Wideman); but the one depicts him as shot from the saddle of a stray horse that he had just mounted, while the other says that he was crouching behind a stump with only the top of his head visible. Obviously both narrators cannot be right, yet both were eye witnesses. The "stranger with a long beard" is not mentioned by anyone other than Thomas Bell, but may have been a French Royalist (not "one of Napoleon's officers").

This freak rebellion forced many a man to define for himself his idea of loyalty. "Country first, Queen afterwards" said the Highlander; but hundreds who, like him, put Canada first, took the Loyalist side. Yet there was wide respect for Mackenzie's courage and consideration for his household.

(5) "That irrepressible patriot" lived at 184 York street, half way between Queen and Richmond; it was a modest two-storey, red brick house, built in 1830, with a large garden, full of fruit trees, stable, woodshed and "a well of the purest water to be found in Toronto." Here the plotters met and decided upon their outbreak; and here, after its failure, the distressed ladies and children of Mr. Mackenzie's family experienced wretched days and nights of doubt and misgiving, first trembling for the fate of husband, father and son; second, fearing for the safety of the important letters and documents pertaining to the rebellion that were in the house; thirdly, in a state of continual apprehension by reason of the oft-repeated visits of the authorities. As soon as the news of an actual outbreak reached the Government officials the York street house was put under the strictest surveillance. A guard was stationed at the door, and patrols

paced up and down before it. Every ten or fifteen minutes soldiers walk in and make the most thorough search from cellar to garret; they look under the beds, thrust their swords through them, peer and pry into every nook and cranny of the building, nor is this attention intermitted by night. Although the only inmates now are women and children, half a dozen civilians are domiciled in the dining room at evening to watch there until morning. Ostensibly they are sent for the protection of the occupants, who, however, decline to receive them in that guise and denounce them as spies. This is continued until Mrs. Mackenzie's grandmother, an old lady of 81 years, appeals to their manly instincts, asking if they are not ashamed to force themselves into the residence of defenceless women, and at this they go away. Some of these men still live in Toronto.

Mr. Mackenzie's papers hung in files from the ceiling in his bedroom at the south side of the house and in his office at the rear. Singularly enough, although the plumes of the officers at times touched them, they were never noticed, and the only ones seized were a few found hidden within the curtains of an old fashioned bed. Immunity from the frequent visits of the soldiery was allowed to the inmates for the first time during church service on the Sunday morning following the outbreak. Seizing the opportunity the ladies kindled fires in four wood box stoves and burned every letter and document in the house. Scraps of charred paper were sailing upward from the chimneys as the people came pouring out of their places of worship; soldiers returning to resume search saw them and rushed in, but they were too late; everything had been destroyed. It frequently happened that prisoners arrested after the rebellion was quelled were marched by the house, bound two by two with stout ropes, and they invariably lifted their hats as they passed. The family remained in the house about a fortnight after the events narrated, Mrs. Mackenzie joining her husband, December 29th, at Navy Island. After the rebellion it was taken by the government.

The age of Mackenzie's mother, (she was *not* his mother-in-law) variously given in Volume I of the *Landmarks* as 81 (p. 7) and 88 (p. 197), is only possible of belief if we scrap the Patriot's story of Culloden, and of a Highlander following his chief into exile. "Facts are chiels that winna' ding", says the proverb, and to pack a long exile, a return to Scotland, acquisition of a farm, marriage and the propagation of ten children, into little more than three years, would strain even a Highland gullet. Yet if Mistress Mackenzie, who certainly died in 1839, is to be confirmed in the advertised age of 90, she must have been born in 1749. And Culloden was fought in April '46. The way out is pointed by a significant fact. The Clan Mackenzie was not "out" in "the 45"; but it *was* out in the Rising of 1715. Exile, return and even ten children then become possible.

At the moment our return must be to '37, where the sad business of stamping out rebellion is "in swing". The story of Lount and Matthews must be told in the words of a man who was confined with them in the heavy jail on the north-east corner of King and Toronto streets.

(6) The hours of April 12, 1838, were the saddest we ever spent. None of us could sleep and we were all early astir. It was a fine spring morning. Looking through the window of our room we saw the scaffold. It was built by the late Mr. Storm. His foreman was Matthew Sheard, then a fine young Yorkshireman, afterward mayor of the city. He was expected to share in the work of building the scaffold. "I'll not put a hand to it," he said; "Lount and Matthews have done nothing that I might not have done myself, and I'll never help to build a gallows to hang them." So, without the foreman's assistance, the gallows was erected near the spot where the police court building now stands. Around the gallows the Orange militia stood in large numbers with their muskets. The authorities dreaded a rescue. While we were watching and talking we heard steps on the stairs, and then the clank of chains. It was poor Lount coming up, guarded by his jailers,

to say good-bye to us. He stopped at the door. We could not see him, but there were sad hearts in that room as we heard Samuel Lount's voice, without a quiver in it, give us his last greeting: "Be of good courage, boys. I am not ashamed of anything I've done. I trust in God, and I'm going to die like a man." We answered him as well as we could, and sorrowfully listened until the sound of his sturdy tramp and clanking chains died away. I don't know why Peter Matthews did not come up with Lount, but I saw him as they were led through the jail yard to the scaffold where two nooses were swinging. They never faltered. I saw them walk up the steps to the floor of the scaffold as firmly as if they were on the pavement. Again I saw them kneeling while Bishop Richardson, who attended Lount, and another clergyman who attended Matthews, prayed. Deputy Sheriff Robert Beard officiated. Lount and Matthews shook hands with the clergymen, and when we looked again their bodies were dangling in the air. Matthews struggled hard but Lount died instantly. When the bodies had been exposed for a short time they were cut down and quietly buried in the Potter's Field.

A pendant of another kind, and dated twelve years after the Rebellion may complete this story of trial and error.

(7) For nearly thirty years William Lyon Mackenzie had been fighting for a principle, experiencing the bitterest poverty, enduring exile, suffering imprisonment, even sparring with death; losing all things but hope, faith in the right and belief in himself. Now after eleven years of outlawry in the United States complete amnesty having been granted to him — the last one to be pardoned — he returns to the city of which he was the first mayor and reaches Toronto in March, 1849. At this time there were four houses on the east side of Yonge street, between what is now Queen but was then Lot, and Shuter streets. The farthest north was a roughcast building and south in order were one frame and two red brick dwellings. They were owned by four members of the McIntosh family, named respectively

Charles, James, Robert and John. These buildings have since been remodelled into stores. John McIntosh's house was of red brick and stood a short distance from the north-east corner of Queen and Yonge streets. Good's foundry extended in the rear of it back to Victoria street, and between it and Mr. McIntosh's property there was a gateway. A portion of Mr. McIntosh's house was occupied at the time by the Rev. Alexander Stewart, the father of Mr. McIntosh's first wife. In the red brick house next north to it Robert McIntosh's family lived until they left Canada. An orchard extended back of it to Victoria street. The houses were probably built about 1822. The land on which they stood was the first ground sold north of Queen street for building lots. Charles McIntosh, who lived in the northernmost house, was the captain of the Cobourg, one of the first steamers on the lake. John McIntosh once represented North York in the Provincial parliament. He was the father-in-law of William Lyon Mackenzie, and it was in his house that the exiled patriot came to visit on his return to Toronto in the early spring of 1849, and his reception was a riot. Rumour had flown around during the afternoon of Thursday, March 22, that there would be trouble in the evening. Mackenzie was in town. With the coming of night, dirty, ragged, intoxicated men and boys began to assemble until several hundreds were gathered. They carried torches and in their midst were borne aloft effigies of Mackenzie, Attorney-General West and Solicitor-General West. Suddenly the mob sent up a shout of "fire" and rushed to a point on Yonge street not far from the McIntosh house. The alarm was false, but it served the intended purpose and swelled the ranks of the rioters.

Then the crowd with all the confused babel of a mob starts down Yonge street. Turning eastward on King street it marches past the old market building, wheels to the right, passes by the doors of the police station, and directing its course along Front street, stops at the residences of the Attorney and Solicitor-Generals West, where it burns the effigies of these officials before their windows. Preserving up to this time as much restraint as could possibly be expected from a mob, that is, no destruction of life, limb or property, cries of "Death to Mackenzie!"; "To McIntosh's!" break the charm. With flaming barrels of tar luridly lighting the darkness this wild wave of humanity surges up from the foot of Yonge street. Peaceful citizens run to their homes, bolt doors and bar windows. Pushing, squeezing for place—there are at least two thousand in the mad mob; they choke Yonge street—splashing and stumbling through mud ankle deep, with ribald songs, a frightful chorus of curses, the most dreadful shouts and imprecations, flaring torches, shrill yells, hideous grimaces, sharp report of fire-arms and above all strident cries for Mackenzie's life, they press forward. Poor Mackenzie! What a welcome to get after all these years in the city that as mayor he first governed; but he must have become pretty well used to almost everything by this time.

By midnight the whole crowd had assembled before John McIntosh's house. Yonge street was full. The tar barrel was set on end in the middle of the roadway and two more barrels were placed by it. The discharge of fire-arms became general: cries of "Colonel Moodie," were fiercely ejaculated mingled with demands for Mackenzie's surrender. Then an attack was made on the house, bricks, stones and sticks were hurled at it; every pane of glass in the windows was broken; stones weighing six or seven pounds were sent crashing through, carrying glass and sash along. Whispers passed among the leaders that if Mackenzie could be got at he would quickly be disposed of. The four policemen at hand were impotent. They arrest a law student but the rioters knock the constables down and rescue their comrade. In the front ranks of the crowd were several aldermen. Hervey Price, barrister, son of the Commissioner of Crown Lands, was attacked, severely cut about the head, and would have been killed but for the interference of one of the policemen. The fury of the mob increasing the constables stationed themselves at the door and prevented it from breaking in. While the utmost lawlessness prevailed at the front of the house some of the rioters made their way to the rear through the gate and made a similar attack in that quarter with every kind of missiles at hand. Great stones were hurled through the windows of Mr. Montgomery's house nearly opposite. At 4 o'clock in the morning the mob left the McIntosh house and went to the residence of Mr. Brown of the Globe, where windows and blinds were smashed.

Friday night another crowd gathered at Mr. Mackenzie's stopping place, but two hundred special constables were on hand reinforced by many private citizens in an attitude of defence, and 60 soldiers who had been brought down from the barracks. Nothing was done beyond noisy demonstrations. Saturday night another rabble gathered, but learning that the McIntosh house would be protected by a strong force, no attempt was made to molest the inmates, the crowd contenting itself with breaking gas-lamps and windows on Bay and Bond streets and in sections of the city where there were no constables. After this no further display of violence was made against Mr. Mackenzie, and in 1850 he brought his family from New York to Toronto and took up his residence here, where he continued to live until his death, Aug. 28, 1861.[2]

[2] There probably is no need to infer from the above account that "hidden forces" and deep political scheming were responsible for Mackenzie's "Welcome Home". Any tavern could have held the pebble of malice round which the snowball of brutality clogged; a published intention to give "the little Rebel" some rough music would be sufficient for the men of the underworld, always in a condition of "mob". And, probably also, the people who started the ball rolling and who profited during the riot, were those who were looking carefully toward a transfer of personal property. Political conditions had altered: Mackenzie was a spent force, or, if not, he could be muzzled. There was no need for intolerance where tolerance could be more deadly effective.

VI. FOUR PROFILES

In a single volume sample such as this it is impossible to note the many references, to men, women and affairs that were important a hundred years since, printed in the four thousand pages of the original *Landmarks*. Yet so much of the fascination of the work resides in just these portraits that a few are here presented. The names of Mr. J. G. Howard, architect and benefactor, and Mrs. Anna Jameson, writer and artist, are well known. Not so familiar are those of Quetton St. George and Joseph Bloor, two worthy citizens from France and England. First, Mr. Howard. He claimed as direct ancestors the Lords of Naworth Castle in the County of Cumberland, northern England. Born in July, 1803, he learned land surveying, engineering and architecture, which last profession he practised in London.

On the 7th of May, 1827, Mr. Howard married Miss Jemima Frances Meikle, a young lady in her twenty-fifth year. Though the couple were not blessed by offspring their marriage turned out a singularly happy one. The union endured for more than half a century when it was severed by the death of Mrs. Howard.

In 1831, owing to the distress of the times, he began to consider emigration, and being impressed by the glowing accounts of an agent of the Canada Company, he resolved to enter this country.

He missed the vessel in which his passage had been engaged, but on the 26th of June, accompanied by his wife, he sailed from London for Gravesend in a steamer belonging to Captain Wallis. After getting the luggage on board the ship Emperor

Alexander, Captain Boig commander, which lay at anchor opposite Tilbury Fort, Mr. Howard and his wife went ashore, and on their return to the beach found that the ship had sailed away without them. Mr. Howard engaged a boat and some men, and after a hard chase the ship was caught. This was the first of a series of misfortunes which befell Mr. Howard on the trip. An account of these is condensed from a journal of the voyage.

A day or two later while Mr. Howard was shooting with his rifle the boom jibed and striking him would have carried him overboard had not the captain seized him by the legs as he was going over the rail. On the same evening he saw a large meteor fall into the sea about 300 yards ahead of the vessel. Two days afterward Mr. Howard and his wife went ashore at Ryde, Isle of Wight and were again left by the ship which they had great difficulty in overtaking with a sail boat. Notwithstanding these experiences Mr. Howard and a party went out shooting and fishing in the morning, a few days later, a hundred miles from land and lost the ship, and did not find it again until night. The next day another party went out in a small boat, and getting out of sight were not found until.eighteen hours afterward, having been drifting about on the ocean all night, unable to see the lights hung out at the masthead or the blaze of the tar barrels set on fire, or hear the booming of the cannon which were fired throughout the night for their guidance. Meanwhile a child had died and a child had been born on board the ship. Nothing else of an unusual character occurred until the ship was about a month out, when at five o'clock one morning all were awakened by a terrible thumping on the deck and cries of fire. A mutiny had arisen. The captain rushed upon deck in his shirt, ran to the fore chains, seized the ring leader, dragged him aft and rope-ended him. The mutineers rushed to the rescue of the man and knocked the captain down. They said they were Englishmen and would stick together, and swore they would shoot him, for they did not want him, as they could work the ship themselves. One was about to deal the prostrate captain a heavy blow when the mate seized him and the captain regained his feet. By vigorous measures the mutiny was quelled, and two hours later quiet was restored. Of this Mr. Howard says, "My wife and myself were both unwell. I kept my pistols and guns loaded by the bedside as we expected to hear the ruffians come down the cabin steps, for a set of greater black-guards never sailed out of England." That evening a storm arose and the four [sic] top-gallant and royal masts were carried away. On Mr. Howard's birthday a wreck was passed. Within the next few days the captain and a passenger fell overboard, but both were rescued. After arriving in the Gulf of St. Lawrence there was another exciting incident one night which Mr. Howard tells as follows in his journal:—"About 10 o'clock I heard an unusual noise upon deck, the captain at the highest pitch of his voice calling to the sailors to brace up the foreyard, and repeating the order at least a dozen times, as if his orders, from some cause or other, could not be attended to. Mr. Hill, the mate, who was with me in my first trip in the boat, came to my cabin and told me to get up and go upon deck, as there was no doubt but the ship would be lost, for the captain and the other mates were drunk, and the ship was driving fast upon the rocks. I dressed myself as quickly as possible and went upon deck. Judge of my feelings when the first object that met my view was the shore, with tremendous rocks running out into the sea, and the breakers dashing over them in a frightful manner. Horror was depicted on almost every countenance, women clasping their children in their arms and their husbands running about the deck like madmen. It was a beautiful moonlight night, and in turning my head I saw the carpenter sitting on the bulwarks with his axe ready to cut the anchor stop if it should be necessary. We had three good boats, but they would have been crowded and swamped, for there were one hundred and sixty-two persons on board, and a great many of them very bad characters." From this pre-dicament, however, the ship was saved by a change in the wind, which, blowing from the land, drove the vessel away from the rocks and into the open water. On Sunday evening, August 26th, the ship being off quarantine, opposite Gross Isle —

the cholera was raging at the time — a lamentable occurrence took place, which Mr. Howard thus relates: — "The
passengers of the Minerva anchored near us had performed
quarantine and were returning on board. When they came
alongside their vessel the ropes of the davits became entangled
with the masts of the boat and swamped her. From the deck
of our ship we could see upwards of twenty persons struggling
in the water, only nine of whom were saved. The agony we
felt at not being able to render assistance, all our boats being
on shore, was extreme. One of our boats returning from shore
went to their assistance and succeeded in picking up four who
were taken to the island. One of them, a fine young woman,
was in a state of suspended animation. She was quite black in
the face when taken from the water, but rubbing her body
with brandy restored her, and by the following morning she was
quite recovered. An old man and his wife were two of the
others who were saved by the crew of our boat. They were
completely soaked, and they wept bitterly for the loss of their
little boy, who found a grave in the ocean. The other was a
little fellow about four years old, brother to the young woman
already named, whose lively countenance beamed thankfulness
while carried about in the arms of the brave sailor who saved
him. The young woman was called upon to lament the loss
of a sister, who sank to rise no more." A child having died
just before reaching Quebec, a party from the ship, of which
Mr. Howard was one, went ashore with the body to bury it
and were directed to the cholera burial ground. Mr. Howard
says: "When there we were obliged to wait for several hours
for a priest. There were no fewer than seven or eight waggons
with rough deal coffins waiting in the hot sun for the same
priest. The coffins were nailed together of unseasoned inch
boards, the lids had shrunk in and warped so that you could
get your hand in, and the stench from them was dreadful. Still
we remained until the child was buried." On the 14th of
September, 1832, Mr. and Mrs. Howard arrived at York, having
been eleven weeks and three days from London. His first
experience in York is thus told by Mr. Howard: "Going up

Church street from the landing place, I was very much astonished to see in a huckster's window a very handsome carving knife and fork for sale, which I had made my brother-in-law a present of before he left England. Going into the shop, judge my surprise to find my wife's sister, whom I believed to be in Goderich. She looked half starved. She had lost one child and the other was in a wretched state." Mr. Howard had a letter of introduction which he presented the next spring to the Hon. Peter Robinson. A few days afterward some of his drawings were submitted to Sir John Colborne, who procured for him the appointment of drawing master at Upper Canada College at a salary of £100 per annum. This was the foundation of Mr. Howard's fortune. Several men immediately gave him orders for buildings, among whom were Dr. Widmer and James G. Chewett. Dr. Stuart, Lord Bishop of Quebec, calling to pay his respects to Mrs. Howard, found her busy washing in the kitchen. She took her hands out of the washtub, and the Bishop, shaking hands with her, remarked that her small hands had never been used to that kind of work, and if the ladies when they came to Canada would unbend as she had done and perform such work whenever it was necessary Canada would have a better name. The next year Mr. Howard was appointed the first city surveyor by William Lyon Mackenzie, the first Mayor of Toronto, and the same year he put down the first 11 foot plank sidewalks on King Street. From this time on for many years Mr. Howard was one of the leading men of Toronto. In 1836 he bought a piece of land containing 165 acres on the east bank of the Humber, to which he gave the name of High Park. On the western side of this the same year he built a residence which he named Colborne Lodge, in honour of Sir John Colborne, who had been his first benefactor and friend in York and had given him the post of drawing master in Upper Canada College which he filled for twenty-three years. On the 23rd of December 1837, Mr. Howard moved from Chewett's building on King street where he had lived to his new residence, Colborne Lodge, High Park. On the morning of the second day afterwards, Christmas, Mr.

COLBORNE LODGE, HIGH PARK

Howard shot a deer and some quail at the rear part of High Park. On Thursday, the 7th of December, before moving from King street, Mr. Howard led the right wing of the scouting party up Yonge street to attack the insurrectionists who had congregated at Montgomery's tavern.

Mr. Howard was a most generous benefactor to this city. He died in 1890 and was buried in High Park by the side of his wife.

It could probably be asserted that John Howard loved Canada. It seems equally certain that Anna Jameson hated it. Nonetheless, her book *Winter Studies and Summer Rambles* is a standard volume of Canadiana. Here follows a profile sketch.

At Dublin, Ireland, in 1794, there was born to Brownell Murphy, an Irish miniature painter, and his English wife, a girl who was destined to share the lot which so frequently falls to persons of talent — to be admired by all the world and yet to live a life of domestic unhappiness. The girl was christened Anna. During the years of her girlhood her parents, who were poor and often in difficulties, moved about from place to place in England. Anna grew up a singular child. When yet but a mere child, of her own accord she worked at modern languages, and even dabbled in Oriental literature, and to such purpose that at an early age she was an accomplished girl; but, as she herself confesses in her writings, with vague and confused ideas of morality and religion. As she grew older the circumstances of her parents improved, and she was not in such distress of mind over domestic difficulties as she had been in her earlier years. As a young lady she had, if not a beautiful, still a singularly attractive face. In 1820 she met Robert S. Jameson, a young barrister, of good family. The young couple were drawn toward each other at their first meeting, and very soon afterward were engaged. But their engagement was followed almost immediately by their estrangement. Anna secured a position as a governess and travelled about Europe, and it would have been well had they never met again. But two years later they were thrown together again by circumstances, the old attachment was renewed, and was followed by their marriage. The ceremony took place on a Wednesday, and the couple went at once to lodgings in London. On the Sunday following the bridegroom proposed that they go to call on a family who were friends of his, but whom his wife had never met. She objected, but he insisted, and at last declared that if she would not accompany him he would go alone. In the most unhappy frame of mind she put on her best gown and started out with him. They had gone but a short way when it began to rain, and her dress was bedraggled by the mud and wet. She pleaded that it was now impossible for her to go on, but he still insisted, and at length, getting into a passion, thrust the umbrella in her hand, and told her to go back to the house. She did so, while he continued his way, and to the inexpressible astonishment of his friends spent the greater part of the day with them and remained to dinner. Such was the beginning of the marital career of a talented young man and a gifted woman. From this time they were in continual strife, but they lived together for four years, at the end of which time Mr. Jameson obtained an appointment to a judgeship in the Island of Dominica; for which he sailed, leaving his wife to roam over the continent of Europe, where she was everywhere welcomed in the highest circles of art and literature. During her four years of married life she had made herself known to a large circle by her writings. At Weimar she became intimately acquainted with Goethe. Mr. Jameson's post in the West Indies proving unattractive, he returned to England in 1833, and soon afterward obtained the Speakership of the House of Upper Canada. He at once sailed for York, again leaving his wife behind. On his arrival here he at first lived in a house near Justice Hagerman's, at the corner of Wellington and Simcoe streets. Dr. Scadding says of him that "his conversational powers were admirable and no slight interest attached to the pleasant talk of one who, in his younger days, had been the familiar associate of Southey, Wordsworth and Samuel Taylor Coleridge." Hartley Coleridge addressed three sonnets to him, under the heading of "To a Friend."

"Mr. Jameson was a man of high culture and fine literary tastes. He was, moreover, an amateur artist of no ordinary skill. His countenance, especially in his old age, was of the Jeremy Bentham stamp." Not long after his arrival at York, Mr. Jameson was appointed Attorney-General of the Province. He then selected, enclosed and ornamentally planted a lot at the west corner of Front and Brock streets, and here he built a house. He then wrote for his wife to join him here. She, however, manifested a great disinclination to do so, and her letters, not only to him but to her friends, show conclusively that all her love for him was dead. Finally, he asserted his authority, and in obedience to his command as a husband she sailed for New York. Here again she was disappointed. There was no one to meet her, and she was compelled to make the journey alone. Even on her arrival at York[1] she complained that she was obliged to walk ankle-deep in mud. Mrs. Jameson arrived at York in 1836, and how she regarded it may be seen from her writing. She says: "It is a little, ill-built town, on low land, at the bottom of a frozen bay, with one very ugly church without tower or steeple, (St. James') some government offices, built of staring red brick, in the most tasteless vulgar style imaginable, (the parliament buildings) three feet of snow all around, and the grey, sullen, uninviting lake and the dark gloom of the pine forest bounding the prospect." She made her home in the house at the west of Brock street until the spring. Meanwhile her husband had been made Vice-Chancellor — the highest position to which he could attain, for the Chancellorship was vested in the crown. Mrs. Jameson, however, had grown indifferent to his successes. In the spring she started on a journey through western Canada, interviewing the eccentric Colonel Talbot in his retreat, shooting rapids in birchbark canoes, and living a half-wild life among the Indians. After two months of this life of adventure, she returned to her husband at York. In the Front street house she wrote letters abounding in merciless criticism of the people, manners and customs of the town. Here she

[1] Note: — So in the *Landmarks*; but York became Toronto again in 1834 [Ed.].

wrote her "Winter Studies and Summer Rambles" and the preface to her "Characteristics of Women". The first-named volume thus concludes: "At 3 o'clock in the morning, just as the moon was setting on Lake Ontario, I arrived at the door of my own house in Toronto, having been absent on this wild expedition just two months." For her daring in shooting the rapids at the Sault she had been formally named by the Otchipways of the locality Was-sa-je-wun-e-qua — Woman of the Bright Stream. Dr. Scadding records the following personal recollections of Mrs. Jameson, gathered during her stay here. He says: 'Mrs. Jameson was unattractive in person at first sight, although, as could scarcely fail to be the case in one so highly endowed, her features, separately considered, were fine and boldly marked. Intellectually she was an enchantress. Besides an originality and independence of judgment on most subjects, and a facility in generalizing and reducing thought to the form of a neat aphorism, she had a strong and capacious memory, richly furnished with choice things. Her conversation was consequently of the most fascinating kind. She sang, too, in sweet taste, with a quiet softness, without display. She sketched from nature with great elegance, and designed cleverly. The seven or eight illustrations which appear in the American editions of the "Characteristics" are etched by herself, and bear her autograph "Anna". The same is to be observed of the illustrations in the English edition of her "Common-place Book of Thought, Memories and Fancies," and in her larger volumes on various art subjects. She had super-eminently beautiful hands, which she always scrupulously guarded from contact with the outer air. Mrs. Jameson was a connoisseur in hands. Fifteen months after her arrival in York Mrs. Jameson bade her husband good-bye and left him. They never met again. She travelled for a time through the United States, and then returned to Europe, over which she travelled extensively. She was, for a long time, an intimate friend of Lady Byron, until by some act she provoked her ladyship's displeasure. The pension allowed her by her husband, with her literary earnings, enabled her to live at her ease. She died in 1860, and was buried in Kensal Green.'

From this talented but most literally eccentric Irish-woman, we turn for relief to a Frenchman. He was one of the first Royalists who, during the French Revolution, came over to England. Among them were numerous officers of the regular Army, all of whom had belonged to the lesser *noblesse*. Since they had suffered the loss of all their worldly goods the British Government offered them grants of land in the newly organized Province of Upper Canada. Among them was a Chevalier of the Order of St. Louis; his name Lawrence Quetton.

It was on St. George's day that he first trod on English territory, and to commemorate the fact he assumed the surname of St. George. He acquired a large tract of land north of York known as the Oak Ridges. He established numerous stations for trading with the Indians, one of which was at Orillia in 1802. For partner he had Gen. Ambrose de Farcy, who kept a store on the road between Niagara and Queenston, in the house of the Comte de Puisaye, a French officer who published a volume of memoirs. In 1805 Quetton St. George established himself in business at York, getting all his wares direct from New York. He prospered so well that in 1807 he built the house now known to all residents of Toronto as the Canada Company's building. For its construction he brought the first bricks ever seen in York from Oswego or Rochester. The street floor and part of the cellar were used by Mr. St. George for carrying on his general mercantile business. The rest of his house was occupied as a residence.

Quetton St. George's first location had been on Yonge St. In the map of 1798 a range of nine lots on either side of Yonge St. is marked "French Royalists, by order of His Honour" (i.e., the President, Peter Russell). These Oak Ridges, intractable land covered with gigantic trees, were beyond the cultural capacity of the majority of the refugees; and they returned to Europe. Quetton St. George, however, burned his boats by migrating to York and going into trade.

He did not ever cease to cultivate his land; and an estate in Whitchurch, one lot distant from Yonge St., was (in 1896) still in the actual occupation of his son — a practical farmer. This profile, however, is of the Chevalier; and the transcription of the several paragraphs devoted to him in the *Landmarks* will both interest and amuse the reader. Even before his descent on York he had seen the advantages of trade, having sent in 1801 a letter to Alexander Wood, a leading merchant of York, wishing to purchase goods. At least 24 yards of white flannel were required, or even the whole of the piece. "Je le prendrai avec plaisir, vu que les sauvages m'en demandent à tout moment". Also he ordered ten or twelve yards of sateen (the colour didn't much matter); and he told Mr. Wood that he could not be in York until November; the letter being written in August.

As soon as Quetton St. George opened his store he gave evidence of an original mind. No other tradesman in York made so much use of the Press; and all the following advertisements are taken from the *Gazette*. He set up a store on King St. East on the corner of King and Frederick: as noted previously it was the first dwelling-house and the second building of brick (the first being the Houses of Parliament) to be built in York. He advertises —

Quetton St. George & Co. — At their store at the house of William Willcocks, Esq., have just received a fresh supply of merchandise consisting of the following articles: — Blue, grey, drab and mixed and chocolate cloths; blankets, white flannel, black Russell and Durants; Irish and Russia sheeting; shirts, ready made; overalls, ready made, and coating; bandana silk handkerchiefs and several other sorts; shawls, pocket handkerchiefs, socks, gloves, and mittens; hair powder; ladies' and men's shoes; moccasins; and an additional assortment of tinware; also a few mechanics' tools; also brandy, spirits and whiskey; besides the assortment they had before, consisting mostly of every article; all of which they will sell cheap for ready money. Approved drafts on England or any part of this country taken in payment; also furs and different country produce. They have also nutmegs, cinnamon, cloves and mace, candles, cotton, wick butter, cheese, chestnuts, hickory and black walnuts and cranberries.

In volume 6 of the *Landmarks* (by an odd coincidence) information regarding the firm is found on pages 306, 311, 333, 344 and 366.

In March, 1803, we read:—

Messieurs Quetton St. George & Co., Being about to leave this town for some time, in order to import a fresh assortment of merchandise, inform the public that they will dispose of their present stock, at nearly first cost. Nothing, however, will be received in payment but cash, bills of exchange or furs.

That must have produced all the excitement that a similar Eaton or Simpson advertisement would provide today.

The "fresh assortment of merchandise" was on view in November, 1803.

Quetton St. George has received from New York a large assortment of Shoes and Buskins suitable to all ages. Also Pig Tail, Ladies' Twist and Cut Tobacco, good cognac brandy, which he will not dispose of in lesser quantity than one gallon. He is in daily expectation of the remainder of his winter supply consisting of East and West India Goods, Ironmongery and Crockery; all of which will be sold cheap.

We now must pass on to June 1806, when we note not only that one or two other merchants (notably Mr. Joseph Cawthra) are competing with advertisements, but also that Mr. Quetton St. George is (a) in quest of some customers who were not as honest as they should be; and (b) doing something with Real Estate.

The second paragraph in his advertisement is very suggestive. He also had trouble with a book borrower.

Mr. St. George has just received wine, Jamaica spirits, Rapee snuff, nails, best Spanish segars.

Mr. St. George having missed two pair of Suwarrow boots, requests those persons who have purchased same from him to let him know, as he is afraid he has forgot to charge them; or should they have been taken on trial, it is requested that they may be returned.

It is also requested that the gentleman or lady who has borrowed a volume of the Revolutionairs [sic] Plutarch, will return it immediately.

He has for sale the following lots of land, viz — Nos. 12, 13 and 14 in the third concession of Whitchurch; 29 and 30 in the fifth concession of Beverley; 19 in the second concession of Whitby; 19 and 20 in the third concession of Whitby; also No. 17 in the Township of Thorold, in the District of Niagara, with the improvements and buildings thereon.

In July 1807 we find him suffering from the malice of some man who appears determined to worry the well-known merchant.

He was a wealthy man, but that did not prevent his customers allowing notes to go to protest. The case is explained by the following "Notice": —

Mr. Quetton St. George had a bill last July from one of his customers, which was some time ago returned protested, for non-payment. Through the politeness of a gentleman of this province the said bill was put into the hands of a lawyer for collection, without having been previously presented to him for payment. To prevent his character being in future injured by the recurrence of a similar circumstance, Mr. St. George requests all those to whom he is indebted in this province to have the goodness to present their account for payment between this and the first of August; and those also to whom he is indebted in Lower Canada, when their respective accounts shall become due (if not previously paid).

To be sued for debt is bad for morale and for credit; especially if the bill has not been previously presented. Then in August 1807 another annoyance descended upon him.

Mr. St. George had had his good nature imposed upon and was determined to oblige none but those who had a claim upon him, for he issued a "Notice" to the effect that:—

Mr. Quetton St. George, to accommodate some of his friends and customers, had given leave to them to send their letters for Europe to one of his correspondents in New York, but finding that some strangers have taken the liberty of doing the same and desired the postage to be charged to him (which they have not yet paid), begs leave to inform all those whom it may concern that he has given positive orders to Messrs. Robert Bach & Co. not to pay anything on his account, and that no letters will be received in future by these gentlemen, except those which he will forward himself or recommend. He also requests payment immediately of the gentlemen who have had the advantage of his friends to correspond in Europe or elsewhere.

For the next five years, to 1814, there are no notices from the *Gazette* reprinted in the *Landmarks*. For interim news of Quetton St. George we must attend the Court of Quarter Sessions, 1813.

When the magistrates assembled on January 25th, which they did pursuant to adjournment, no less a person than Mr. Quetton St. George was hailed [haled] before them to show cause why he had failed to assume the duties of collector for the town of York, to which office he had been duly appointed. Mr. St. George's answer was a very ingenious one, namely — that he had received no official notification of the fact that he had been so appointed, until he was called upon to answer the charge of neglecting his duties. Such a reply would be creditable even now to a certain illustrious statesman, whose replies to awkward questions are as mystifying as they are lengthy. But in the case of Mr. St. George the court went straight to the point, deciding then and there that the excuse was insufficient, and enquiring if he was willing to do his duty. Hearing he was not, they straightway fined him two pounds "for such refusal", and then proceeded to "name and appoint Stephen Jarvis Esq., as a fitting person to serve as collector for the town of York." The court then adjourned *sine die*.

And then, next year, in the *Gazette* of December 24th, 1814, we have the happy ending of all romances, commercial wedding bells.

Quetton St. George & Co. Mr. St. George begs leave to return his thanks to his friends and the public for their very liberal support to him since his first establishment in business at this place and also to inform them that he has now taken Messrs. Julius Quesnel and John S. Baldwin into co-partnership and that the business of the concern will be in future carried on under the name of Quetton St. George & Company.

The new firm takes this opportunity of expressing their hope that Mr. St. George's old customers will continue their favors towards them, and of assuring them that every attention shall be paid to their wishes and commands; and also at the same time to inform them and the public at large, that they have now an extensive assortment of goods of the first quality immediately imported from England, from whence they will continue to import a constant supply, they flatter themselves that their prices will not be higher than those of other merchants.

N.B.—Mr. St. George requests those indebted to him to make their payments without delay, and that all those to whom he is indebted will present their accounts immediately, or at farthest before the first day of May next, as he proposes to make a voyage to Europe in the course of the next summer.

And so we say farewell to Mr. St. George, again in Paris, after Waterloo; again, it may be, Monsieur Lawrence Quetton, and (we suppose) resuming the activities of a Chevalier de St. Louis.

A few lines on a pleasant unassuming Englishman must round off the chapter.

The brewery of Joseph Bloor, after whom Bloor street is named, was situated in the ravine north of the First Concession Road (Bloor street), and midway between Sherbourne street bridge and Huntley bridge. The brewery was on the south bank of Severn (the brewer's) Creek, which had its rise north of St. Clair avenue, and following the ravine, crossed Yonge street at Tannery Hollow and finally emptied into the Don at Winchester street. It was in operation in 1833. The blockhouse on the right stood in 1837 exactly at the junction of Bloor and Sherbourne street, on the east side at the south end of the first bridge.

Until 1830 or thereabouts Joseph Bloor kept an inn near the market place of York, conveniently situated for the accommodation of the agricultural public. This inn, which was called the Farmers' Arms, was situated on the north-west corner of the lane leading northward from the north-west corner of Market Square and King street. The lane was formerly known as Stuart's Lane from the Rev. George Okill Stuart, once owner of property there. It was afterwards called Francis Lane, and is now known as Francis street. That section of the city, in Mr. Bloor's time, was known as the Devil's Half Acre. On retiring with a competency from the proprietorship of the Farmers' Arms, Mr. Bloor moved to Yorkville about 1830 and established a brewery in the ravine. This brewery was a low, red brick building one hundred feet long and fifty or sixty feet wide. It stood at the bottom of the ravine, a little to the east of the present [in 1896] iron bridge at the head of Huntley street. The stream, which was larger then than now, was dammed up at this point to give water power for grinding. A big pond several acres in extent was thus made and in the spring the water would back up nearly to Yonge street. The brewery was reached by a roadway running down the ravine from Bloor street at the head of Huntley street. Picturesque as the spot is even now it was still more so at that time when the woods were thicker and Nature in her primeval beauty. At the top of the hill on the northern side stood the cottage of Charles Jarvis, from which steps led down the steep declivity. There was an entrance to the brewery at the south side and also on the east side. About this time all the sand used in Toronto for building purposes was drawn from the Island. Mr. Bloor kept a team of horses for carting, and in attempting to cross from the Island on the ice with a load of sand, the team broke through and was drowned. Mr. Bloor kept the brewery but a few years. In conjunction with Sheriff Jarvis he entered into a successful land speculation, projecting and laying out the village of Yorkville, which narrowly escaped being called Bloorville. That name was proposed as also was Rosedale after the sheriff's homestead, and likewise Cumberland, from the native county of some of the surrounding residents. Dr. Scadding suggests that Bloor, the name of a spot in Staffordshire, famous for a great engagement in the wars between the houses of Lancaster and York, would have been a happy appellation. Yorkville was at last selected, a name which preserved that discarded in 1834 for Toronto. Mr. Bloor accumulated a large amount of property on the first concession road, stretching along the northern side from its eastern end as far west as Gwynne street and back to the creek in the ravine. He subsequently sold this property. The first concession road was afterward known as St. Paul's road and Sydenham road. That Mr. Bloor's name should finally have become permanently attached to it in Bloor street is a fact which may be compared with the case of Pimlico, the well known west end quarter of London. Pimlico has its name from Benjamin Pimlico for many years the popular landlord of a hotel in the neighbourhood. Mr. Bloor was a quiet, pleasant Englishman, widely esteemed and respected.

For many years he was identified with the Bloor St. Methodist Church, to which he gave largely, both during his lifetime and by legacy. Up to the time of his death he lived in a cottage on the site of what was later 100 Bloor St. East. The brewery continued to be run for a few years by Mr.

John Rose, then it fell into disrepair and was long supposed to be haunted.

Among other activities, Joseph Bloor went into partnership with George Cooper in an undertaking to remove the old Island Blockhouse which stood where Hanlan's Hotel was later built, mounted one 24-pounder gun, and saw but was powerless to avert, the taking and pillaging of York in 1813. Messrs. Bloor and Cooper thus erased an inglorious memory.

AN INTERLUDE OF NAMES

It is to be lamented [says John Ross Robertson], that the records of where many of the pioneers of the city were buried in the first twenty years of its existence, appear to have been utterly lost. As regards scores of the old-time worthies, "no man knoweth their sepulchre", not even their direct descendants, while the graves of some who did noble service for their king and country are not marked by even the slightest memorial. *Sic transit gloria mundi.*

Ecclesiastical records to many people present a most fascinating study. Such records of births and baptisms, of marriages and of deaths, to be found in all church archives, though in the great majority of cases bare statements of fact, are interesting to read, as they carry the readers back in imagination to the times when their ancestors were in the flesh. To stand, for example, and contemplate the grave of Stephen Jarvis, in the churchyard of St. James', is to touch hands with the eighteenth century. Stephen Jarvis was born in 1756 and died in 1840, being at that time one of the very last survivors of the U. E. Loyalists. His name is to be found in the Registers of the great Cathedral, with those of many others who have helped to shape Toronto from the earth of an Indian encampment. The Historian may note entry after entry that recalls the spacious days when England was pouring men and treasure into Upper Canada, and the new Canadians — their feet set upon the rock of determination — lifted hearts above their foes from the south, their winter from the north, and the forest that surrounded them.

But our immediate purpose is to look through these Registers for entries that are odd or amusing. Among the baptisms, for instance, ignorance, fancy and nervousness on the part of the parents; with delay in making the entry and consequent forgetfulness in the case of the officiating clergyman — provide some quaint combinations. Sometimes the names of the parents are omitted or wildly mis-spelled, sometimes the feelings of the clergyman at the moment are given in a comment that is quite audible to the spirit a hundred and fifty years later. Archdeacon Stuart goes out of his way to note "The six children in the above registry are the offspring of parents who are Africans." Evidently "the ingathering of the Gentiles." A little later we find — "Child's name, Sarah: an adult and African; parents not given." Adult and African — but a child in the eyes of the Church.

Over the spelling of some surnames much doubt appears to hang. "Quantz", for example, is written Squants, Quanze, Quants, and Quanst. But much of the early spelling is provocative of doubt. What can be made of "George Lentz Saigien"[1] to whose record of baptism this note is appended "sponsors, could obtain no sponsors"?

A query of a different kind is raised by the baptism of William McGinnis. His parents belonged to the 49th Regiment, and no godfather could be found for William, "the Reg't having left the place". Apparently also having left the baby: a regimental habit, traditionally.

One meets odd surnames in these records: Rolannoin, John Canis, Tilgara, Sypes; and "Jibbet" — which may really be Jobbitt, recorded later. "Settisbett" provokes speculation; so does "Millenicum" as the Christian name of a bride — who coyly shortens it to "Millie". A name that is difficult to place is "Wait Swut". One asks "Who gave you that name?" "Soul Hale" is satisfactory if a little unusual, and "Salina Serviner" can be reduced to a probable — "Selina Seraphina". Her surname is Pool, and a note follows — "From the Thames".

There seems no reason for spelling Helena "Hellener".

One entry gives the name of the child as Alextian Abbit, and the only sponsor as Shristian Abbit; who also appears

[1] Perhaps an Indian, of Saugeen.

to have been his mother. None could sponsor better. There
is a pleasant note to the christening of Mary Diver (one of
whose sponsors was Jacob Clock) "Aged 17, and just going
to be married".

On the same page we find "Tresive Mercer" and "Crinard
Cloak"; we also find the information that "Robert McGuinis
was a large storekeeper": exact size not stated.

One entry has the promise of sadness. The child was John
Williams. "Parents — Father absent, a soldier. Mother dead".
One hopes that young John was especially commended to
the notice of Heaven.

There are a number of interesting marriage records in the
Registers of St. James' Cathedral; and they are printed
verbatim in volume three of the *Landmarks*. The first is
in 1800 when Jepe Bennett married Catharine Hoover; and
they cross the century to 1896. Name after name recalls the
great pageant of history that has happened to Upper Canada.
Here is Jenny Thompson, daughter of the first settler in
Scarboro, marrying James Elliot, himself a pioneer. Here, in
1803, is recorded the wedding of George Rippebarrack and
Catherine Clock; with a note: "The name of the bridegroom
is in the register exactly as it appears here". Jesse Ketchum's
marriage to Nancy Love is noted in 1804; and Jordan Post's
to Melinda Woodruff in 1807. He was a watchmaker, a
wealthy, tall, and much respected New Englander, who carried
on business on the north side of Duke St. near Jarvis, which
was then New Street. He owned much land, and Jordan
St. and Melinda St. commemorate the pair. Then, between
the notices of George Quantz and of Hiram Kendrick comes
"Albert Hagerman, an African, and Nancy Long, an African".
Bond or free one does not know; but married in St. James'
none the less.

A little later in the same year (1807) the witnesses to a
marriage were Henry Hebnet and Hinreh Pingel; and we
come to Rolannoir, Oresho, Ginioz and Druyard — contracting parties and witnesses. Almost as odd are the four that
succeed — Castedder to Kaffer, "Witnesses Wm. Drmonsy and

Jofermun Yminner". They probably made their marks. After this "Prime Fobey" (a witness) seems almost English. But almost certainly a number of names were those of Dutch settlers from Pennsylvania who allowed the officiating clergyman to use his imagination in spelling. But who was responsible for "This marriage was solemnised between us, J. P. Radermiller and Magdalene *and Henry* Borkholder"? A little later "Relief Welder" is the name of a bride, not a trade. In 1813 we find a member of the Quantz family spelling his name "Quantis"; and Mussoin Fissense is a witness. "In many places the spelling in the register is more than erratic". We agree.

In 1814 Aaron Eyres "a black man" is married to Elizabeth Long "a black woman". Then in the next year we note "Desive" and "Archarge" as the supposedly Christian names of brides. John Kake of Etobicoke should be noted now for later reference; and "Chimham Himay" as a matter for wonder and query. A bridegroom in 1816 is recorded as "A Menial servant of the 82nd Regiment", meaning (we suppose) that he was not a fighting man. More first names for ladies are "Zyelia", "Jouth", and "Elethean" (probably Althea). Certain names of course recur frequently, marrying and giving in marriage; and some that at first seemed "out of town" become modernized and recognizable. However, there are always enough folks with private notions of spelling to prevent the search from becoming dull. We come across "Merrogh", a word well-known in Irish folk-lore: Jane Merrogh became Mrs. Knott. In 1821 Archibald Riddle married Battice Marr, who would now, we expect, be Beatrice. (She came from Aberdeen, so was not French.)

Then come two more despairing efforts at spelling the hated word mentioned on page 219. "Chinquaceuchy" writes John Strachan, and thinks "Oh dear! I'm sure that isn't correct"; so, next time, he tries "Chinquacosay". A pleasant name for a wedding is Cake. In 1822 Manuel Cake married Nancy Christner, Andrew Cake married Zebra Prentice, and Adam Cake married Zebra's sister Hannah. Zebra Cake was a witness to that wedding, but we find her, a year later, spelling her name "Sebry". Her husband married again, as a widower, in 1832. "First worn down and then worn out" one could probably say. A little earlier James Upthegrove was wed to Delehia Wyant, spinster — and probably called her Delia.

Well, this may be considered of sufficient length for an interlude. "Calling names" is one of the blood-sports of childhood; and it must be a long while since the writer indulged himself so far.

VII. THE COURSE OF JUSTICE

I. THE ASSIZES

"The charge is prepared; the lawyers are met,
The judges all rang'd — a terrible show!
I go undismayed, for death is a debt,
A debt on demand — so take what I owe."

The Beggar's Opera

The instruments of British justice, and of its Canadian
equivalent, are a judge and a jury. Their implements are
(or were, in the early nineteenth century) the pillory, the lash,
the stocks, the gallows, and the jail; with a branding iron as
a convenient accessory. Inhabitants of Toronto not only heard
the penalty of branding ordered, but actually saw it inflicted
in open court; the iron being heated in the great wood stove
that warmed the room, and the culprit made to stretch out his
hand and have burned thereon the initial letter of the offence
committed. The early "Courts of General Quarter Sessions"
were held at the Government Buildings; but after their
destruction by the U.S. troops in the War of 1812 the court
house was removed to the south side of Queen Street; a two-
storey plain frame building erected, and occupied at first as a
residence, by Alexander Montgomery. Though situated nearer
Queen Street than Richmond Street it faced and was
approached from the latter.

Within the Court House on Richmond Street took place,
in 1818, the celebrated trial of a number of prisoners brought
down from the Red River Settlement on charges of "high
treason, murder, robbery and conspiracy", as preferred against
them by Lork Selkirk, the founder of the Settlement.

At a Subsequent Court of Oyer and Terminer, held at York, a true bill against Earl Selkirk and nineteen others was found by the grand jury, for "conspiracy to ruin the trade of the North-West Company". Mr. Wm. Smith, under-sheriff of the Western District, obtained a verdict of £500 damages for having been seized and confined by the said Earl when endeavouring to serve a warrant on him in Fort William; and Daniel McKenzie, a retired partner of the North-West Company, obtained a verdict of £1,500 damages for alleged false imprisonment by the Earl in the same fort.

Besides the legal cases tried and the judgments pronounced within the homely walls of the Old Court House, interest would attach to the curious scenes — could they be recovered and described — which there occurred, arising sometimes from the primitive rusticity of the juries, and sometimes from their imperfect mastery of the English language, many of them being (as the German settlers of Markham and Vaughan were indiscriminately called) Dutchmen.

Peter Ernest, appearing in court with the judgment of a jury of which he was foreman, began to preface the same with a number of peculiar German-English expressions which moved Chief Justice Powell to cut him short by the remark that he would have to commit him if he swore. When Ernest observed that the perplexities through which he and the jury had been endeavouring to find their way, were enough to make better men than they were express themselves in an unusual manner, the verdict, pure and simple, was demanded. Ernest then announced that the verdict which he had to deliver was, that half of the jury were for "guilty" and half for "not guilty". "That is," the judge observed, "you would have the prisoner half-hanged, or the half of him hanged?" To which Peter replied, that would be as his Lordship pleased. It was a case of homicide. Being sent back they agreed to acquit.

It became evident before long that "a plain frame building" was not adapted for continued public service, and in April

1824 the foundation stone of the new gaol and court-house
was laid by the Lieutenant-Governor. Followed an interval
of two and a half years — an interval still not unknown where
public works are concerned — and on October 21st, 1826
(Trafalgar Day) the Canadian Chief Justice Campbell delivered this charge to the Grand Jury.

After the lapse of so many years that the accommodation
of the courts for the administration of justice to this district
have been suffered to remain in a state (to say the least of it)
not very creditable to the country, I with pleasure embrace
this first opportunity to congratulate you on the prospect at length
afforded us, of being speedily relieved from so indecorous a
predicament. The building in which we are now assembled, and
which is so near completion, appears to be well adapted for
all the purposes for which it is intended — the arrangements are
judicious, and on a scale of ample accommodation, becoming
the opulence and the respectability of the Home District, and
highly creditable to the Committee of Magistrates who have
planned and superintended the structure. The corresponding
edifice in its vicinity, intended for a jail, planned and erected,
I believe, under the management of the same gentlemen, and
still nearer completion, I am happy to observe, is on a like
liberal scale of extensive and well arranged accommodation,
in which the health and comfort of the unfortunate persons,
debtors and criminals, whose destiny may be to occupy it, seems
to have been properly attended to, so far as those important
objects are consistent with the main design of the building —
that of absolute security of the custody of the persons; but as
to its perfection in this latter respect the sheriff is the best judge,
as having the whole responsibility, and therefore has been doubtless occasionally consulted on that point. It appears to me, however, that this building should long ere now have been ready
for the reception of the prisoners now confined to the old jail.
Should you think so, gentlemen, it will be your duty to enquire
into the cause of the delay. The miserable state of the place
in which those unhappy beings are confined and some of them

for a great length of time, has long been considered not only as insecure, but as extremely injurious to health. Any unnecessary continuance of imprisonment in such a situation is as repugnant to the dictates of humanity as it is contrary to the intention of the law — for, however rigorous the punishment which our laws have assigned to the different degrees of crime — foul and unwholesome air or other unnecessary treatment, forms no part of it — nor is recognized or allowed by our excellent Constitution.

These are circumstances which I would not have thought necessary to obtrude on your attention, gentlemen, on the present occasion, were it not to account for the extreme astonishment with which all respectable strangers, as well as all persons of superior minds and intelligence in this province, are invariably struck on viewing the mean and ruinous condition of the wooden cottage in which the Supreme Court has been compelled to hold its terms, sittings and Assizes during a period of thirteen years — a building not adequate in any one respect for the accommodation of any court of justice, but also in such a state of irreparable decay and dilapidation as to be unfit for human residence. Yet this indecent and long-continued neglect has taken place amongst a civilized people, distinguished (with few exceptions) for loyalty and attachment to the British Crown and Constitution, and I feel warranted in saying that this view of the subject, and a serious consideration of the consequences naturally resulting from so degrading a predicament, unparalleled in any part of his Majesty's dominions, must have determined his Excellency speedily to remedy an evil fraught with much latent mischief, and to remove a stain on our provincial character which strangers might be apt to consider as indicating a want of due respect and attachment to our Government and institutions, or, at all events, as no very flattering mark of our sense of decency and common propriety.

After which exordium His Lordship turned to a review of the cases on the calendar; not of especial importance "except in one instance, which is a case of rape of unusual atrocity, there being no less than three men implicated in the commission of this act of brutal violence; to all of whom it may prove fatal should the charge be supported by evidence."

Capital punishment for this particular crime has only recently been removed from the statute book; but it is a comment on the severity with which offences against property were punished that later in the same charge to the jury it was stated: "One of the (larcenies) appears to be to a large amount, but whether simple or compound does not say; if the latter it will be attended with fatal consequences to the parties accused, who appear to be husband and wife." This distinction was underlined at the first Assizes for the Home District in the Rural Court House, held in October, 1827.

After a sitting of more than ordinary length the assizes terminated on Thursday afternoon; the following is a list of the convictions and sentences:

Hiram Losee, manslaughter, twelve months' imprisonment and pay a fine of ten pounds.

Jason Bryant, grand larceny, six months' imprisonment, and to be publicly whipped on the first day of the ensuing quarter session, 39 lashes.

Edward Devlin, grand larceny, same sentence.

William Jones, killing cattle, to be hanged on Saturday, the 17th November next.

William Jones was originally charged with "maliciously killing a cow", Hiram Losee with murder; yet it is Jones who has to lose his life, and Losee, his offence whittled down to manslaughter, gets off with twelve months' imprisonment and a light fine. To us, in this day, it would appear that the sentences should have been transposed.

Prisoners at that time could not give evidence on their own behalf, and were not always defended, except by the prosecutor; as witness the next case.

On Friday, the 14th, came on at Niagara, before the Hon. Judge Allcock, the trial of George Nemiers and Mary London, alias Mary Osborn, for the murder of the late Mr. Bartholomew London, of Saltfleet, by poison. The trial commenced at half-past nine in the morning and took up about eight hours. The Attorney-General in a pathetic address to the jury called their attention to the solemn duty before them. He said that although he prosecuted for the Crown, it should be seen that he urged no matter that appeared doubtful; he was as much their [the prisoners'] advocate as their prosecutor. The fact being fully proven, the jury delivered them in guilty, and the judge, who had throughout the trial judged with mercy, now with mildness proceeded to pass the dreadful sentence of the law, to be executed on the 17th, which was accordingly executed pursuant to sentence. A numerous concourse of people attended the execution.

It is easily seen that the proceedings were full of decorum; the accused were mildly sentenced to be hanged, and probably some of the *best people* "attended" at their taking-off.[1]

II. THE SCAFFOLD

From the early days of the city until public executions ceased, the death of a man on the gallows was held to be an occasion for the people to enjoy themselves. The descriptions that follow are taken from the First, Third and Sixth volumes of the *Landmarks*; and are here presented for a more inhibited populace who, themselves deprived of seeing final agonies, must now obtain their thrills vicariously from the word pictures of "crime reporters" in the daily press.

Among the many emigrants who arrived in the infant town of York between the years of 1793 and 1807 was a young Irish

[1] And in England, at that time, men of the same integrity and breadth of view were interpreting substantially the same laws — with similar fatal consequences.

tailor, named John Sullivan. He was accredited with being a good workman, but was very ignorant and dissipated. In the beginning of the year 1798 he fell in with a man named Flannery,

EXECUTION OF LOUNT AND MATTHEWS

who was nicknamed "Latin Mike," because of his penchant for making Latin quotations, learned probably at church. The two occasionally got on the spree together. In June, 1798, Flannery wrote out an order for three shillings and ninepence, and put the name of one Fisk to it, then prevailed upon Sullivan, while he was intoxicated, to get the order cashed. They then spent the money in whiskey, and Flannery finding that the forgery had been found out, fled across the lake, leaving poor illiterate John Sullivan to pay the penalty. The latter was arrested, pleaded not guilty, but was convicted of having uttered the note, knowing it to have been a forgery, and was sentenced to death. He was confined in the "old log jail," a primitive looking structure situate on the south side of King street, on the site of the Leader building, nearly opposite Toronto street, until about October 11, when he was led into the yard, the place of execution. The scaffold consisted of two pieces of scantling set upright with a stout cross-piece nailed, over which was thrown a rope; while one end was held by the executioner, a man named McKnight, the other was adjusted in a noose around the doomed man's neck. The common, for the whole vicinity was but sparsely settled, was crowded by men, women and children, who were dressed up in holiday attire and looked as if they intended to thoroughly enjoy the occasion. At a given signal the hangman pulled on the rope, and with a sudden jerk suspended Sullivan in the air. It was but for a moment, however, the rope having broken or the knot having got twisted. The executioner coolly proceeded to readjust the rope, and as he finished Sullivan as coolly exclaimed, "McKnight, I hope to goodness you've got the rope all right this time." And then his soul was launched into eternity, without prayer, and without hope, for having uttered a forged order for less than a dollar.

In 1816 open murder occurred in "Muddy York," the criminal being a farmer named Elijah Dexter, and his victim James Vanderburg. The two men had a quarrel, and for several months were deadly enemies. Finally, on the 8th or 9th of July, the two met on Yonge street, near the Rosedale ravine, and after an exchange of some hot words and a blow given by Vanderburg, Dexter presented a gun and shot Vanderburg dead on the spot. There was a great deal of excitement over this trial, many being of the opinion that Dexter acted in self-defence. However, he was convicted, and was sentenced to die on the 10th August following. A scaffold, the first proper one that had ever been built in the neighbourhood, was erected, and on the day of the execution Dexter was led forth by the jailer, the Rev. John (afterwards Bishop) Strachan accompanying him. There was a great crowd of people surrounding the yard, and when Dexter was led out a great cheer went up. Farmers had driven their families for miles to witness the sight, and business for the time was entirely suspended. When Dexter reached the foot of the scaffold he paused, and, eyeing the dread structure, solemnly shook his head. The jailer tried to prevail upon the doomed man to ascend, but the latter firmly refused. The Rev. John Strachan then approached, and in a tender sympathetic voice exclaimed, "Oh, Mr. Dexter, do please come up; do come up, please." But Mr. Dexter remained obdurate, and the jailer was in a quandary, not wishing to use force on such a solemn occasion. However, a happy thought struck him, and procuring a horse and cart, he placed Dexter in the vehicle with his back to the scaffold, and conveyed him under it. The noose was then adjusted around his neck, and when all was ready the horse was lashed, and, starting forward, left the unfortunate murderer hanging by the neck. When the jail yard was being extended, some time afterwards, the remains of a man were found in a pine box, and they were supposed to be those of either Sullivan or Dexter.

For some years after the execution of Dexter things in this district were very quiet, but on the morning of the 15th February, 1819, the community was horrified by hearing of a most diabolical murder which occurred near Whitby. The murderer was a Frenchman named De Benyon, a dissipated farm hand, who lived in a log cabin on a side road. With him lived a step-son about 13 years of age, and one bitterly cold night this demon first turned his stepson out of the house, and when he crawled in half frozen, De Benyon tied him in front of the fireplace, and, piling more wood on the fire, literally roasted him to death inch by inch. When the poor lad's legs were burned almost black and were unable to support him, the in-human stepfather pushed him forward into the flames until his hair caught fire, and in this position he was roasted, the murderer all the time gazing on his work. De Benyon attempted to escape, but was captured near the Don, where the G.T.R.

bridge now crosses the river, and was summarily disposed of by being hanged to a tree. This is the only case of Judge Lynch which is known to have occurred in Ontario.

In 1829, Charles French, an apprentice to William Lyon Mackenzie, paid his first and last visit to a theatre performance, as a sort of double celebration of two important events in his life, the termination of his apprenticeship and his coming of age. Mr. Richard Watson, who accompanied French to the theatre that evening, has related to the writer the melancholy issue of this fatal visit. One night in the autumn Mr. Watson and French went together to the theatre, and there met quite a number of their youthful acquaintances. With them French drank freely. On taking their places for the performance Mr. Watson saw in the seat directly in front of him a big burly labourer by the name of Nolan. Now, this Nolan was a quarrelsome bully, who had beaten some of French's companions, for which they swore to have revenge. Nolan carried about with him as a weapon a pair of tongs, and this evening the iron ends could be seen protruding from the pocket of his big coat. Among the visitors to the theatre on this occasion were three young fellows, named Gosling, Dr. Forest and Getz, friends of French, who with him had sworn to be revenged on Nolan for his brutalities. Gosling carried a pistol. Between the acts French and his companions went out and drank heavily. Somehow the pistol of Gosling came into the possession of French. At the close of the performance as the people were coming out from the theatre, French stepped up to Nolan and said: "Is your name Nolan?" "Yes," was the reply. "Well, take that, then!" exclaimed French, drawing the pistol and firing as he spoke. The ball struck Nolan in the right side. He walked to the hotel where he boarded, at the corner of Front street and West Market Square, and entering the bar-room cried out: "I am shot; squint-eyed French has shot me!" "Nonsense!" returned the man behind the bar. "See here, then!" and withdrawing the hand that he held pressed against his side, the blood gushed out in a stream over the counter. The next day Nolan died in the greatest agony. After the shooting French walked to the Black Bull inn on Queen street west and went to bed. The next morning Mr. Wiman, the chairmaker, went to the Black Bull and arrested him. The young man asserted that if he shot Nolan he had no remembrance of it, being so stupefied with liquor. He was tried, convicted of murder, and condemned to be executed . . . Mr. Mackenzie did everything in his power to save the young man's life, and of his exertions to this end Dr. Scadding relates the following incident: "On the steps of the court-house we once saw him — Mr. Mackenzie — under circumstances that were deeply touching. Sentence of death had been pronounced on a young man, once employed in his printing office. He had been vigorously exerting himself to obtain from the executive a mitigation of the extreme penalty. The day and even the hour for the execution had arrived, and no message of reprieve had been transmitted from the Lieutenant Governor, so he came out of the sheriff's room, after receiving the final announcement that there could be no further delay. The white collars on each side of his face were wet through and through with tears that were gushing from his eyes and pouring down his cheeks. He was just realizing the fact that nothing further could be done, and in a few moments afterwards the execution actually took place." The scaffold on which French was hung, in front of the Toronto street jail, was left standing, a grim structure in the heart of the town, until the execution of murderer Christy, some time afterwards. In the same year another man, by the name of Lemon, was executed here on the same gallows. The murder of Nolan and the execution of French dealt a blow to the Colborne street theatre from which it could not rally, and it was soon afterwards discontinued as a place of amusement . . . Gosling, Dr. Forest and Getz were tried for complicity in the murder. The latter escaped, but Gosling and Dr. Forest were each sentenced to six months' imprisonment.

At this point the *Landmarks* are contradictory, volume to volume. Volume I asserts that French was hanged in 1829 for the murder of Nolan, and that he went to the gallows alone. Volume III reads:

In the year 1828 Charles French and James Christie were hanged in the rear of the second, or what was then known as the new, jail, near the corner of King and Toronto streets, opposite the site of the old log jail, and on the former site of the establishment of Messrs. Rice Lewis & Son. There were present at the execution over ten thousand people, and the greatest excitement prevailed. They [the condemned] ascended to the platform together, and their souls entered into eternity simultaneously.

Charles French was a printer, in the employ of William Lyon Mackenzie, and, but for his sporting proclivities, would have made a steady workman. He was in the habit of attending the theatre on Church street regularly, and one evening meeting with a man named Thomas Joslin, the two had some drinks together, and before the performance was concluded had a quarrel. The fight was renewed near Colborne street, in which French drew a pistol from his pocket and deliberately shot Joslin. He then ran away and took refuge in a tavern on Queen street west, where he was arrested. A great deal of influence was used to secure his acquittal, but in spite of this influence he was convicted and sentenced to death.[2]

There appears to be no doubt as to the time or the manner of death of Julia Murdoch. On the 14th December, 1837, she was hanged for having wilfully murdered her mistress.

The murderess was a woman about 21 years of age, unmarried, and worked as a servant for a Mrs. Harriet Henry. She was well thought of by the family, and when Mrs. Henry

[2] Reference to the actual account in the *Gazette* shows that the trial of French took place on Oct. 17, 1828, and he was hanged, solus, on Oct. 23. Christie suffered on Oct. 30.

"Joslin" is probably an error for "Gosling", who was a friend of French and not his victim. It is difficult to know how the second account came to be written; it bears no relation to fact.

became ill Julia was called in to wait on her. For a time everything progressed favourably with the invalid, but one evening she died very suddenly. At the time it was not suspected that Mrs. Henry had been murdered, but shortly after Julia Murdoch was discovered selling some silver spoons and other articles, which had belonged to her mistress. She was arrested for larceny, and it was then that the first suspicion of foul play was entertained. It cannot now be ascertained if Mrs. Henry's remains were buried and the body exhumed, or whether the burial had not taken place; but at any rate, a post-mortem examination was made, when it was discovered that Mrs. Henry had been poisoned with arsenic. The girl was charged with the crime, and although she strenuously denied all knowledge of the poisoning, yet it was brought home to her. The poison had been mixed in some fish which had been prepared for dinner. The girl Murdoch denied her guilt. The day of execution was cold, snow on the ground, and the scaffold was erected on Toronto street, where now stand the York Chambers, near the old jail. The day before her execution she stated that she considered the dreadful circumstances in which she was placed as a merciful arrangement of Divine Providence for the purpose of leading her to a true repentance of her misimprovement of early religious advantages. She readily submitted to be pinioned. The Christian Guardian of that date says that the utmost decorum marked the conduct of the vast assemblage of persons who witnessed the fatal result. "It was, however, exceedingly revolting," says the Guardian, "to see among the spectators a number of females." On the day of her execution fully four thousand people congregated about the jail yard, a large proportion of them being women and children. The prisoner was dreadfully agitated, and as she walked to the gallows leaned for support on her spiritual comforter's arm. When she arrived at the platform she appeared to regain courage, and after prayer had been offered up she knelt on the trap-door, and was hurried into eternity. A portion of McGrath's troopers surrounded the scaffold, and by hard work succeeded in keeping the crowd away from the structure. This was the first and only woman hanged in this district.

After the execution of Lount and Matthews, which is described elsewhere, Toronto had no excitement of the sort for almost five years. Then, on July 30, 1843, Thomas Kinnear, "a Scotch gentleman of good family and fortune was found brutally murdered in his home at Richmond Hill". With the apprehension of the murderers will always be associated the name of Frederick Chase Capreol, who was sent to Canada in 1828, at the age of twenty-five, to assist in settling up the affairs of the North-West Fur Company. In 1833 he married, came to "little York" and, later, "conducted an auction room" on the ground floor of a building at the corner of Yonge and Melinda streets. It was while he, with wife and family, was living in the upper part of this house that the murder was committed.

The report which reached town was that Thomas Kinnear and his housekeeper, Ann Montgomery, had been assassinated at Mr. Kinnear's residence, a solitary dwelling lying back near the woods, a little beyond Richmond Hill, on the west side of the Yonge street road. The woman's throat had been cut from ear to ear. She was found in a wash tub, and Mr. Kinnear had received a blow on the back of the head from some heavy instrument, fracturing his skull. There was evidence to show that the work had been done by at least two persons. It was believed that a large sum of money was in the house, recently taken there by Mr. Kinnear, and that robbery was the motive for the murder. As the people came from their respective places of worship that Sunday evening, they met excited groups at the street corners discussing the affair, for the murdered man was well known in Toronto. The news spread quickly through the city, and many were the eager questions asked: "Who were the murderers?" "How many were there?" "Was a woman connected with the work?" "Where had they fled?" Such were some of the inquiries, but none could answer them. Among the last to hear of the murder was Mr. Frederick C. Capreol, one of the most prominent citizens of the day and an intimate friend of Mr. Kinnear. His children brought the news home on their return from church, and detailed all the particulars they had heard about the crime. Hurriedly putting on his hat, without a word to any of the family, he rushed from the house on Wellington street, and hastened to King street in the hope of finding some one who could give him more news of the tragedy. But the streets were almost deserted and he met no one who could impart additional information. He then went to the police station, where he found an officer and a detective on duty.

"Are you doing anything about this murder?" Mr. Capreol asked excitedly.

"No," replied the officer, sharply. "What is your name, sir?"

"You know very well who I am," cried Mr. Capreol, angrily. "This murdered man was a particular friend of mine and that is why I am so anxious about the matter."

"We have nothing to do with the case," said the officer, curtly, proceeding to make an entry on the slate, as if to say "The interview is at an end."

But Mr. Capreol was not thus to be bluffed, and he asked "Do you intend to do anything about it?"

"Couldn't say; could tell you better in the morning," was the answer.

"But the morning will be too late to start about it. The rascals could be in the States by that time."

"We shall do our duty, whatever that may be. We have no authority in the matter," was the officer's response.

Seeing he could obtain no satisfaction from the police, Mr. Capreol left the station. At this time the founder of the Northern Railway of Canada was strong and agile and bold as a lion, and must have been a man of undaunted courage to conceive the plan he undertook that night. On leaving the station he walked rapidly to Yonge street, questioning every person he met in regard to the murder, and gaining the additional information that on the day before a suspicious looking man and woman had been seen in a much-bespattered waggon driving at a furious pace along the Vaughan road. For a few moments Mr. Capreol stood undecided at the corner of Colborne and Yonge streets. Then the determination seized him to pursue and capture the murderers alone if possible. At this moment Mr. Stevenson, a mutual friend of the murdered man and Mr. Capreol, came along.

"Hello! Capreol, what are you doing here? Did you hear about Kinnear?" he exclaimed.

"Yes, and you are the very man I want to see; I propose to follow the murderers and catch them and I want you to go with me."

"Me?" cried Mr. Stevenson in surprise.

"Yes, why not! You have plenty of time. You are strong as a giant. I have just made up my mind to go. You were a personal friend of Kinnear. So come along."

"Of course I will not. Let the authorities take the matter in hand."

"The authorities? What do they care? I have just come from the station and nobody there knows anything about the affair or will take any action until to-morrow."

"Well, Capreol, perhaps the whole affair is a hoax, and we may see Kinnear to-morrow morning laughing over his own resurrection."

"It is not likely."

"Well, there's plenty of time."

"Plenty of time? Why, my dear man, they will be far away then. If once they get into the States they will be safe enough."

"Oh, I guess they will not get as far as that. Good night," and laughing pleasantly Mr. Stevenson hurried home.

Astonished but not in the least turned from his purpose Mr. Capreol rapidly walked to the house of the Hon. Henry Sherwood, then mayor of the city. On arriving he found it in darkness, the family and servants having retired for the night. He rang the bell and after a time a man servant came to the door.

"I want to see Mr. Sherwood at once," said the caller.

"You cannot see him; he has gone to bed."

"I must see him immediately."

"But he has gone to bed."

"Then call him."

"But, I tell you he has gone to bed."

At this moment the window over the front door was raised and the nightcapped head of the Hon. Henry Sherwood was thrust forth.

"Who's there? What's all the disturbance about? Why, is that you, my dear Capreol?"

"Yes, I want to speak to you. Will you give me credentials to pursue the murderers of Mr. Kinnear and his housekeeper?"

"Credentials! Credentials! I don't understand, Capreol, credentials did you say?"

"Yes. If you give me authority to pursue the murderers I feel confident I can bring them back within two days. All I ask is your authority. I will bear all the expense myself."

"Wait until the morning, I have gone to bed." At this the man in the hall chuckled.

"Yes, so your servant has told me half a dozen times, but if I don't get authority until morning the murderers will escape."

"Oh, no. I'll see about it then and the detectives shall be placed on their track."

"But why not place me on the track now? In two hours I will be on the lake in 'The Transit' and in six hours I will intercept them at Lewiston, for they have probably gone that way."

"I can't do it now, Capreol, I am going to bed. Good night," and the window was closed. At the same time the hall door was shut, but not before a voice was heard exclaiming exultingly: "Didn't I tell you he had gone to bed!"

Disappointed, but more determined than ever, Mr. Capreol turned away from the Mayor's house and hurried to the Church street wharf where the "The Transit" was lying. Here he found a man sitting on the rail enjoying a pipe.

He greeted him with the inquiry: "Are you Captain Richardson?"

"Why?" was the monosyllabic question in return.

"Because if you are, I want you to get up steam immediately," cried Mr. Capreol. But Captain Richardson, did not move or appear in the least excited. Striking a match he deliberately re-lighted his pipe, which had gone out. Then he calmly asked:

"Have you got one hundred dollars about you?"

"Yes," answered Mr. Capreol, "I will give you a cheque right away for the amount if you must be paid in advance, although I think the charge extortionate merely to go across the lake."

"Is it a bogus cheque?" asked the doubtful captain, without moving his position.

"No; it is a good honourable cheque. I am Mr. Capreol and I want to get over to Lewiston before 3 o'clock to-morrow morning. You have heard about the murder on Yonge street, I presume? Well, I am pursuing the murderers, and I hope to intercept them at Lewiston. Come, move like a good fellow and get up steam."

"What did you say your name was?" queried the captain.

"Capreol."

"Capreol! Capreol! I don't know that name. How do I know you are not the murderer yourself, trying to cut the country?"

At this Mr. Capreol grew indignant, but restraining his anger he said: "Do you suppose, captain, I would take this course if I were the murderer?"

"I don't know; it is very likely; it is not a bad idea; but I guess it is all right, only I want cash, not a cheque. How do I know the cheque is good?"

"I assure you the cheque is good."

"Well, I am not going to risk anything; I want cash."

Checked again, Mr. Capreol thought a moment, then taking from his pocket-book all the money he had with him — about $13 — he gave it to the captain, saying: "Get up steam and be ready for me in one hour from now. In the meantime I will go and get the balance."

"All right," returned the captain, "but if you don't come

back in an hour with the money I don't move, and you don't get this back either."

But where to get the balance at this time of the night was the next problem that confronted Mr. Capreol. Leaving the wharf at the corner of Front and Yonge street, he nearly ran against Mr. Carruthers, a wealthy friend, to whom he appealed for help.

"I am sorry, Capreol," said that gentleman, "but I don't exactly care to advance money on such a hare-brained scheme as yours. I am thinking more on your own account. I would not go if I were you. The whole city will be talking about you. Your family do not know anything about it, you say. Come along with me, and leave the matter to the authorities."

"A curse on the authorities. Good night to you, and thank you for nothing," cried Mr. Capreol in a rage as he dashed up the street, leaving Mr. Carruthers standing amazed at the corner.

At Melinda and Yonge streets he paused, feeling almost baffled. But suddenly an idea occurred to him. "I'll try Mr. Ogilvie," he exclaimed to himself. Mr. Ogilvie then lived over his store on the south side of King street, a few doors west of Yonge . . . In two minutes Mr. Capreol was rattling away at the front door of his store. But on this night circumstances seemed to thwart the amateur detective at every turn. It happened that Mr. Ogilvie's chamber was upstairs at the rear of the building, and knock as loudly as might be he could not be aroused . . . Mr. Capreol went around to Melinda street with something like despair in his heart, for he knew that solid gates and a high brick wall barred the entrance to the yard in the rear. A few moments was spent in examination of the formidable-looking barrier, then, realizing that every moment was precious, he essayed the feat of scaling the wall, a feat which even Jean Valjean might have despaired of. Time after time he fell back the ground. Once he heard or thought he heard footsteps approaching from Jordan street. In dismay he crouched by the wall, not knowing how to account for his suspicious actions f a policeman had discovered him in the attempt to climb over

the wall. But no one approached, and re-assured he again set
to work at his almost impossible task. The wall was as smooth
as brick and mortar could make it. There was not the slightest
hold for hands or feet. At length taking out his penknife, by
dint of hard labour, he managed to dig out mortar sufficient
to give him the scantiest holes for his toes and the tips of his
fingers. After several heavy falls, with torn clothes, bleeding
hands, bruised and scratched limbs, without a hat, he finally,
half an hour before midnight, had the satisfaction of sitting
exhausted astride the top of the wall. On recovering his breath
he prepared to descend, a rather dangerous feat, as the ground
within the wall was several feet lower than the sidewalk. At
length he found himself in Mr. Ogilvie's back yard, his trials
near at an end, as he thought, but indeed they had only fairly
commenced. At the rear of the store was a door. Upon this
he rapped and pounded and kicked for nearly ten minutes, but
all to no purpose. Mr. Ogilvie was a sound sleeper and his
windows were closed. Then he began a search for a stone
or a piece of wood to throw against the glass, but neither could
be found. The yard had been newly planked and swept and
was as smooth and clean as a billiard table. Not until now had
he lost heart, his condition was worse than before, for now he
was a prisoner, as it was impossible to scale the wall, higher
as it was on the inside than on the street side. Then it rushed
upon him that Mr. Ogilvie was probably not at home. Sitting
down on the steps he gave himself up to despair. Suddenly the
recollection of his murdered friend arose. "They must, they
shall be brought to justice," he exclaimed and springing up he
began anew an examination of the premises. All at once his
eyes lighted upon the pipe which carried water from the roof
This pipe was fastened perpendicularly to the wall about five
feet from Mr. Ogilvie's chamber which was about twenty feet
from the ground. It was a desperate chance, for how could
the window be reached at that distance from such a precarious
position as one clinging to the pipe would be placed in. Mr
Capreol did not hesitate long. Clutching the pipe desperately,
hand over hand up he went. The frail tube shook and trembled

and bent as if about to fall away from its fastenings. The bands holding it quivered and creaked as if strained to their utmost. The perspiration stood out in great drops all over the face of the

MR. CAPREOL CLIMBING INTO MR. OGILVIE'S WINDOW

bold climber. Once looking down he was seized with vertigo, and might have fallen . . . Finally looking westward to the window five feet away, he saw that his feet were nearly on a level with the sill. The venetian blinds were open and held back against the wall by strong old-fashioned staples. This helped him in one way as it gave him a better hold than the pipe furnished, but the projection of the blind increased the difficulty of reaching the window sill with his foot. At length panting, utterly exhausted and nearly fainting, he obtained a foothold on the sill. Then with the blade of the knife, he raised the lower sash of the window so as to get his fingers under it. The next moment he had pushed up the sash and stepped into the room. There on his bed lay Mr. Ogilvie in sound sleep. Sitting down for a few moments the intruder watched his sleeping friend while he recovered his own composure. Then advancing to the bedside, he gently shook the sleeper. The effect was magical. In an instant Mr. Ogilvie had sprung to his feet, seized the supposed burglar by the throat with an iron grasp that choked him and rushing him to the open window, was about to hurl him out when he recognized the face of his friend.

Releasing his hold, frightened and pale, Mr. Ogilvie stood in astonishment looking at his strange visitor who stood before him bareheaded, with bloody hands and torn garments. Rapidly Mr. Capreol explained the situation while Mr. Ogilvie dressed.

"A hundred dollars? Certainly. There are twenty-one sovereigns," and the merchant counted the gold in his visitor's hand.

Borrowing a pair of trousers and a hat, Mr. Capreol hastened to make his return to the boat, which he found waiting ready for operation.

It detracts little from the foregoing story to add that the whole adventure was unnecessary. A warrant for the apprehension of James McDermott and Grace Marks, Mr. Kinnear's servants, had already been made out and was in the hands of Mr. Kingsmill the High Bailiff.

It was found that the two suspects had been at the City Hotel in the morning, and had gone on the steamer to Lewiston with a horse and wagon, the property of Mr. Kinnear, and lots of luggage. James McDermott was of slender build, swarthy and of a forbidding aspect. Grace Marks, although wholly devoid of education, possessed good features and in personal appearance was much superior to her paramour.

As soon as the High Bailiff discovered where they were stopping at Lewiston, he cautiously proceeded (with one of the crew of the steamer that had brought them over, and who could identify them) to their bed rooms. Going into the room where McDermott lay Mr. Kingsmill softly approached the bed to see if he could identify him according to the description given. The murderer's heart at that time (according to the High Bailiff's description) was heaving violently, his countenance looked almost black, and he had the appearance of a fiend. There was another person sleeping at the same time in the room, who, after being informed of the murder, immediately got up and appeared in every way disposed to render assistance. The girl, who asked repeatedly what was the matter, with affected surprise at being disturbed, was made to dress first. Having given her in charge of the person with him, the High Bailiff then went up to McDermott's bed; he, from the motion of his eyelids, appeared to be only feigning sleep. The following dialogue then took place:

High Bailiff (rousing up prisoner) — "Come Mac, I want you, get up."

Prisoner — "What, what do you want me for? What's the matter?"

High Bailiff — "How came you not to pay the dues on the horse and waggon?"

Prisoner — "Because I had not got the money."

High Bailiff — "Well, get up and dress yourself, I want you."

The prisoner up to this time, as the High Bailiff was in plain clothes, appears not to have recognized him, but the young man who had been sleeping in the room with him, pronouncing the name of "Kingsmill" the truth of his position seemed to flash across his mind.

Prisoner — "Ah, I see it now. I know what you want me for. But have you found Nancy yet?" [Nancy was the housekeeper.]

High Bailiff — "No; where is she?"

Prisoner — "Have you offered any reward for her?"

High Bailiff — "No."

Prisoner—"Well, you find Nancy out. You get hold of Nancy. She'll tell you all about it. It was all owing to her. She was at the bottom of it."

The High Bailiff then having taken a variety of keys, a gold snuff box and other things out of the prisoner's pockets, tied them up in a handkerchief. As soon as McDermott was dressed he handcuffed him, and got him downstairs. Several then being in the bar-room he very prudently took the prisoner into another room. Upon the passage to Toronto the girl Marks voluntarily made a statement. Both parties, however, denied all knowledge of Nancy.

Both McDermott and the woman Marks were convicted of murder on their trial, which took place on Friday, 3rd November, 1843. William Hume Blake for the Crown, John Duggan for the friends of Kinnear and Kenneth McKenzie for James McDermott. McDermott was executed 21st November, 1843, in the old Berkeley street jail. Grace Marks was sent to the penitentiary for life.

Apart from the satisfaction of aiding in the capture of a murderer Mr. Capreol seems to have been "a foul way out", for he was never repaid his considerable monetary expense; owing (one supposes) to his amateur status.

The next notable murder took place four years later. Here is the account, as published.

If Wm. Turney had not received a good education he probably never would have been hanged, but his fondness for letter writing betrayed him as a miserable murderer, and he expiated his crime on the gallows in the year 1847, at the old jail on Berkeley street, hooted and jeered at by a crowd of over three thousand people. The executed man was a discharged soldier and resided at Markham, where he spent the greater portion of his time in consuming bad whiskey and quarrelling with his neighbours. One day he called at a store kept by a Mr

Logan, and instructed the clerk, a man named Walter McPhillips, to draw him a jar of whiskey. The latter stooped down to the barrel to get the liquor, and while in this position Turney quietly slipped up behind him and struck him on the back of the head with a heavy club, killing him instantly, his brains being scattered over the barrel. Turney then stole about $11 from the till and escaped from the store unnoticed. Shortly afterwards the murder was discovered, but at the time the authorities were at a loss on whom to fix the guilt. Turney, who had been drinking to excess, was suspected, and was taken into custody. A few days before the trial he managed to have delivered to his wife a letter, in which he informed her that she would find the money he had taken from Logan under the floor of a water closet on the premises, and to use it in his defence. The wife was unable to read, and took the letter to a neighbour to read for her. This neighbour at once informed the authorities of the contents, and on these statements, backed by a chain of circumstantial evidence, Turney was adjudged guilty, and suffered on the gallows, along with James Hamilton, another murderer. In his dying speech Turney stated that he had been a trooper in Sir De Lacy Evans' corps in Spain, and said that he and four other troopers some years before went to the house of a Spanish grandee, and forced the wife and two daughters to get them something to eat. While they were carousing one of the troopers attempted to kiss one of the daughters, and the son resented the insult and struck him. The troopers, half crazed with liquor, then murdered the whole family and escaped.

On the 14th day of November, 1849, Robert Smith, a private in the Rifle Brigade, stationed at the Old Fort, was hanged at the jail on Front and Berkeley streets, for the murder of Richard Eastwood, a private in the same regiment. It appears that these two men were not on friendly terms, and were continually "chaffing" each other. Eastwood was spoken of as a well-behaved soldier, but Smith was somewhat dissipated, and of a jealous disposition. It was proposed to draft Eastwood into the Royal Canadian Rifles, and upon hearing this on the 13th

August previously, Smith said sneeringly to the other, "So you've got to go in with the — Canucks; I'm — well glad we're rid of you." Eastwood made some retort to the effect that Smith was not fit to be in a Canadian regiment, and then left the guard room. He returned in about an hour, and as he entered the room Smith got behind him, and, raising his rifle, deliberately shot him through the back, the bullet passing through the unfortunate man's body, and lodging in the bed-post. Smith was immediately taken into custody, and was handed over to the civil authorities. He was tried, convicted and sentenced to death, the sentence being carried out on November 14. Before his execution Smith made a confession, blaming whiskey as the cause of his ruin. He ascended the scaffold with a firm step, and when he reached the platform he drew up to "attention," and saluted the great crowd beneath him, who were shoving and justling one another to get near the doomed man. He muttered something inaudible, and then, turning to the fatal trap door, drew himself up to his full height, and gave a signal of readiness. He neither blanched nor quivered, and looked more like a soldier on parade than a man about to face his Maker.

On Tuesday, October 24, 1854, Martin Richard Kehoe was placed on his trial charged with the murder of his wife, Ellen Kehoe, on the 30th July, 1854. The trial took place before the late Mr. Justice Burns. The prisoner resided on Power street with his wife. The woman's throat was cut in three places in such a manner that it would have been impossible for her to have committed the act herself. No evidence was called for the defence. Mr. Dempsey, in defending the prisoner, claimed that it was most improbable that in the middle of the day, with a slight partition dividing the house from the next one, and no property or money to induce the prisoner to murder, that Kehoe should have committed the deed. Mr. Dempsey urged the stronger cases of circumstantial evidence which had been tried before and acquittal secured; he, however, admitted that the medical testimony was strong. The jury found a verdict of guilty. On Saturday, November 4th, Kehoe was placed at the bar and asked what he had to say prior to sentence. The prisoner said: "I call upon the Supreme God, before whom I am probably shortly to appear, to acknowledge my innocence. I had neither hand, act nor part in the matter, notwithstanding the evidence of the medical gentlemen to the contrary. I know not how the act was committed."

His Lordship — "The jury have found you guilty of the crime with which you were charged, and I have no doubt they came to a proper conclusion. The crime is that of murdering her whom you led to the altar and promised to love, honour and cherish. There is no discretion allowed to the court, no punishment save one. It is that by which your life is forfeited. I can hold out no chance of mercy this side of the grave. Only this remains with me, to give you time to make your peace with God.

"The sentence of the court is that you be removed to the common jail, and from that, on the 4th December, you shall be brought to the place of execution, and there hanged until you are dead."

Upon this conclusion the prisoner again protested his innocence.

On Monday, 4th December, Kehoe was led to execution. The scaffold was erected on the west wall of the old jail on Front street. The execution was a public one, and thousands were present, notwithstanding the extreme cold weather. Shortly after 10 o'clock Kehoe, accompanied by two Roman Catholic clergymen, the sheriff, the governor of the jail and others, was pinioned in his cell and led out for execution. He walked to the gallows with a firm step and an unflinching look that betokened none of the bearing of a hardened criminal, or a would-be hero, but the demeanour of a humble penitent. He ascended the steps which led to the scaffold, and standing on the front part addressed those assembled . . . He spoke for several minutes; said he was innocent of or unconscious of having committed the crime for which he was now wrongfully about to suffer. He exhorted all Catholics and others who were present to pray for his soul and be liberal to him in their opinion; spoke of the course of his past life as one that should be guarded against; was thankful to the governor of the jail for his considerate and suitable treatment; begged them to be good men and temperate, and said it was to liquor he owed his present misfortune. Having concluded his "dying words," which he delivered with a fluency and theatrical manner that ill befitted the occasion, he bowed his head, and the executioner immediately covered him with a cloth, adjusted the fatal noose and led him back to the trap door. Here he knelt down composedly, the clergyman bent toward him and after he had uttered some inaudible words retired. The spring bolt was pulled by the hangman and Kehoe was in the other world. While the body dangled in the air the blood spurted from the dead man's mouth and eyes, to the horror of all present. He confessed to having been imprisoned in the States for having stabbed the wife he afterwards murdered.

John O'Leary and William Fleming were executed together on March 4, 1859, for separate slayings, each with a knife. "An immense number, a large proportion of which were women, witnessed the execution at the old jail." O'Leary's statement on the scaffold included the phrase, "I would not at this moment change my situation for that of the Queen of England, because I feel confident that I am prepared."

The next dying speech was uttered on March 10th, 1862, when James Brown suffered for the murder of Mr. J. S. Hogan, M.P.P. It appears probable that such a trial in these days would have a different result. Brown's words come across the years with a ring of truth.

The victim had disappeared at the beginning of December 1859, but about 16 months afterward a human skeleton having yet some flesh on the bones and enveloped in male attire, was found in the marsh. The clothing was identified as that of Mr. Hogan, and an abandoned woman, one of the old Brooks bush gang, named Ellen McGillick, made a statement to Detective Colgan which led to the arrest of Brown. She stated that she had witnessed the murder of Mr. Hogan on the

King street Don bridge one night in December, 1859, by another
abandoned woman named Jane Ward, Brown, and two other
men named Sherrick and McEntameny, the last-mentioned of
whom had meanwhile died. Brown, Sherrick and Ward were
arrested, and McGillick's evidence was to the effect that Ward
had struck Mr. Hogan on the head with a stone tied in a
handkerchief, when Brown and Sherrick robbed him and then
threw him in the river. Her evidence was partially corroborated
by Maurice Malone, Dr. Gamble, and others. Police Magistrate
Gurnett committed the three for trial, which took place before
Chief Justice Draper in April, 1861. Mr. James Doyle, counsel
for the prisoner, succeeded in establishing an alibi for Sherrick,
several witnesses swearing that at the time at which the murder
was alleged to have been committed he was living at Clover Hill,
50 miles from Toronto. The result was that the jury acquitted
Sherrick and Ward. Mr. Doyle offered the same evidence to
show that McGillick's statement was unworthy of credence,
but the Chief Justice ruled it out. The jury found Brown guilty,
but Mr. Doyle succeeded in getting a new trial, when Brown
was again found guilty and sentenced by Mr. Justice Burns to
be hanged on March 16, 1862 . . . When sentence was passed
upon him Brown declared his innocence. He had a dogged
and sullen aspect, which was made more obnoxious by a scar
on his nose caused by disease. He was born in Cambridgeshire,
England, and was 32 years of age when executed. He expressed
contrition before his death, but declared his innocence un-
swervingly to the last, and with such earnestness that the ministers
who attended him expressed their belief in it. He was executed
at the old jail, before a large concourse of people, whom he
addressed as follows:

"This is a solemn day for me, boys. I hope this will be a
warning to you against bad company. I hope it will be a lesson
to all young people, old as well as young, and rich and poor.
It was that brought me here to-day to my last end, though I am
innocent of the murder I am about to suffer for. Before my
God I am innocent of the murder. I never committed the
murder. I know nothing of it. I am going to meet my Maker

in a few minutes. May the Lord have mercy on my soul. Amen. Amen."

The "Amen" was echoed by a few near the scaffold. When he was launched into eternity three or four strong spasms shook his frame and then all was over. The body was delivered at the request of deceased to Mr. Irish for burial. The crowd was not as large as that which witnessed the execution of Fleming and O'Leary. The fair sex was largely represented.[3]

Two singular cases follow.

Robert Coulter was convicted on 17th April, 1863, of having murdered James Kenny on the night of the 18th November, 1861, and was sentenced to be hanged on the 1st June ensuing by the late Chief Justice Draper. During a fight between Coulter and Kenny, on the south-west corner of Edward and Yonge streets on the night mentioned, the latter had six ribs broken and received such further injuries that he died some days after. It was proved that the deceased was an habitual drunkard, and Dr. Sipple swore that he died from natural causes, while Dr. Aikens gave the opinion that his death was caused by inflammation of the lungs, resulting from the injuries he received. Coulter was born in County Fermanagh, Ireland, and was 35 years of age when executed. He married at 30, and settled in the village of Angus. Subsequently he left his wife and came to Toronto, where he lived a loose and dissipated life. A mistress of his who lived in Yorkville disappeared, and never was heard of after, while he was suspected of killing an Indian about ten years previous to his execution; had served two years

[3] Gradually in Canada the feeling was growing that the death of men should not be regarded as a popular amusement. The time was not yet, but it was not far away, when "the long drop", in the decent half-light of the jail, without curiosity or public hate, would terminate the murderer's earthly existence. John Traviss, in 1872, was the first to be hanged in this less spectacular fashion. He had shot a man in the back of the neck for the love of a lady; and we need not disturb his bones. Nor need we dwell on the deeds of Robert Du Coursier, who shot his brother and poisoned himself; except to note that only at the second attempt, while actually in prison and under sentence of death, did he procure poison sufficient to cheat the gallows.

THE FIRST JAIL IN YORK, 1800-24

in the penitentiary for a murderous assault on a policeman, and afterwards joined a gang of horse thieves in the vicinity of Barrie; also killed a man named Coots, of Angus, on the occasion of a quarrel caused by Coulter's intimacy with Coots' wife. He escaped to the woods, and, so desperate was he known to be, that no one could be got to follow him, especially as he was armed with a rifle. Rewards having been offered, he was subsequently arrested and tried but, strange to say, was acquitted. He was, however, convicted of robbery, and sentenced to three years in the penitentiary therefor, which was commuted to two years; on the expiration of which he joined the Brooks bush gang. In the fall of 1861 a man named Rebbell died on Centre street, his death being attributed to a kick received from Coulter. After the Kenny murder he escaped to the county of Huron and got married a second time. He then went to Michigan, where he was afterwards arrested. He was a powerfully built man, and died hard. He made no confession. Between 2,000 and 3,000 witnessed the execution, being a much smaller crowd than attended that of O'Leary and Fleming.

William Greenwood, who committed suicide while under sentence of death, was charged with having murdered Catharine Walsh at the cottage on the west side of Sayer street (now Chestnut), two doors north of Elm street. He was the late Mr. J. Hillyard Cameron's gardener, and lived in a cottage on Mr. Cameron's grounds, Queen street west. Subsequently the cottage was removed and his wife went to live with her mother on the Kingston road, while Greenwood remained at Mr. Cameron's. Catharine Walsh had also been a servant at Mr. Cameron's, but had got married to one McNuty, who afterwards left her and went to the States. According to evidence of Dr. Aikens, death was caused by strangulation, the marks of a man's thumb being visible on deceased's cheek, as if a hand had been held firmly across her mouth until she was quite dead. The body of a child whose mother was said to be a woman named Marshall, was also found in the cupboard of the house; after the first deed was done. The medical evidence went to show that the child was smothered. Greenwood was tried on October 3, 1863, before the late Chief Justice Adam Wilson and a jury. Mr. Stephen Richards, Q.C., afterwards Chief Justice, prosecuted, and Mr. M. C. Cameron, afterwards Chief Justice, defended the prisoner. Mr. Cameron made a lengthy and powerful speech, and the jury returned a verdict of not guilty, but the prisoner was then detained in custody on the charge of being accessory to the death of the child of Agnes Marshall. (Mr. Duckett, a coloured man, who lived next door to where the murder occurred, swore that Greenwood had a peculiar tooth, whereupon Mr. Cameron instructed the accused to open his mouth, which he did, but there was no peculiar tooth. Mr. Cameron dwelt on this discrepancy, and it no doubt had a great effect on the jury. After the trial it was discovered that two teeth had been recently extracted.) At the next Assizes he was tried for arson, convicted and sentenced to seven years in the penitentiary. [This account does not explain what was burned.]

On the 22nd January, 1864, he was tried for the murder of the child of Agnes Marshall, and was convicted and sentenced to be hanged on the 23rd February following. He declared that he was innocent. On the night before the day fixed for his execution he hanged himself by means of a towel, thus cheating the gallows, as in the subsequent De Coursier case. In order to kill himself he had to crouch on the floor, the bar to which the towel was attached not being sufficiently high to enable him to produce death otherwise.

The case of John Williams, of Weston, now comes before us.

On the night of the 21st September, 1877, an unfortunate woman named Annie Williams, *née* Bennett, was virtually pounded to death by her drunken husband, John Williams, in a humble cottage in the vicinity of Weston. Williams was a Welshman, who was employed by Mr. Eagle, of Weston, in making bricks, at a price per 1,000. He was very frequently under the influence of liquor and, when so, invariably thrashed his poor, patient, hardworking wife; the blows inflicted on her on the night mentioned having been but the finishing touch of numerous poundings she had previously received at the hands of her inhuman husband. When arrested he brutally remarked "She's a goner this time." The body of the unfortunate woman, when found next morning, presented a horrible spectacle, having been pounded black and blue, her features being smashed out of recognition. She was the mother of fifteen children, all living except one. A man named Stone, who was employed by Williams, had an altercation with him in the cottage, both being drunk, and also a scuffle when Stone went to the hay loft near the cottage, where it was his custom to sleep. Williams maddened by the dispute with Stone, then turned on his unfortunate wife, and at intervals during the night bestowed blows and kicks on her which caused her death. The children were powerless to prevent him, and Stone and one Chapman were lying in the hay loft stupefied with liquor. The actual cause of death was a rupture of the liver, effected, it is surmised, when Williams jumped on his wife, as stated by a child of tender years. He was convicted at the Assizes held here on the 29th and 30th October, 1877, before Chief Justice Hagarty and a jury, *who made a strong recommendation for mercy.*

The attitude of the jury would appear to have been, "If a man cannot beat his wife who *can* he beat?" It is difficult to understand such a mentality, unless it arose from the conviction that with "The Aggrawater" out of the way her husband would become an exemplary citizen and the support of his numerous family. In the event, he was executed on the morning of November 30: the hangman on that occasion, a man named England, scorned to wear a mask.

The execution was witnessed by about 150 persons, admitted by passes procured from the sheriff. At midnight preceding the execution the Rev. Mr. Johnston wrote a letter to Williams' children and his friends, at his dictation, in which he inculcated the duty of attending church, the violation of which principle had brought him to the gallows. Some days before the execution his four daughters, only one of whom was of tender years, bade him a last and tearful farewell, which was described by Governor Green as the most affecting he had ever witnessed. He was attended on the scaffold by Mr. Johnston, who linked arms with him as he was escorted from his cell to the scaffold, where, with the aid of some prompting, he spoke as follows:

"I would wish to thank the Governor of the jail, the Deputy Governor and all the officers under his charge for the kindly way they have used me. I also wish to thank my counsel for the way they have defended me. I am happy that I got a fair trial, and I thank the public at large for what they have done for me. I am also deeply grateful to my clergyman. That's all." And then he was launched into eternity.[4]

This section on early Canadian crime and punishment closes with one of the most celebrated cases of the 19th century in Canada.

On July 23rd, 1880, George Bennett, also known under the alias of George Dixon, made expiation on the gallows for the murder of Hon. George Brown, managing director of the Globe Printing Company. When Bennett secured work as assistant engineer at the Globe office he was living with a young woman named Mary McGowan, who alleged that she was married to him. He was in the habit of abusing her, and finally, after

[4] Allow the time of which this *Landmark* treats to obtain a mitigation of opinion. We plead that the conditions under which most people lived would today be called intolerable; that whiskey was puddle-cheap and that life was nothing much to lose. Also, that the Law concerning the payment to be made for murder was known and respected (in general), and accepted — by the individual debtor. You "took the law into your own hands" through envy, lust or hate; and the Law then took you into *its* hand and exacted payment. You had your moments, especially the one that found you standing on a platform like a college professor, exhorting several thousand attentive people as to the way that they should walk not to follow your example. And you were in a "state of grace" — almost unbelievably so — and so sure of Heaven just across the line that you wouldn't change places with the Queen. Better surely to die that way, since you *must* die, than drunk in a ditch or drowned in the Don.

they had separated several times, she had him arrested for having neglected to support her. Previous to this it had been stated that Bennett was the son of a coloured man, and on this point he was exceedingly sensitive. He accused Banks, the chief engineer of the Globe, of having "given him away," and cherished against him a feeling of deadly enmity. When Bennett was discharged on account of his carelessness and drunken habits, he blamed Banks for having secured his discharge, and he openly threatened that nothing less than Banks' death would satisfy him. For several days, and after he had been released on bail in the case of neglecting his wife, Bennett had been drinking to excess, and had haunted the Globe lane with the avowed intention of killing some one. On Thursday, the 25th March, at about four o'clock in the afternoon, he entered the Globe office by a side door, and immediately proceeded to Mr. Brown's private room, from which shortly afterwards came the report of a revolver. When the employees ran to see what was the matter they found Mr. Brown and his visitor in a deadly struggle, the revolver lying on the floor. It required but a few moments to overpower the assassin, but the bullet had sped, and accomplished its deadly work after Mr. Brown had suffered a long painful illness. The coroner's jury sent Bennett to the Assizes, and on 22nd June he was sentenced to death. Upon hearing his doom pronounced the prisoner did not appear to be greatly concerned, but, quietly folding his arms across his breast, remarked: "I have nothing to say except I would rather you would make the sentence a little shorter; it would suit me better." A very strong feature of the evidence against the prisoner as to felonious intent was a letter found with others on him at the time of the arrest, in which he threatened to kill Banks and his late master for fancied ill-treatment and to complete the tragedy by committing suicide.

The unfortunate man did not seem to have many friends, or, if he had, they were very careless as to his condition. His brother and two sisters called at the jail for the purpose of taking a last farewell with him, but he refused to see them, saying that he had taken leave of all things earthly, and did not wish his attention to be distracted from what was before him. He wished to be certain of his peace with God. During the early hours of the evening he spent most of his time in reading and writing occasionally addressing a common-place remark to the two watchmen. All the officials who had anything to do with him were very kind, which fact he appeared to appreciate. At midnight he retired, and for a time slept quite soundly. He occupied the cell in the east wing, from the windows of which could be seen the scaffold, and although Bennett did not seem the least concerned, Governor Green considerately had him removed to the west wing, and placed him in the cell known as the debtors' room. At about two o'clock the doomed man started suddenly up from his bed and commenced to rub his neck vigorously, and then with a ghastly smile and a muttered word sank back on his pillow and was soon asleep again. He had been dreaming that he had been hanged. Just as the first streak of light dispersed the shadows from the room he again sat up and repeated the motion of rubbing his neck, his head falling to one side as if he had already taken the fatal drop. Although but half awake, he seemed to at once detect the delusion, and the look of relief which overspread his face showed how much he appreciated the short reprieve. At five o'clock he arose, and, making a careful toilet, took his Prayer Book and commenced to read his prayers in an earnest manner, occasionally varying his position by walking up and down the room. He was dressed in a suit of black broadcloth and a blue silk necktie, his beard, which had been allowed to grow, half covering the latter. At 5.30 he was notified that his breakfast was ready, but he declined to eat anything, saying that he felt perfectly well and in good spirits without partaking of any nourishment. About 6 a.m. his spiritual advisers arrived, and they continued in prayer with him until the arrival of the sheriff. England, the hangman, had arrived at the jail the night before, and was accommodated with a cell. At seven o'clock he commenced his preparations. When he hanged Williams he neglected to wear a mask, but walked out before the spectators and coolly pulled the lever which sent the doomed man to eternity and then turned his

face to the spectators as if for approval. A few days afterwards
a mob attacked him with bricks and stones, near the Don, and
he had to flee for his life. On this occasion he probably remembered the lesson, as when he appeared in the corridor he
wore over his head a mask of black glazed linen with small
apertures made for his eyes. With a couple of leather straps in
his hand, which he swung jauntily as he walked, he proceeded
to the debtor's room, apparently little moved by his surroundings
or by thoughts of his part in the approaching scene.

At 7.45 Mr. Sheriff Jarvis entered the condemned man's
room, followed by the executioner, Mr. Langmuir, the Government Inspector of Prisons, Dr. McCollum, the jail surgeon, and
the representatives of the Globe, Mail and Telegram. Bennett,
as the door was opened by Governor Green, was taking a few
short steps up and down the floor and conversing with his
spiritual advisers.

The sheriff said: "Well, Bennett, my poor fellow, are you
ready?"

"Yes, sir, quite ready." The hangman then brought his arm
straps out, and pinioned the arms of the doomed man. When
it was nearly done, Bennett said: "Don't make it so tight; it's
not necessary, is it, to hurt a fellow?"

"It's all the better for you, my friend," said the hangman.

"All right, if you think it necessary," replied the prisoner,
and the pinioning was completed.

Bennett had in his right hand an ebony crucifix. All being
ready, Mr. Bright, who had gone outside to lengthen the rope
a foot, as Bennett intended to stand on the drop, returned and
reported to the sheriff, who directed the procession to the
gallows . . . In the walk Bennett was firm, and stepped out
as confidently as if the occasion was an everyday one.

As the solemn procession passed through the winding corridors,
a few of the spectators who had not gone into the yard, crowded
forward to catch a glimpse of the doomed man. Few there were
who did not feel a thrill of admiration for the manner in which
the murderer conducted himself. Linked to the arm of a constable, he walked with his head thrown back, not a trace of

fear being discernible in either his deportment or in his features. For fully an hour before the doomed man left his cell members of the press, officials and spectators had been arriving, and even up to the last five minutes the door bell continued to tinkle, announcing fresh visitors. Hardly a word was spoken above a whisper, and all the spectators appeared to be deeply impressed with the sombre surroundings.

When the sheriff appeared at the top of the stone steps leading to the yard, followed by the reverend fathers, a low murmur went up from the spectators, and more than one face blanched as they caught sight of Bennett, who continued to walk with firm and unfaltering step. At the foot of the gallows he paused a moment, and, sighing heavily, turned his head to one side. Taking a momentary glance at the spectators, who numbered about seventy, he proceeded upwards, not failing to change his step so as to walk in time with the constable. Immediately upon reaching the floor of the scaffold, Bennett stepped forward and addressed those present, speaking without faltering, and holding a crucifix upraised in his hand:

"Gentlemen, I am going to die, and I am innocent of the crime. By no words that I can possibly say can I clear myself, and I cannot say more than that I am innocent, as the act was beyond my control. The act by which Hon. George Brown met his death was done in an excited moment. I suppose he could not foresee the consequences. He thought I was going to use the revolver when I drew it from my pocket, and he grasped at it, and it caused the act which caused his death. His hand must have struck the trigger, as the shot was fired simultaneously with his catching it. I am going to meet my God now, and it would be a foolish thing for me to die with a lie on my lips. What I say here you may accept as a fact. I would not likely speak false when I am about to die. I am possessed of spirit enough to have acknowledged the crime if I did it . . . I am not false at heart nor a coward. It would have been a shameful thing to have done such an act, as Mr. Brown did not deserve it. He was a most popular man throughout the world, and he went to his death through an oversight on my part. I went to him for a very simple reason, and not to commit a crime. I could not control the event. There was liquor in me, and the accident occurred, and the result — was the fatal act."

Bennett then turned his back to the spectators, and, motioning with his right hand, in which he held a crucifix, remarked quite coolly, "I am prepared to die. All I have to say is, 'May God have mercy on my soul.'"

Quietly stepping on the trap door, Bennett made a motion with his hand, and the hangman stepped forward, secured his legs by placing a strap around them between his knees and ankles; the noose was fastened about his neck; the sheriff gave the signal; rapidly England drew back the bolt, and, a moment later Bennett's body was suspended in mid air, having taken a drop of about eight feet. For a moment the body remained limp and motionless, turning round and round, then there was a convulsive twitching and drawing up of the legs, repeated at intervals for about eight minutes, and then all was still.

As a footnote to criminal history, we here print two letters; the first, which may be marked as "unsolicited", from Mary McGowan, the young woman whom the executed man repudiated as his wife, but who said she was married to him at Yorkville about five years before:

Sir: — I take the liberty of writing these few lines to express my sorrow that my husband has spoken so falsely about me. I see by the papers that he says I was false to him; but the God in the Heaven knows that I was not. He will certainly be punished for the wrongs he has done to me, and any sins that are on my soul he has driven me to it. I have done no wrong to him or to my sister that they should try to ruin me for ever, and I hope God will forgive them. While with him my life was a burden, and although I endured terrible sufferings I clung to him till he cast me aside, and then attempted to take my life. He said that after we parted that I tried to get him out of the situation, but he knows that to be untrue. Often I have gone down to the Globe office with his supper, in the pouring rain, and after he had taught me the gauge of steam, I used to put coal in the furnace and light the gas, while he lay drunk on the table. This is a terrible confession for a wife to make against her doomed husband, but in justice to myself I must tell the truth, and show the public how he has treated me. He denied his own father and mother because one of them was coloured, and would he not deny me?

The other letter is from Bennett: it was handed to Governor Green:

Toronto Jail, July 23, 1880.

I here express my sincere thanks to the officials of Toronto jail. I have received from them the kindest attention and utmost civility in contributing to my wants during my confinement here. It is remarkable the discipline that is exercised in the discharge of the various duties to be performed, and the caution, promptitude and despatch which accompanies all work done within the building. The persistent watchfulness with which innocent and guilty alike are regarded when once beneath the shadow of this roof makes Toronto Jail a credit to the city and the country at large. I have found Mr. Green a kind, shrewd, observant man. Nothing can escape his notice. The manner in which the business of the place is conducted is worthy of all praise.

Farewell, Toronto Jail,

GEORGE BENNETT

Nearly three-quarters of a century are between us and this flowery testimonial. Psychiatric investigation of the criminal mind is now fashionable, but one doubts if there is much to the purpose in determining whether George Bennett was genuinely impressed by Toronto Jail, or was acting under pressure, or felt that by thus adopting the manner of a Patron he raised himself to a superior position. At any rate there is no compulsion upon us to enquire too curiously.

VIII. TOM, DICK AND HARRY

The *Landmarks of Toronto* were published at intervals over a period of twenty years, 1894 to 1914. As articles in the *Telegram* they had first attracted public attention in 1886. It is therefore inevitable that as emphasis comes freshly upon buildings, persons and incidents mentioned earlier in another connection, the same names, the same characters in slightly different focus, are presented again and again. Such men as John Strachan, William Lyon Mackenzie, Mr. Secretary Jarvis, Parshall Terry, Jordan Post, William Helliwell, John Montgomery and Quetton St. George, swim continually into our ken — until we are ready to acknowledge them as "old acquaintance". Here is a handful of Mr. Secretary William Jarvis, in various guises, annoying or annoyed. Appointed in 1792 as Secretary and Registrar of the Province of Upper Canada, Mr. Jarvis found that there were inconveniences in having a responsible post. On one occasion indeed he came very near to the loss of his place: —

It was during the administration of Governor Hunter, a man very peremptory at times. The Quakers from up Yonge street sent a delegation, headed by Timothy Rogers and Jacob Lundy, to the Governor complaining of the difficulty and delay they experienced in getting the patents for their lands; whereupon Mr. Jarvis and several other officers of the province were ordered to appear the next day before the Governor, together with the deputation of Quakers. Pointing to the Quakers, the Governor exclaimed, "These gentlemen complain that they cannot get their patents." Each of the officials tried to exculpate himself, but it appeared that the order for the patents was more than a year old, and Mr. Jarvis was found to be the one most to blame.

The unfortunate Secretary could only say that the pressure of business in his office was so great that he had been absolutely unable to the present moment to get these particular patents ready. "Sir," was the Governor's reply, "if they are not forthcoming, every one of them, and placed in the hands of these gentlemen here in my presence at noon on Thursday next, by George I'll un-Jarvis you!" It is hardly necessary to remark that the Quakers returned with their patents.[1]

Something more than an inconvenience happened to Mr. Jarvis in 1796. On December 7, the Upper Canada *Gazette* announced: —

About eight o'clock on Saturday evening last the dwelling house of Wm. Jarvis, Esq., of this town [Newark] was discovered to be on fire, which had made such progress as to render all attempts to extinguish it almost abortive, notwithstanding which the assembling of the people was so speedy and their exertions so well directed that the province records, the most valuable house furniture, and the right wing of the buildings are saved. The conduct of several, of Miss Vanderliep in particular, in rescuing two of Mr. Jarvis' children, is spoken of with much applause, and credit in general is due. We are authorized to mention with gratitude the friendly exertions of the officers of the United States Garrison, and other strangers who rendered essential service.

But alas! The goodness that induced some persons to exert themselves in salvage was accompanied by a strange loss of memory; as witness the next advertisement: —

Mr. Jarvis takes the earliest opportunity of returning in this public manner his sincere thanks to the gentlemen and others

[1] Mr. Secretary Jarvis had been in trouble once or twice before because of acting without sufficient authority and having to be disowned. In any case, Governor Hunter was a peremptory man who thought nothing of dismissing an underling without notice — and then providing other employment for him.

who so gallantly exerted themselves in the preservation of his family and property, at the fire on Saturday evening last. He assures every individual that the uncommon solicitude shown on the occasion has made the most lasting impression on his feelings. He will thank those whose goodness induced them to carry articles to their houses to inform him where to send for them.

Next, a really annoyed proclamation: —

Five Guineas Reward — Taken away. On Saturday evening, the 3rd inst., from the subscriber, during the fire, two beaver blankets — one very large, the other small. Whoever will bring the said blankets to the subscriber shall receive one guinea reward for each; or [whoever will] give such information that they may be procured on prosecution of the offender or offenders to conviction, shall receive the above reward.

And, finally, in the *Gazette* for December 21, Mr. Jarvis refers to a further sorrow he had experienced in addition to the theft of his blankets; he advertises: —"In the loss sustained by Mr. Jarvis was also a buffalo skin, which, if returned, with or without the beaver blankets, will be thankfully received and no questions asked."

Another annoyance that brought the Secretary into court was the conduct of his servants. One, named Marshall, cut his throat in an outbuilding through a disappointment in love.

Also, following the custom of the time, he was a slaveholder, and in the early part of March, 1811, he complained that a negro boy and girl, his slaves, had stolen silver and gold from a desk at his house and escaped from their master, and that they had been aided and advised by one Coachly, a free negro. The accused having been caught, the court ordered that the boy, named Henry, but commonly known as Prince, be committed to prison; that the girl be returned to her master, and Coachly be discharged.

Secretary Jarvis died in 1818; and a few years after, his
residence met the fate that so frequently befalls old houses: —

The property was cut up by his son. A man by the name of
Lee took the house. He was an Englishman and conducted an
English chop house and billiard room in part of the building.
He also put up a small addition on the Sherbourne street side.
Early in the twenties James Padfield rented a portion of the
building from Lee and started a school.

When the school was broken up in 1824 Isaac Columbus
came into possession of the house, part of which he converted
into workshops of various kinds, for he was a jack of all trades,
using the remainder as a residence. Columbus, who was a
native of France, was one of the characters of early York,
peculiar in many respects, but good-natured, good-hearted,
charitable, and a very clever workman. During the war of
1812 he was employed as armourer to the militia stationed at
the Garrison, near which he had a forge. Many of the swords
carried into battle by the officers were manufactured by him,
and although perhaps not Damascus blades they did excellent
service. Before moving into the Jarvis house he lived on the
west side of Sherbourne street, a little north of Duke, and
in both places he was still patronized by the soldiers of the
Garrison, who, in order to get their work finished expeditiously,
would come down in a small troop and post themselves at the
door, through which they allowed no one to pass until Columbus had completed their orders. As remarked, the talents of
Columbus were very versatile. In the Jarvis house he opened a
gun shop, a jewellery shop, a blacksmith shop, (which for a time
afterward was occupied by Paul Bishop), and a factory for the
manufacture of stove pipes, he having obtained a contract for
a quantity of these. In such varied occupations he employed
quite a number of men, among whom were James Bright and
Paul Bishop, both blacksmiths by trade and both of whom
married daughters of Mr. Columbus. The gun and jewellery
shop was at the corner of Duke and Sherbourne streets. The
stovepipe shop was further down on Sherbourne. Columbus

was equally at home whether required to make a service of plate, pull a tooth, make and insert a new set of teeth, jump the battered axe of a woodsman, make skate blades or the irons of an ice boat, put in order a surveyor's theodolite, or replace an instrument lost from a draughtsman's case. He was the schoolboy's friend, and they used to flock to him in great numbers to get their little matters attended to. Dr. Scadding once having left an article for repairs, with instruction that it must be made at a specified time, Columbus retorted that "must" was only for the King of France. He was an out-and-out royalist, and refused to have anything to do with the York Liberals who were then beginning to agitate reform, on the ground that the modern ideas of government hindered the King from acting as a good father to his people. The expression "first quality blue," used by him to indicate an extra quality for which an extra price was to be paid, passed into a sort of proverb among the schoolboys of the time who grew into the habit of applying it to persons and things held by them to be of a high order of excellence. Mr. Columbus moved into the Jarvis house in 1824 and left it about 1832, when it was taken by Mr. James Kidd, the father of Mr. John Kidd, who lived there until 1837, when he built a one-storey and attic dwelling across the way on the south-west corner of Jarvis and Queen streets. This building is still standing [in 1896] but elevated to two stories and an attic. Mr. Kidd died here in 1844. During the cholera epidemic in Toronto it is said several persons died of the dread disease in the Jarvis house. Either from this story or from the tale of suicide, the old mansion after a time acquired an uncanny reputation and was commonly reported to be haunted. During Mr. Kidd's occupancy strange, unearthly noises were heard at night in the big room formerly used by Secretary Jarvis as an office, and no one could be persuaded to occupy it, so it was left vacant. On several occasions in the dead of night Mr. Kidd, during one of these ghostly outbreaks, would creep down to the deserted chamber, lamp in one hand and pistol in the other, to solve the mystery if possible; but on his approach the noises would cease and no trace of any visitor could be found.

Once a man by the name of Baxter, recently arrived in Canada, came to the house to spend the night. He, being ignorant of the reputation of the house, was assigned to the haunted room. Several times during the night he was heard tossing restlessly on his bed. The next morning he appeared at breakfast pale and haggard, and declared he would never pass another night in that room. In 1848 Paul Bishop, who had acquired the property, tore down the old house.

Paul Bishop was a French Canadian and established himself as a blacksmith and wheelwright. For many years he was the principal workman in his trade in the town; but eventually he failed in business and left Toronto. Mr. T. D. Harris obtained possession of the shop which he altered considerably. Mr. Harris had established a hardware store in 1829 and had done an extensive business for many years. Money being scarce he issued scrip redeemable by himself and this passed current through the town. The notes were about the size of the present Dominion bills and were popularly known as "shin plasters".

His store was supposed to be fire proof. This belief prevailed to such an extent that during the great fire of 1849 no effort was made to remove the contents of the building at 124 King street east. For a long time it resisted the flames, but at length fell a victim and everything was destroyed. After this disaster Mr. Harris retired from business. In the year 1841 a great fire had raged in the western part of the town destroying the western half of the block bounded by King, York, Pearl, (then Boulton) and Bay streets. Mr. Harris at the time of that conflagration was chief of the fire brigade and had been for several years, but immediately after the fire he resigned his office, and Robert Beard was appointed as his successor.

On very many pages in the *Landmarks* we meet the phrase, "The old house (or shop, or store) was torn down." It is hard now to realize the appearance of these places of business;

and harder still to enter into the kind of life that they sheltered. Take, for example, the dry goods business of Messrs. Archibald Laurie and Company, at the corner of King and Yonge where now stands the Dominion Bank. When the brothers Laurie retired to the Scotland from whence they came, Mr. William Harris Dow pursued the same business in a retail way at the same spot.

Rigidly conservative in his procedure, a portion of Mr. Dow's stock eventually became so antiquated as to approximate to the contents of a veritable curiosity shop, and prove attractive merely to customers possessed of archaic notions or hypercritical particularity, who could generally succeed in "ticking off" their list of wants, however unique, by recourse to the Dow emporium. Mr. Dow's trade becoming inactive, and embarrassment setting in, he was compelled to abandon his business not long anterior to the acquirement of its site by the Dominion Bank for the erection of a head office. Closely coincident with Mr. Dow's retirement his health declined, and death occurred after a short illness. Socially Mr. Dow led quite an isolated existence, and was exceedingly methodical in his habits. Although by no means inappreciative of humour, he was reserved to the verge of eccentricity in his intercourse with employees or the public. During a residence in Toronto covering a period of over thirty years, Mr. Dow is not known to have extended his visits in a social capacity to more than one or possibly two houses, where of a Sunday evening he occasionally joined the family circle over a cup of tea. When Mr. Dow had charge of Messrs. Laurie's establishment, as was not unusual at this period, all the employees, including the manager, were boarded and lodged on the premises, and although the proprietors were anything but inconsiderate of the comfort of their clerks, the business was rigidly conducted by "rule and line." Every lawful morning at six in summer and seven o'clock in winter the whole staff had to report personally at the retail department and register their names in a journal provided mainly for that purpose. After the expiration of fifteen minutes, the book was securely laid aside, and in the course of the day the circumstance of any absence at roll call was duly noted on the pages, with a caution attached by the assistant manager, for the edification of the delinquent; to which his attention was pointedly directed on the following morning, when the journal again came into requisition. The doors of the residential portion of the house were locked by one of the younger hands at 10 p.m., and the keys delivered to the assistant manager, any irregularity in the matter of ingress on the part of employees being recorded by that functionary. On alternate Sundays one of the two youngest employees mounted guard at 5 p.m., and, in accordance with regular custom, all the clerks to be found in the house at 9 p.m., including the manager, assembled at that hour in the dining room to hear a portion of Scripture read by a junior.

This dining-room was necessarily situated in the third storey, at the end of a long corridor, and the culinary operations were performed, unavoidably, at a remote distance in the basement of the building; an arrangement, in the absence of elevators, rather inconvenient to all concerned. To secure at all times attention to the calls of customers, the staff was divided into two detachments, known as the first and second parties, these weekly alternating.

There was no porter, so the sweeping of the store, cleaning of windows, managing shutters and shovelling snow, fell to the lot of the two youngest assistants; together with the delivery of parcels. But the whole establishment, from the manager downwards, took part in a ritual cleaning of boots, each for himself, every morning in the attic. (Except for the two youngest assistants, who, having other things to think of in the mornings, cleaned their boots last thing at night.)

That apprentices were not of much value in York the following advertisement appearing in the Canada *Gazette* some years earlier, will painfully show: —

Sixpence Reward — Ran away from the subscriber, about four weeks since, an apprentice boy, 17 years old, stout for his age, fair hair, dark complexion, short, flat nose, broad face, grey eyes and flat feet; had on when he went away striped overalls and shirt, a short brown coat and a white handkerchief about his neck. Any person returning the said boy shall receive the above reward.

Slaves were, of course, another matter; the advertisements that follow reveal their place and value in Toronto society: —

Indian Slave. All persons are forbidden harboring, employing, or concealing my Indian slave, called Sal, as I am determined to prosecute any offender, to the utmost extremity of the law; and persons who may suffer her to remain on their premises for the space of half an hour, without my written consent, will be taken as offending, and dealt with accordingly. Charles Field.

A Slave For Sale. To be sold — A healthy, strong Negro woman, about 30 years of age; understands cookery, laundry and the taking care of poultry. N.B.— She can dress ladies' hair. Enquire of the printers.

Other advertisements give the impression that in those early days a woman's place was often elsewhere than the home. Sometimes it was the pillory: — "In 1804 Elizabeth Ellis for being a nuisance was sentenced to six months' imprisonment and to stand in the pillory on two market days for two hours at a time."

There is also a cryptic reference to a Miss or Mrs. Day who appears to have been deported: — "Paid Captain Earl for taking down Mary Day, four days, ditto for provisions furnished by him to take her from Kingston to Lower Canada, £2.0.0. Paid William Hunter his account for keeping the said Mary Day, £10."

That is a quotation from York's assessment rolls.

Sometimes the ladies left home of their own volition, followed by the blessing (or otherwise) of deserted husbands. As witness these cases:—

Whereas Deborah, my wife, eloped from my bed and board, and improperly resides with Charles Wilson, of this town, innkeeper, and refuses to return to the duties of her family, all persons are, therefore, strictly forbidden harboring or trusting her, as I will pay no debt, that she may contract or occasion.

Advertisement — Whereas my wife Nancy refuses living with me with out any manner of cause, she being influenced by her vile parents to pay no regard to her marriage covenant, but violate the laws of God and man, therefore I forewarn all persons not to credit her on my account, or to harbour or employ her on any pretence whatsoever; if other wise they shall be dealt with as the law directs. John Anderson.

Some husbands were as nice as they could be about it.

Whereas Bathsheba Cameron, wife of Archibald Cameron, of the town of York, Upper Canada, has without any just cause or provocation whatever eloped from his bed and board, behaved in an unbecoming manner, and after absenting herself from the 1st of January, 1799, although solicited to return without effect, which he can prove, has again returned to this town; he is therefore at last under the disagreeable but absolute necessity of thus giving public notice that the said Bathsheba Cameron may not be credited nor harbored on his account, as he is determined to pay no debts of her contracting. Archibald Cameron.

And some were *not*: —

Notice; — Whereas my wife Mary has eloped from my bed and board and stripped my house of everything valuable, and carried them off in the absence of myself and son while at work in the field, for which she can assign no reason, excepting my checking of her by speaking for frequently getting beastly drunk, striving to barter her daughter (near 16 years of age) to a half Indian for three gallons of rum, and for her bad example to her two younger daughters, one 14 and the other near 5 years old. I therefore caution all persons from crediting or harbouring her on my account, as I will not pay any debt of her contracting. Given under my hand at No. 17 north side of the Township of Toronto, Upper Canada, this 29th day of May, 1815.

But occasionally the lady took her turn and hit back. Catherine Tip, having been advertised as a deserter "without provocation or sufficient reason" replied a fortnight later: —

Whereas William Tip has endeavored to pass himself upon the public for my husband, and has lately presumed to declare himself such in the Upper Canada *Gazette,* I conceive it a duty which I owe to the welfare of my children and to my own future happiness to assure the world that I never was and never will be united in wedlock to that unworthy man. Catherine Camp.

Another lady (well, a female, anyhow, for so she signs herself), having observed in the *Gazette* a paragraph which said "a tax is to be laid on scolding wives" thinks it no more than just and equitable that a similar one be imposed on drunken husbands: —

"The manner in which they are to be rated is as follows: — For getting drunk in the morning, £30 per annum; twice a day, £40; three times a day, morning, noon and evening, £50; every alternate day, £20; once a week, if not on Sundays, £15; on Sundays, £60; for beating his wife once a day, £200; twice a day, morning and evening, £400; every alternate day, £100; once a week if not on Sundays, £80; on Sundays, £500; coming home from the tavern drunk and beating his wife into a fit of hysterics, consumption or giving her a pair of black eyes, £700. Getting drunk and being in consequence confined to his bed a week or two, £1000."

"The usage of a spaniel," says she, "many of our sex experience from their malignant husbands"; and are they then to renounce the use of their only weapon? Perish the thought.

In 1817 John Venzente came before the Court of Oyer and Terminer, indicted for having shot Peter Harris, "a young man whom he had just reasons to suspect was endeavouring to disturb the peace of his family by coveting his young and handsome consort." Venzente prayed that his trial might be postponed "as his principal evidences had not yet arrived." (One wonders what they were). The Chief Justice addressed to the jury "a very eloquent and feeling charge"; the jury (all married men, no doubt) were absent as much as half an hour; and their verdict was manslaughter. A decent newspaper veil is dropped over the sentence; a young and handsome consort should not be left alone too long.

This may be the place to reprint what the *Landmarks* call a "Unique Birth Notice".

Birth — At Prescott, on Thursday night, the lady of Captain Loring, A.D.C., and Private Secretary to his Honour Lieutenant-General Drummond, was safely delivered of a daughter. The happy father had returned from a state of captivity with the enemy but a few hours previous to the joyful event.

No comment!

Two somewhat bizarre items may end the first part of this chapter; one amusing but of no particular point — another of interest for the family name.

February 6th, 1823. The Register of this week records the birth of the first triplets in York. The notice reads: Birth: On Sunday last Mrs. Lee, wife of Francis Lee, of Yonge Street, of three fine children, two boys and a girl."

A Mr. Endicott of York, wanted to trace a long-lost brother, and inserted in the *Gazette* this notice: —

Appeal to the Public — A young brother of the subscriber, named William Endicott, a native of Axminster, in Devonshire, left England in the year 1796 for Bermuda or the West Indies, since which the subscriber has received no correct account of him, but understanding lately that he died a few years ago in some part of America, in affluent circumstances, the subscriber, who is heir-at-law, would be most grateful for any information respecting him, and readily reward any person who may possess it for the trouble of communication. He lives in the town of York, in the Province of Upper Canada, North America. Any letter addressed to William Allan, Esq., postmaster at York, will be safely received by him. John Endicott, York, 7th June 1822.

Finally, a tantalizing paragraph taken from the middle of a chapter on "The Corner". That is the north-east corner of King and Yonge, stated to have been "a business centre — one of the best known sites in the City of Toronto, for nearly a century." As the Crown granted the first patent for the lot in 1801 (to Charles Field who was so vexed about his straying slave) we have to add two and fifty years of progress toward a second century. Well, in the middle of the story and at the end of a page about Mr. Samuel Ridout's office and Mr. Joseph Dennis's children, we have two paragraphs: —

Mr. Charles Lord Helliwell, who resided in Toronto in 1818, states that in 1830 the two-storey dwelling on the north-east corner of King and Yonge streets was occupied by a man named Bosworth, as a tavern. Mr. Helliwell recognizes, even after so many years, the engraving of the two storey building in Robertson's *Landmarks*. He says he does not remember the original cottage which stood on the corner, but has a vivid recollection of the house with the fine willow trees on both fronts of the curb of the sidewalks.

He says that in the rear of Bosworth's tavern was a stable. In 1831 a man, driving a load of pork down Yonge street, was followed by a bear. It was in the evening and the man did not observe the bear. He arrived at the tavern, unhooked his horses, and went to bed in the tavern. In the night the inmates were aroused, and found that the bear had gotten into the horses' stall and was creating quite a sensation.

I have wondered for twenty years what became of that bear? [2]

THE FIRST FERRY HORSE BOAT

II. STRUGGLE AND RELEASE

One of the virtues of the *Landmarks* is that a century is seen as a very little time, during which men and women appear, endure, and pass on; leaving to others a place in the front line — and, usually, a better chance in the fighting. That Englishman or that Scot who came to Upper Canada may have started with a few illusions, but a month's resi-

[2] Those animals were far more plentiful around York in the days of our ancestors (would it be wrong to murmur something about "bears and fore-bears"?).

dence left him without them. Take the case of Thomas
Helliwell. When he left the Old Country he did so in
secret, for the law prohibited the emigration of manufacturers:
so he sailed from Sunderland on the north-east coast and
his family, a few weeks later, embarked from the north-west.

They had much to endure and no small amount of hard-
ship to undergo. They sailed from Liverpool in the ship Abeona,
belonging to Portland in the State of Maine, U.S.A., in
June, 1818.

Coming out of port the captain of the ship and the pilot
disagreed, and through the neglect of one of them, or possibly
of both, the ship ran aground in the Mersey, and as the tide
went out was left high and dry. She was at last got off, but
was found to be making water very quickly. Her crew were
greatly alarmed and refused to proceed, so that there was
nothing for the captain to do but put back to Liverpool, which
he did, the vessel's pumps being kept constantly at work.

At Liverpool they remained for three days to effect repairs,
then again set sail for New York, which after a voyage
extending over six weeks was at last reached. Here, however,
fresh troubles beset them, as the captain of the ship failed to
fulfil a portion of his engagements with his passengers. Of
these the whole of them, with one single exception, were
emigrants. It is to be feared that the solitary cabin passenger
must have had anything but a lively time.

Many of the Abeona's passengers, instead of at once resuming
their journey to their destinations either in Canada or the
United States, remained in New York for the purpose of taking
legal proceedings against the captain, but the Helliwells did
nothing of the kind. They obtained a small boat from the
captain, into it put themselves and their goods and soon landed
at Pertham Bay, N.Y. From there they sailed to Albany and
from thence to Schenectady. From the latter place they shipped
in Durham boats for Oswego and reached that port after a
tiresome journey of several days' duration.

While on their journey from Schenectady to Oswego, when evening approached the boat halted and was moored fast for the night, the whole of its occupants camping on the river bank.

After a very brief rest at Oswego the Helliwells shipped for Lewiston, which was safely reached after a very stormy passage. At Lewiston they were met by Mr. Eastwood, who crossed with them to Queenston, from whence they went to Lundy's Lane. It was getting towards the latter end of August, and Mr. William Helliwell relates how greatly interested he was in all he saw, and how well he recollects the day. One circumstance he vividly remembers, and that is that there was at the time a wild beast exhibition which consisted of one single elephant, and that people had come from miles around to see it.

More than probably there were some other exhibits of a less sensational kind, but the elephant comprised the show's only real attraction.

The family lived first at Lundy's Lane, but in 1826 migrated to Toronto. They had been in the brewing business in Drummondville and "Mrs. Helliwell drove all the way seated in a large chair which was placed inside a huge kettle used in the brewery; and so protected she rode all the way to Toronto."

On the east bank of the Don, where now is Broadview Avenue, a road known as the Mill Road led to Parshall Terry's Mills. After he was drowned while attempting to cross the Don on a floating bridge, Colin Skinner and John Eastwood owned the mills. Both these men married into the Helliwell family, and near their mills Thomas Helliwell senior built a brewery.

This was a building of two stories, about fifty feet square, constructed of stone, brick and wood against the side of the hill so that the eaves on one side touched the hill after the manner in which farmhouses in the old Dutch settlements of New York State were built. Connected with the brewery and

in the same building was a distillery. On the first settlement
of Upper Canada before distilleries were established here,
Jamaica rum was the principal drink. In those days the pure
article was obtainable. Helliwell's brewery had a capacity for
making one hundred and twenty bushels of mash from three
to five times per week and the distillery put from fifteen to
twenty bushels a day into whiskey, rye whiskey being the principal liquor made. The region about the mills at this time
was a secluded spot in the modest state of nature, a favourite
haunt for wolves, bears and deer, a spot presenting difficulties
peculiarly formidable for the new settlers to grapple with
from the loftiness and steepness of the hills and the kind
of timber growing thereabouts: massive pines for the most
part. Mr. William Helliwell, one of the brothers managing
Helliwell's mills and later Fishery Commissioner for the county
of York, with his residence at Highland Creek, has stood at
the door of the brewery and seen bears, wolves and deer
moving about in the adjacent forest. One night wolves killed
a dozen of his sheep, one of them being killed on the door-
step of his house. Returning home one day from the town
he came upon a huge bear in the road near the Don bridge
and at other times he frequently met these and other wild
animals on parts of the road farther removed from the town.
Thomas Helliwell, senior, died in 1825. After his death
his sons Thomas and William managed the brewery, which was
burned down in 1847 and never rebuilt.

Mention above of Parshall Terry may excuse a note here
that his twin daughters, Augusta Deborah and Sarah Maria,
were baptized by the Reverend George O'Kill Stuart, in
the year 1808, they being then "aged eleven years and
upwards". About that time, in this city, an exceptional
number of twins seem to have been baptized. The early
registers of St. James' Cathedral are full of surprises, and
of cryptic references that the *Landmarks* copy but cannot
resolve. For example: "was baptised, John, a foundling laid
at Mrs. Cockburn's door on the evening of the 8th inst."

That entry is by John Strachan, who underlines a fact apparent, in baptizing the son of John Brown and Eliza Fee, by adding "the child illegitimate". To the entry of baptism for Martha, daughter of Samuel Sluder, is appended: "No friends in this country". It sounds bleak, and probably was still more so.

One of the Rector's crosses must have been that people would come to him from Chinguacousy, a word that he could not spell. So we have Chinguacushy, Gincagushie, and even a despairing variant Chingueaisgnas. "And Heaven it knoweth what that may mean." Or this: "Child's name Robert, Elizabeth, Wilks. Parents, George, Sponsors, Susan Highland; Date, Tecumseth." And why should Mark Burnham, the son of Zaccheus and Mrs. Burnham have been baptized on 2nd October 1818, and again, but with different sponsors, on November 11th? (Perhaps it didn't "take" the first time!)

This matter of names has been enlarged in another section[3]; it can scarcely be justified under a heading "Struggle and Release". We are on safer ground with the report of a trial in 1800. Before the Court came "— Ricks, for a grand larceny of which he was acquitted. The indictment appeared to be founded upon the inhuman principles of spite and malice". That is what the Grand Jury said of a charge laid by Mr. John Dennis against Reuben Riggs; and as the said John Dennis had also published a libellous article in the *Gazette,* the printer was anxious to "get out from under". In the next week's issue he apologizes, and so does Dennis, completely. He says: —

By desire we now insert the following document which we hope will exonerate us from any appearance of malevolence:—
"Whereas Mr. Reuben Riggs of York, carpenter, has been indicted in respect of a certain trespass of which I complained against him and having been tried on such indictment and honorably acquitted.

[3] See p. 156.

"Now, I do hereby certify and declare unto all whom it may concern that I never did intend directly or indirectly that the said Mr. Riggs should be charged with, or arrested, or accused, with anything, crime or misdemeanor, other than trespass of which I complained, and that my only object was compensation for a trespass. I do certify and make known to whom it may concern or these presents may come, that as far as I have known him, which has been altogether after or since said tryal, by what appeared on said tryal, that said Reuben Riggs was innocent as to any the least intention of felonious intent, as I now understand the word; having supposed what I signed a form in such cases, and that I do believe him to be an honest, sober and industrious man. John Dennis. Acknowledged and signed in presence of A. Macdonell, Seneca Ketchum." (Verbatim from the original, points excepted.)

Now dip for a moment into darker matters; accident, scandal, death.

A market place had been established in 1803 by Governor Peter Hunter. It was a wide square on which subsequently a wooden building arose; and its boundaries were King, Church, Market and New Streets.

In 1831 the wooden market building was torn down and in its place was erected a quadrangular brick building with arched gateway entrances at the sides. Around it were set posts with iron chains dependent. This building filled the whole square with the exception of roadways on the east and west sides. Around the four sides of this new market above the butchers' stalls ran a wooden gallery. Here in 1834 occurred a frightful accident. A political meeting was being held and the gallery was overcrowded. While one of the speakers was haranguing the assemblage part of the balcony gave way, precipitating the people to the floor below. In the descent many were caught upon the sharp upcurved iron hooks of the butchers' stalls. Some of the wounded on this occasion were: — Son of Col. Fitzgibbon, injured severely; Mr. Mountjoy, thigh broken; Mr. Cochrane, injured severely; Mr. Charles Daly,

thigh broken; Mr. George Gurnett, wound in the head; Mr.
Keating, injured internally; Mr. Fenton, injured; Master Gooder-
ham, thigh broken; Dr. Lithgow, contused severely; Mr. Mor-
rison, contused severely; Mr. Alderman Denison, cut on the head;
Mr. Thornhill, thigh broken; Mr. Street, arm broken; Mr.
Deese, thigh broken.

These were only the more prominent citizens. There were
others; and for a city of Toronto's size it counted as a
major misfortune.

The next incident comes under the heading of "struggle".

Andrew Mercer came to York at the beginning of the century,
and acquired large tracts of lands. His cottage stood at the
south-east corner of Bay and Wellington streets. This is an
epitome of a once celebrated case growing out of his large
accumulation of property, and it may be observed as a curious
circumstance that the property which he obtained gratuitously
from the Crown at the commencement of the century when
it was comparatively worthless, returned to the Crown in the
latter part of the century when it had grown valuable. In
1871 Andrew Mercer died in his Bay street cottage at a very
advanced age, leaving an estate valued at about $150,000. As
no will was found at his death, and as no legal heirs were known
to the authorities, his property escheated to the Crown from
which it had come. Subsequently however, Andrew Mercer
Jr., a reputed son of the deceased, and a law student by the
name of Reynolds, found hidden away between the leaves of
a book in the Bay street cottage, a paper which purported
to be the will of Andrew Mercer. That document was simply
a scrap of paper about two inches wide by six inches long.
The writing was in pencil. It reads: — "June 7, 1871. In
case I should die before my son should return or before I will
have time to make my will, I wish James Smyth and Charles
Unwin to have my estate divided among my wife and son.
And. Mercer." The chirography, tremulous as with age,
resembled that of Mr. Mercer. On the discovery of this paper,
Messrs. Smyth and Unwin, the executors named in it, brought

suit in the Court of Chancery before Vice-Chancellor Blake to determine the validity of the instrument and to have probate issued. On the trial, which lasted through the 13th, 14th, 15th, 17th, 20th and 21st of January, 1876, the following counsel appeared: — Messrs. Boyd and Thorne for the executors, C. Moss for Andrew Mercer, junior, P. McGregor for the housekeeper of the late Andrew Mercer, who claimed to be his widow, Mr. Small for R. D. Mercer, London, England, who claimed to be a nephew of the deceased, and C. Robinson and J. D. Edgar, for the Attorney-General, the Hon. Oliver Mowat. The case excited the greatest interest not only in worldly but in religious circles, for in connection with the suit to determine the validity of the will, another question arose, the two being tried together. This was as to whether Bridget, the housekeeper, who claimed to be the wife of the deceased, was Mrs. Bridget Mercer or Miss Bridget O'Reilly. Her assertion was that she was married to Andrew Mercer, June 25, 1851, by the Rev. Father O'Reilly, whom she had brought to Mr. Mercer's house for the express purpose of performing the ceremony, and that her son was born a month later. Father O'Reilly, who was dead at the time of the trial, had been the parish priest at the Gore of Toronto at the time of the alleged marriage. The parish book was examined and in it, on the date specified, appeared the record of the marriage. The priest being dead, the late Archbishop Lynch was called to testify as to the validity of the record. He said that Father O'Reilly was a priest at the Gore of Toronto at the time and that the entry of the marriage was in his handwriting. An examination of the writing of the record was made on the other hand[4] with the result that the record was not credited. The result of the trial was a decree made January 21, 1876, declaring that the paper writing propounded by the executors for probate in the Surrogate Court of York as being the will of the late Andrew Mercer was not the will of the said Andrew Mercer and that the said decree decided all issues in the suit in favour of the Attorney General. Another litigation was induced

[4] i.e. for the Crown.

by the decision, for afterwards when the Crown undertook to take possession of the Bay street house, Andrew Mercer, jr., refused to go out, and the case finally went before the Privy Council of England who decided that the Province had a right to all its escheated lands. The Crown, however, voluntarily made a grant of certain monies and properties, being part of the estate, in behalf of Andrew Mercer, jr., and his wife and family.

Return for the last note to the unknown, the men who had left their homes to better themselves, who came here to live and were called to die: Tom, Dick and Harry. In 1848 Toronto was scourged by ship fever (typhoid) and cholera. Hundreds of emigrants died on the wharves, and in the hospital on the lot at the north-west corner of King and John streets. Perhaps in order to give people something amusing, to turn their attention from the risk of sudden death, John Ritchie built and fitted up a theatre, which he named the Royal Lyceum.

For more than a dozen years Toronto had now been a city, but as yet the people had seen neither a theatre nor a player that would be dignified with the name according to modern standards. The amateur companies had provided most of the entertainments in the theatrical line, assisted now and then by such professionals as could be induced to visit the by no means attractive town.

However, in some manner and regardless of risks, whether patronage or sickness, a company was brought here; and Mr. Alexander Jacques, of Ottawa, thus relates an incident:—

In the company, under the assumed name of Brown, was a clever actor, a Philadelphian, of Quaker extraction, who boarded at Mrs. O'Keefe's hotel, on the north side of Wellington street, nearly opposite the head of Scott St. Brown was up for the benefit on the Monday night. I had promised to assist, and was to appear as Harry Hamen, and Brown as Jeremy Twitcher, in the old English drama of "The Golden Farmer". On Saturday night after the performance was over, we had all the arrangements fixed for Monday night, as we walked down King to the corner of Yonge street. I was to visit Brown on Sunday morning at ten o'clock, to get a copy of my part for the farce. On entering the hotel I was met with the startling news "Brown's dead." Sure enough I found the news too true. On visiting his room, there, what but a few hours before was a living being full of life, hope, and high aspirations, (for he was a good versatile comedian), was the inanimate form of poor Brown. Mrs. O'Keefe was in dread of the news getting out that a man had died of cholera in her house, so matters were kept quiet. Potter was told of the sad end, and at once made arrangements with Mr. Williams, undertaker, to have the body buried in Potter's field, Yorkville, that Sunday night. The weather was sultry, and towards evening a thunder storm, with rain and lightning, set in. About ten o'clock, Potter and one or two others, with the writer, proceeded up Yonge street on our melancholy errand. During the trip to the toll-gate the rain had ceased, but from over Wells' hill wicked flashes lit up the scene. Just as we lowered the body into its final resting place, Potter took off his hat, all following his example, and in a dignified, and quite clerical style, appealed to the great Author of the universe for the peace of poor Brown's soul. Just at that instant flash after flash, peal after peal, of the lightning and thunder rolled over us and vividly lit up the last scene. The rain poured in torrents, and, having filled in the mother earth on top of the other, we departed from that lonely home of the dead of early York, a spot now unknown as a graveyard.

IX. PASSING THROUGH FIRE

Charles Dickens wrote of a little city in Upper Canada that it looked as if half of it had recently been burned down and the other half not yet built up. This pulse of death and rebirth, of construction, destruction and reconstruction, beats for a hundred years through the history of Toronto. The volumes of the *Landmarks* reiterate the tale. Streets are laid out, houses built — wood, brick, stone; and along each street goes traffic and into each store flows trade. Then some merchant tears down a store and rebuilds to a size more consonant with his hopes, his ambitions or his needs. At once a different standard is set: before long his lead is followed by competitors or friends, and gradually the face of the street is lifted, the look of the city is changed. The account of the notable houses of Toronto is punctuated thickly with the words "It was torn down"; and even more often "It was destroyed by fire". Look back to the period 1830 to 1850 and we find that the combination of wooden houses and crude fire fighting gave "the devouring element" every advantage. In 1800, when Toronto was sparsely settled and the gaps between houses were wide, regulations were issued as to the possession of water-filled buckets by every householder. We know that, from their earliest experiences of the calamity, the inhabitants of Toronto were anxiously concerned with the necessity of obtaining such equipment as would aid them to save at least some of their goods when fire showed itself in their homes.

In 1820, and for some years subsequently, the law was that every householder should keep two leather buckets hanging in a conspicuous place in front of his house. On an alarm, which

THE BRITISH AMERICAN INSURANCE BUILDING,
N.W. Cor. Church and Court Sts.

THE FIRST FIRE HALL IN TORONTO,
Church Street, near the Old Kirk, 1827

was sounded by shouting and ringing the bell of St. James' Church, then the only bell in the city, a double row of citizens was formed from the burning building to the Bay, or to the nearest cistern, and along one line were passed the buckets full of water, and down the other the empty buckets.

In 1826, eight years before York became Toronto, the first fire department of the town was organized, and the first fire engine company was instituted. It was composed of some of the most respectable merchants and tradesmen of the town.

When hand fire engines came into use the bucket brigade passed out of existence and water was conveyed to the engines in large barrels, filled at the bay and drawn to the fire on wagons. This "puncheon system" continued down to 1861.

The puncheon was a large cask, capable of containing from sixty to eighty gallons of water, or about what would fill three ordinary flour barrels. One of the conditions on which the carters of those days obtained their licenses was that each man be provided with at least one puncheon. The system of rewards offered to those carters first at fires with their puncheons was a sufficient inducement to guarantee a punctual service. To the carter who was first at the fire with his puncheon, a prize of four dollars was given, to the second man three dollars, to the third man two dollars and to the fourth man one dollar; all coming later received a York shilling for every puncheon brought, and the same price was paid to the prize winners for every additional puncheon. As might have been expected, disputes as to the relative time of arrival were frequent, and in such cases the contesting parties went with their claims the next day to the chief engineer's office, where the question was decided. The carters were not paid in money at the time of the fire, but on the arrival of each puncheon its carrier was given a check of tin or lead which entitled him on presentation to the proper officials to a shilling for every check. These checks were round, the size of a silver half dollar, and bore on them the number of the company issuing it. Sometimes they were stamped with a fancy device like an engine. In consequence of the provision of the law, every carter had his puncheon and some of the more wealthy ones had several puncheons, one for each of the carts. A few carters made it their business to keep puncheons filled on the carts, at all times ready in the event of an alarm. Others, when the day's work was done, put their puncheons on their carts, filled in readiness for fires during the night, and it is shrewdly suspected that many a building was set on fire by the carters themselves, in the expectation or hope of obtaining one of the rewards. So keen was the rivalry that although the cartsmen started from home or from the bay with their puncheons full, yet, on account of their mad haste to get to the fire over the rough roads of the town, when they reached the engines there scarcely would be a pailfull left, all the rest having been splashed out.

The person who discovered a fire was supposed to rush to the nearest bell and ring it; but as the members of the volunteer Fire Brigade were all employed during the day and, equally, scattered about the town at night, it usually happened that the cartmen with their puncheons arrived at the fire in advance of the engines. Thence came opportunities for "salvage" that storekeeper and householder alike deplored.

Hand engines continued in use down to 1861, and were drawn to fires by the firemen. In that year the brigade was re-organized with steam engines, but the members of the department still continued to practice their ordinary avocations, going to fire halls only on the alarm. Although the city had steam engines it did not at first have horses at hand to pull them, and whenever there was a fire the nearest horses at hand were drafted into the service. The old hand engines [after the introduction of steam] were sold to small municipalities in the province, the last one to be disposed of being the Phoenix, which was purchased by the village of Oakville.

In 1866 there were fifty-five fires within the city limits and fifteen of these were probably incendiary. The alarm bells in use were not particularly effective. "There is no lookout or watch kept at any of the engine or fire alarm stations, and it often happens that fires do occur for which some of the principal bells are not rung at all. There are many parts of the city in which should a fire break out, a messenger, to convey the intelligence to the nearest engine or alarm station may have to travel nearly two miles . . ." Picture the scene: an elderly citizen, leaving a rapidly burning house behind him and making his way on a winter's night over awful roads, to one of the two fire halls that the city owned: a mile or more ere the alarm could be sounded, the firemen gathered from their resting beds, and one of Toronto's two steam engines prepared to move. And he would have a terrible knowledge to clog his steps, knowledge almost certainty: "When they get to the house they'll find no water." And 1866 is less than ninety years ago. What Toronto's people suffered earlier can be gathered from the *Landmarks* more easily than it can be imagined. It is indeed "a thing imagination boggles at": a suggestion that the young city owed as much to arson as it did to architecture. Let us pass through fires for the twenty years 1838-1858 — a selection only — as the Devil went through Athlone, in standing leaps; and let us glance at earlier days of primitive innocence.

The first fire engine was presented to the town in December 1802, Governor Peter Russell being the donor. "As a very small token of their sense of this indulgence, a subscription was most cheerfully set on foot — for the erection of a proper building in the town for the preservation of the engine." The location of the first fire hall and the value of the first fire engine are alike unknown; but, as to the latter, an announcement a week later may be reprinted without comment: "On Sunday last the house of Mr. James Playter on Yonge street was entirely consumed by fire, together with every article contained in it." Plundering Yankees, in

THE FIRE AT GOODERHAM'S, 1869

1813, carried off the engine owned by the town; but whether as a curiosity or for subsequent use in Washington it is impossible to say. The Parliament Buildings in York, at that time destroyed, were burned a second time, in 1824, through the prosaic overheating of a flue; and

early in the summer of 1829, the historic residence of the first Lieutenant-Governor, General Simcoe, was burned to the ground. Castle Frank, for so the house was called, was on the western bank of the Don, at the northern end of Parliament street. It was not in use at the time of its destruction, and was supposed to have been set on fire by some fisherman.

In 1838 one fire on King Street broke out at mid-day on the premises of William Musson, "when most of the members of the fire companies were at their dinners. Consequently they were speedily on hand". The *Colonist,* Toronto's newspaper, murmurs, "It is a matter for regret that some employers are reluctant about allowing men to leave their work for this very necessary service".

In August, 1838, the hat manufactory of Mr. Joseph Rogers was burned.

The damage was £1000 and the houses adjoining were scorched. In this fire the new hook and ladder apparatus did such good work that the City Council decided to purchase a similar one if the old one could be sold to some other corporation. Mr. Rogers, it is recorded, was on a buying trip to Montreal at the time. An advertisement in an adjoining column states "that notwithstanding the fire, Mr. Joseph Rogers will resume business as soon as a convenient and satisfactory building can be obtained." Thus it is to be seen that even at that early day Toronto merchants were alert and progressive. [A Ross Robertson comment of 1896.]

In 1839, St. James's Cathedral Church was wholly destroyed. It was new, built of stone, and complete all but the tower. Flames burst through the roof, suddenly, and soon all the interior was burned including the fine new organ. The *Palladium* (newspaper) grieved:

"It is not the pecuniary loss alone, which is not less than £12,500 but the almost irremediable inconvenience it must occasion for a great length of time. Had the long-intended new church been erected, at the west end of the city, concerning which so much has been said and written, and which ought to have been commenced long ago, this inconvenience would not have been felt, as it now must be. As this calamity has occurred it may be well now to consider whether it would not be of more benefit to the public generally to erect several small churches, even though they should be of wood, say one in each ward, than to lay out a large sum of money upon one only. A wooden, or even a brick building, of much elegance and of sufficient extent, by proper management could be erected for £2,500, so that for the £12,500 which it is said was the entire cost of St. James' church now in ruins with its contents, five churches of moderate size, one in each ward, could be built."

On this occasion it is said Dr. Strachan was seen standing by, watching the destruction of his beloved temple, and whistling the while as a means of relieving his sorrow. Another loss, not mentioned by the *Palladium,* was the destruction of a very large triplet window of stained glass over the altar of the church, containing three life-size figures by Mr. Craig, a local, historical and ornamental painter, not well skilled in the ecclesiastical style. As home productions these objects were tenderly eyed, but Anna Jameson, accustomed to the cathedrals of Europe, in her work on Canada, denounced them as being "in a vile, tawdry taste".

The church, it may be presumed, was fired by accident; but in the previous year there was an incendiary blaze — the police made diligent but unsuccessful efforts — and from now on the fire-bug takes command.

On May 6, 1842, Metcalf's machine shop, on the south side of Lot (Queen) street, between Yonge and Victoria streets, formerly occupied as the House of Industry, was damaged to the amount of £250. The origin of the fire is unknown, but the Colonist stated that several suspicious-looking coloured men had been about the vicinity some time ago. They had asked for work, but, not being practical men, they were refused. The police arrested a coloured man the next day on a charge of being one of the incendiaries, but, it being impossible to prove anything against him, he was let go. Mr. T. Armstrong, the secretary of the hook and ladder company, received such injuries at this fire that he was laid up for twelve months.

At a later fire, corner of Richmond and Church Streets, "one of the dwellings was occupied by a Capt. Masterson, who was very ill, and who had to be carried to the street with only a blanket thrown around him. The *British Colonist* says that the sick gentleman suffered no injury, the weather being very warm." "No injury" but, one presumes, a slight amount of inconvenience.

In December, 1844, the Post tavern and its stables on Yonge Street were partially destroyed. The incendiary, William Ross, was sent to the penitentiary for five years. (He could not have had any fun in Portsmouth; the penitentiary was fire-proof.)

Fires seem to have been attracted to the premises of certain men. The same William Musson who was let off lightly by his dinner-hour blaze in 1838 became again a victim in 1845. He was a tinsmith on King Street between Church and Yonge, and about 2.15 p.m. on May 9 an outhouse was seen to be on fire. Flames spread

rapidly to Messrs. Smith & McDonell's storeroom, which was filled with oils, groceries and spirits, including about 100 barrels of whiskey. The exploding of these casks caused the flames to spread over the adjoining vacant lots, which burned for some

time. There was at that time a very wide space between
King street and the next parallel street towards the bay; Market
street. The intervening space was occupied, from Church to
Yonge streets, with wooden buildings, some of them very old.
In the centre of these buildings the fire originated. The flames
had spread to an alarming extent before the fire engines arrived
on the scene, and when they did arrive the supply of water
was very limited. Before long Mr. Brewer's book bindery was
enveloped in flames, and from thence the fire ran south towards
the post office, burning Mr. Berczy's stables, and placing the
post office building in great danger. It was hoped that the
progress of the flames would be stayed at this point; but, in spite
of all efforts

six more merchants lost their premises. Three other large
stores were all on fire but were ultimately saved.

The inadequate supply of water caused general indignation,
which was increased by the absence of the garrison. Soldiers
had been useful on several occasions: once they even had
extinguished a blaze before the brigade arrived; but this time
they were confined to barracks — and Toronto didn't like it.

Almost monotonously the records repeat themselves. "No
cause could be found", "Incendiaries suspected", "Supposed
to be the work of incendiaries"; but none is caught. A servant
maid leaves a shovel full of live coals on the floor; four houses
were destroyed but we are not told that anything happened
to *her*.

In March 1846, Mr. Helliwell, the brewer, and the Hon.
H. J. Boulton lost their houses. "One fireman, whose name
could not be ascertained, earned great praise by his courageous
conduct at this fire." Great praise and anonymity do not
usually go together.

Sunday evening, January 10th, saw the first fire of 1847,
when the grist mill, brewery and distillery of Messrs. Thomas
Helliwell & Bros., on the Don River, were completely destroyed:
also the dwelling house of Mr. Jos. Helliwell. The fire was

first discovered about 11 o'clock, when the roof of the cooler
was seen to be in flames, which spread with amazing rapidity
to the brewery and distillery, consuming them both. The
flour mill caught next, and was, with the stone dwelling
house of Mr. Joseph Helliwell, completely destroyed. Mr.
Eastwood's paper mill was scorched, and was only saved
from destruction with great difficulty. The loss was estimated
at about $80,000, of which $5,000 only was covered by insurance. Many of the workmen employed by Mr. Helliwell
had all their clothes burnt, and all had a narrow escape from
being burnt to death, as the stairs in the house where they slept
were consumed before they woke.

Sunday appears to have been a fatal day for fires in
Toronto. John Doel's brewery caught on April 11; but
"The fire engines were soon on the spot and about 200
barrels of beer which were stored in the cellar, were saved".
A very noteworthy fact. Then, a week later, on Sunday
morning, a fire consumed the premises of Mr. Piper, tinsmith, Mr. Green, gunsmith, Mr. Love, druggist, and others.
Nothing is said about the prompt arrival of the fire engines,
this time.

The next Sunday fire occurred on May 31, by which more
than twenty families were rendered homeless. The flames were
first discovered shortly before twelve o'clock, issuing from a
frame building on the north side of Richmond street west,
near the corner of Yonge street, occupied by James Wiley.
As the wind was blowing strongly at the time, the fire soon
spread in all directions. The east end of Knox Free Church
was soon in flames, and in one hour the edifice was burnt to
the ground. Meanwhile the rear of the houses on Yonge street
had caught fire, and in two hours the whole range of brick
and frame buildings from Richmond to Queen streets, with
the exception of one brick and one wooden store, were completely destroyed. The loss by this fire was estimated at about
$10,500, of which not more than $5,000 was covered by

insurance. This fire led to a meeting being called by the Mayor to consider the subject of getting a better water supply, which, it seems, was badly needed.

That is a rare example of journalistic understatement.

By this time it was apparent to some of the citizens that adequate prevention might be better than inadequate cure; so, after the workshop of Mr. Harper, a builder on Richmond street west, was found to be on fire — a watch was set on the premises. Two days elapsed.

On Friday morning, about 3 o'clock, a man was seen to climb the fence, and proceed towards the shop. One of the watch, James Mullin, followed him with a gun in his hand. Mullin met the man returning, and called on him to surrender, but receiving no answer, and perceiving a flame in the direction of the shop, he raised his gun and fired. The fire was speedily extinguished, but on examination the man was found to be quite dead. The body was identified as that of William Somerset, of York township. [Amateur but determined arson.]

The first fire of any importance in 1848 happened on Tuesday, February 1, when a block of buildings, from Rennie's tavern on the north side of Front street, just west of Church street, to Colborne street, were completely destroyed. The fire originated in one of the outbuildings of Rennie's tavern, and, as the wind was blowing a hurricane from the west at the time, it quickly extended to the surrounding houses, until the entire western part of the block on Front, Church and Colborne streets was levelled to the ground. Twenty-five houses were destroyed, besides outbuildings, and there was but very little insurance on either houses or furniture.

The usual scarcity of water was complained of, and the firemen displayed their usual energy and activity.[1]

[1] Two interesting points about this fire are (1) that the Chamberlain of the City lost two houses but had insurance; and (2) that "The land on which this property stood belonged to the Corporation; the leases had just expired and arbitrators had been appointed to value the improvements upon the lots, according to the terms of the lease. The fire thus relieved the Corporation of all liability."

DESTRUCTION OF THE GLOBE BUILDING,
S.W. Cor. Yonge and Melinda Sts., 1895

In 1849 Mr. George Leslie lost his large greenhouse, "over 4000 valuable plants, including some rare exotics"; and soon after came the enormous blaze that destroyed St. James' Cathedral (the rebuilt stone Cathedral — with a vulnerable wooden spire), the Old City Hall, Post's Tavern (for the second time) and the *Patriot* (newspaper) office. With many more: half a million dollars damage, and one man's life. "Mr. Watson, who had been publisher of the Canadian and of the Upper Canada *Gazette,* was upstairs in the top storey of the *Patriot,* trying to save some type, when the floor gave way under him; he was burned beyond recognition."

This was the largest fire that had taken place in Toronto since it came into existence. During 1850 the usual scarcity of water operated to remove a number of wooden buildings. Supposed incendiaries started a blaze in the back kitchen of a small frame house, on the north side of Adelaide Street, near Yonge. This spread rapidly and ate two taverns, a machine shop, a shoe shop, a grain store and numerous small frame dwellings, houses, homes.

"Mr. Robinson, cabinet maker, everything destroyed . . ." There were a number of smaller losses which are not stated. The fire brigade is not mentioned in connection with this fire, or the water supply: though neither could have been very good, or the fire would not have spread as it did.

We may reflect, of course, in mitigation of horror, that damage by water to the contents of those buildings was almost as non-existent as the buildings themselves. Such as was saved, by volunteer exertions, was usable.

On May 7, 1851,

a fire started in the livery stables on Wellington street, near York, owned by Mr. Grantham, and destroyed them utterly, together with eleven horses occupying them. A tavern occupied by Mr. A. Archer, on the same street, was also destroyed. Again the short supply of water rendered it impossible to make much headway against the flames, and it was only by everyone helping to carry water in pails that the fire was stopped at all.

A number of small fires occurred during the latter part of June, 1852, and grave suspicions were entertained as to their cause. One on June 29, on Princess street, just north of King, destroyed three or four frame buildings. Attempts were made while this fire was in progress to start others in the neighbourhood, but fortunately without success.

In July, 1852, an "indignant remonstrance" was sent in to Mayor J. G. Bowes and the Council by the leading insurance companies of the city, asking for more stringent by-laws for the prevention of fire, in the matter of forbidding the erection of wooden buildings within the city limits, allowing steamers to come to the wharves without proper precautions being taken, a greater number of hydrants, etc., etc. The petition was signed by a number of leading insurance men and others, but *did not have much effect* [the Editor's italics], for, on the occasion of a small fire in Richmond street shortly afterwards, we find the papers calling attention to the fact that had it not been for the extreme stillness of the night, the fire must have consumed a considerable portion of the adjoining blocks, as the means of extinguishing the flames were altogether inadequate in the case of a large fire.

In June 1854 numerous attempts, most of them successful, were made to start fires in Toronto. One, on the 14th, is notable for the fact that the Rochester, U.S., firemen were then on a visit to their Canadian colleagues. Eighteen or nineteen wooden houses were destroyed, most of them the property of Mr. Crawford, a baker, who had no insurance on them, or on sixty barrels of flour which were also consumed.

It must have been an excellent fire for the visitors to watch. Their comments are not printed.

The deepest alarm was now felt at the great number of fires which were occurring, and the citizens anxiously demanded that the authorities should enquire into the state of affairs. They were likewise anxious that the water question should be thoroughly looked into, and a requisition was sent in to the Mayor and Council to awaken them to a sense of their duties in the matter. There is no record, however, of anything particular being done about it at that time.

On Sunday evening, Nov. 12th, 1854, a fire in Duffy's frame tavern, on the north side of Stanley street, near Nelson, caused considerable alarm to the people in that locality. Although there was a strong gale blowing at the time, the firemen worked with such vigor and efficiency that they succeeded in confining the fire to the house where it started. The loss on this property is not stated.

The largest fire Toronto had seen for years broke out in Jacques & Hay's great cabinet factory on the bay front, nearly opposite the end of York street, which was the largest establishment of its kind in Canada. A man named Tilley discovered the fire about 10.30 in the evening of Thursday, December 28th, 1854. The flames were then confined to the painting and varnishing room in the south end of the third storey of the old factory. He tried to put it out with two pails of water, and thinking he had nearly extinguished it, went down stairs for more; when he returned he found the flames were beyond control, and that it was necessary to give the alarm, which he immediately did. The engines arrived promptly and took up a position near the water, and began to play upon the south end of the building. It was hoped that the progress of the flames would be stayed in the old factory, but the fire had got too complete a hold upon the combustibles within, and it was all in vain that the firemen gallantly exposed themselves. The flames defied all their efforts, and soon had spread all through the old place into the immense new building. After that further efforts were useless, and the firemen turned their attention to saving the piles of lumber. The wind was very high however, blowing from the north-west, directly on the great piles lying between the buildings and the wharf. The terrific heat soon drove the firemen away from the engines, which lay at the water's edge. The whole stock of finely-seasoned lumber — the collection of years of labor and care — was entirely consumed. The dwelling house of Mr. Jacques was saved, the wind not blowing in that direction. A quantity of made-up furniture was also got out of the factory by the active exertions of the workmen, but the greater part of the stock and the fine and valuable machinery shared the fate of the building.

In connection with the amateur attempts to deal with fires a century ago, the *Landmarks* reporter occasionally uses the phrase "incredible stupidity". The two words should not be used together: with Rational Man stupidity is never incredible. As witness the fire

which originated in the shed of Mr. J. G. Joseph's house on the west side of Church street, opposite St. Michael's church, destroying the houses of Messrs. Meudell, Holdsworth, Childs and Rice Lewis. It seems that the supply of water was so very limited that before a full measure could be had four brick buildings had been burned. The hose had to be taken to a Yonge street hydrant before anything like a full stream of water could be obtained, the nearest hydrant, on the corner of Richmond and Church, being found to be useless. This fire was the scene of some disgraceful conduct on the part of the firemen. When the houses were opened for the removal of the furniture, the cellars were ransacked, and liquors freely distributed, rendering the men ready for anything desperate. Two firemen began fighting, and their comrades gathered round, some trying to separate them and others assisting in the contest. The [two] constables, who came to do their duty by carrying off the combatants, were assaulted by the firemen, who drove them off the ground, injuring them so badly that they were confined to their houses for some time afterward. Another constable, Booth, shortly after came on the ground, and was immediately assaulted, struck on the head with an axe, and kicked severely.

The matter was investigated by the Police Magistrates and several persons were fined for fighting and assault, but no great harm was done in the fighting to any one.

As a pendant to the rowdy firemen we next have the mob:

On Friday, July 13, 1855, when a travelling circus was performing on the old Fair Green, on Front street east, a mob of rowdies attacked the tent in which the show was proceeding. They first threw one of the waggons belonging to the company into the bay, and then two or three more after them. Next they set fire to one of the remaining waggons and attempted to pull down the tent and burn it also. Fortunately the fire was put out, though great damage was done to the property of the circus company.

We continue with such moving pictures. One, at Browne's Wharf in 1856, where Murphy's cooperage caught fire,

but before assistance arrived the fire had spread to the adjoining sheds. By some mistake when the engines arrived, the hose was brought to play on the ruins of the old cooperage, where the fire had first broken out. The result was that a few staves were saved at the expense of a long range of sheds on the wharf, besides placing a large and valuable warehouse in considerable danger. An amount of machinery which was stored in the sheds was destroyed.

A very destructive fire occurred on Saturday, Jan. 26th, 1856. The fire was first discovered by a watchman who had charge of some stores near the Phoenix foundry, on the east side of Yonge street, No. 58, in a large brick house fronting on Yonge street. Thinking the family might be up, he took no notice, but went on his rounds, and when again passing he saw flames issuing from the building; he at once gave the alarm. The engines arrived in a short time and were quickly placed in an advantageous position, and began to play on the fire, which, in spite of all efforts, consumed the Phoenix foundry and the large brick house in front. It was with very great difficulty that the fire was kept from spreading any further. The loss to Mr. McGee, owner of the foundry, was $30,000, totally uninsured.

To underline the last word — "uninsured" — and then to add "This was the third time the foundry had been destroyed or greatly damaged by fire," is to comment rather helplessly upon human error.

In July 1856 the fire was kindled that led to the extinguishment of Jacques and Hay.

It will be remembered that the old factory was destroyed by fire about a year and a half previous, but a new and larger fabric had been erected on the old site, filled with machinery and material, and peopled with workmen. At three o'clock on the day in question the establishment was in full and successful operation, 300 people labouring in the various departments, aided by all the appliances which ingenuity and skill could devise, and an hour afterwards it was a heap of ruins — buildings and machinery and stock destroyed, and the occupants compelled to flee for their lives, leaving seven of their fellows overwhelmed amidst the flames. With the exception of a few chests of tools and barrels of oil and varnish, nothing of any value was saved from the flames. The fire, and the flames soon spread to the brewery and to the piles of lumber. Mr. Jacques' house soon followed. The roof of the brewery was of shingles set in mortar, and it resisted the flames a long time. A little help from the engines would have saved it, but, unfortunately, they could not be got to it in time. The following is a list of the killed: — James Minns, a carver. He was supposed to have gone up stairs to save something and to have perished in the effort. John Watson, cabinetmaker, married, one child; Anthony Ellis, cabinetmaker, had been married only a few days; Charles Drummond, carver, left a wife and family; — Cole, carver, little known of him; Ives Leguerre, a Frenchman, stranger in the city; Thomas Gobert, a German, was also a stranger.

One of the badly injured was named J. Hurtso.

On Friday, September 25, 1856,

the stables of Mr. Jones, on the corner of Duchess and George streets, were burned to the ground. It is not so much the damage that was done by this fire as the barefaced way in which the buildings were set on fire by an organized band of incendiaries, which makes it noticeable.

The fire was first discovered by constable Patterson, who was on duty on Jarvis street. He noticed flames issuing from the building, and on going towards it, he saw two men running from the stables. He made an attempt to secure them both, and succeeded in capturing one, named Thomas Caldwell. In the meantime the alarm had been given, but the engines arrived too late to do any good. The place was completely destroyed. The night watchman employed by Jones was arrested for complicity in the crime. Another man named William Kelly was also apprehended. The reason for attempting to burn the stables was that Mr. Jones had established a line of omnibuses, which had the effect of injuring the cabmen's business to a great extent. Another attempt to burn a new omnibus was made on November 19, which fortunately proved unsuccessful.

Another case of suspected arson occurred on April 22, 1858.

The fire broke out in a stable on the southwest corner of Church and Crookshank (now Wilton Avenue) streets, adjoining the house of Mr. John Harrington, one of a block of three. The flames soon spread from the out-buildings to the main structure, and although the fire engines were soon on the spot, they were quite powerless in consequence of the scarcity of water. The nearest hydrant was on Queen street, and the only way in which water could be got was by placing one engine half-way between it and the fire and pumping the water into the engines at the fire. In spite of all efforts the three buildings were entirely destroyed, with their contents. A few minutes before the alarm was given two men were seen, running from the direction of the fire, by the constable on his beat, and that, coupled with the fact that no light had been used in Mr. Harrington's stable, gave force to the belief that the property had been fired. The buildings and furniture were partly insured.

The year 1859 was unlucky for Toronto. Fire after fire took place. "The city was now thoroughly alarmed as it was felt that an organised band of incendiaries was at work. Steps were taken to patrol the streets at night and a reward of $1000 was offered for any information that would lead to the capture of the guilty." Result there was none; and the mere repetition of details, "the law of diminishing returns", must operate to destroy interest in subsequent disasters. Still, it would be easy to tell of the destruction of the Government House on King street west (January 11, 1862); and one cannot resist the fire that followed a week later. Says the *Reporter*: —

The Government House hardly had time to cool off after its scorching when another public building, the new jail north of Gerrard street, east of the Don, then in course of erection, was all but destroyed by fire. About 2 o'clock on the morning of Friday, January 17th, 1862, the caretaker of the jail was awakened from his slumbers by the reflection of a brilliant light on the windows of his bedroom. Hastily quitting his bed and running outside, he saw that the upper portion of the centre building of the jail was on fire. He immediately ran round to the main entrance, and to his astonishment found that the padlock and hasp had been wrenched off the door and carried away. He endeavored to ascend the stairs, but was prevented by the dense volume of smoke, and he at once ran off to the city to give the alarm, shouting "Fire at the new jail" as he went along. The bell at Berkeley street gave the alarm, and he returned. However, after the engines turned out the bell ceased, and, as no indication of the fire could be seen from the city, the engines returned to the stations. The alarm was given again from St. Lawrence Hall, but not until much valuable time had been lost. The engines again turned out, but there was great difficulty in hauling them, owing to the depth of snow, and it was not until five o'clock in the morning that they reached the spot. By this time the roof of the centre building had fallen in, and the chapel was a mass of flames. The firemen, under Chief Ashfield, went to work to lay the hose, but after they had laid down several lengths it was found that they had not sufficient to reach from the Don to the building. Some of the hose carts had not arrived, and another long delay took place, as messengers had to be sent to the city to bring forward the hose, and it was not until 7 o'clock that a stream could be brought to bear on the burning building, and by that time the centre building was completely gutted, so the efforts of the firemen were directed to prevent the fire spreading to the wings. The steam fire engine poured a steady stream of water on the burning embers, but after it had been at work two hours, it was found that one of the plates or tubes of the boiler had got burned by allowing the water to get too low, and the engine ceased work. In the meantime the other engines commenced work, and, after working hard and steady until 1 o'clock, the centre building was completely gutted and the walls scorched and cracked.[2] The damage done was estimated at $30,000; insured for $20,000. It was supposed that a gang of bushmen had gone inside the building to get shelter from the piercing cold, and either wilfully or accidentally fired the premises.

And as a final comment upon Rational Man — in 1866

a blaze broke out in the wholesale hardware store of Mr. W. R. Harris, situated on the west side of Yonge street, between Front and Wellington streets, and did considerable damage. The fire broke out about 5.30 in the evening, and had gained a good hold when first observed. The two fire engines were on the ground almost immediately, but the water supply was very limited, and beyond a few jets of mud and water, nothing

[2] A repetition which may imply that the wings of the building were saved.

could be got. Of course, the fire, left to itself, soon gained the third storey, and forced its way out of the front windows, threatening the stores on the opposite side of the street. Fears were also entertained for the safety of the adjoining premises, and as Harris' store was the centre of a large and valuable pile of buildings, the destruction of them would have involved a great deal of damage to trade for some time. The scarcity of water caused matters to look still more serious, and the engines ran wildly about from hydrant to hydrant in search of a stream sufficient for the occasion. After considerable delay, one of them managed to get a decent supply; but hardly had it started when the hose gave out, several breaches having occurred in it. Meanwhile the flames were burning wildly in Harris' store, which seemed to go like tinder, and showed themselves in an adjoining hoop skirt factory, from which, however, they were driven after some difficulty, and much damage to the stock. It was only by the crowd passing up pails of water that the latter store was saved from destruction. The fire seems to have burned itself out without spreading any farther, having entirely destroyed Mr. Harris' store and all his stock, the damage amounting to about $16,000 or $18,000 most of which fell on Mr. Harris, who fortunately was insured for the full amount. The cause of the fire was unknown. The building was owned by Mr. John Crawford, and was insured for $2,400. At the enquiry, which was held to find out the origin of this fire, great complaints were made at the inefficiency of the waterworks, evidence being put in to show that it was almost impossible to throw two streams of water at one time, owing to the limited supply, and that sometimes the water was entirely turned off at the time of a fire. After a long investigation the jury returned the following: The Jury, having completed their investigation of the late circumstances connected with the fire which took place on the premises occupied by Mr. W. R. Harris, on the afternoon of July 26th last, feel it to be their duty to call the attention of the corporation to the evidence given to the fact that the insufficient supply of water placed in jeopardy a valuable block of buildings, on which the insurance amounted to over one million dollars. The jury are also surprised to learn that some portions of the city are entirely without a water supply at night. The jury are, therefore, of opinion that the full power of the water-works should at all times be at the immediate and entire command of the fire department, and they would urge upon the corporation to insist upon a full discharge on the part of the water companies of their obligation.

Bigger and better fires were soon to occur and the city as continually renewed itself. We may doubt that the men concerned with setting fires had any vision of the Toronto that was to be; but their efforts after destruction only met with a more durable will to resist and to rebuild better. Loss of life, loss of treasure, loss of property, of trade and of time — all were subsidiary to the idea of a greater Toronto.

And even the firemen of a century ago, continually thwarted in their efforts by men and by the elements, were conscious obscurely of being on the winning side. At the Exhibition of 1858 they held high carnival and gave a great demonstration. With the fire brigades of London, Hamilton and Cobourg our scarlet-coated firemen marched in procession, inspired by Mullaney's Brass Band.

No one wishes for a moment to go back to the days of the hand engines and voluntary firemen. Yet there was a picturesque side to the old-time firemen that does not now attach to the much more efficient body possessed by Toronto. There was a rivalry then between the various companies as to which could turn out in the smartest style and whose engine could throw a stream of water the highest. The various engines were all part and parcel of the life of the town, and at a fire it was considered no small privilege by youths and men to be able to take a hand at the breaks. "Good old Rescue, well done, No. 2," would resound from the crowd surrounding that engine during the progress of a fire, while perhaps from a similar congregation around the

"Phoenix" or "Deluge" would be heard the cry of "Break her down, boys; you're higher than No. 2; break her down."

Requiescant in pace

It may be of interest to note here that insurance against fire began in Canada at an early date. There is some record of insurance in 1771. The Phoenix Fire Assurance Co. of London began in Montreal, 1804; the Halifax Fire Insurance Co. in 1809; and the British American Assurance Co. in 1833.

X. RECREATIONS AND DIVERSIONS

In previous chapters glimpses have been caught of how Toronto was born and how orderly she grew; the names and
noted deeds of some of her citizens; the way that she worshipped God and the ceremonial with which she hanged men.
The last item (for want of better) must head the doings of
this chapter: a public hanging seems to have been the only
pleasure that the hard-worked inhabitant of early days could
share: almost his only opportunity of witnessing a cathartic
emotion in his fellows. Class that occasional "splurge" as
a diversion: what were his recreations? He did not read;
his parlour, if he had one, housed a Bible, his kitchen a
copy of Scobie's Almanac and an occasional news sheet —
what need of more? The poet says: —

> "They eat, they drink, they sleep, they plod,
> They go to church on Sunday."

But the rural Canadian probably only heard a church service
when a Methodist knight-errant came to a neighbour's house
some three or four times a year. A hanging was ordained, by
the very fact of its publicity, for the attendance of the public.
It was a focal point for the corporate spirit. To rise at
five or earlier, to jolt for hours over infernal roads, to stand
with many others under the lash of wind and rain — to
see a bundle of clothes that shortly before had been a man,
twist and swing at the end of a rope, made a fine advertisement for law and order. The times were hard, of course,
and life was nothing much to lose. Its expectancy was less,
though the sense of its continuity — that it could be driven
into and drawn from the soil by swink and sweat — was
perhaps greater than it is today.

The man of Upper Canada had no theatre, concert, cinema, or community hall; often he had no church. But he was able, indeed he was invited, to come to Muddy York once or twice a year and to become a super at a grand Farewell Performance.

Apart from this, what did he do? On Sundays he pitched horseshoes, in winter he skated (if he were young enough). In spring and summer there was often a circus to which people came for miles around. From about 1830, George Bernard's circus took an annual tour through Upper Canada, and that tour lasted at least five months.

"Mrs. Bernard was quite an equestrienne and consequently a drawing card. Leading members of the troupe were Cadwallader Stone, Rockwell, Gossan who played the clown . . . and a boy named Frank, an apprentice to the athlete business. Frank was a clever youth, a good horseman and tumbler." "In after years," according to the late Alexander Jacques, "he was the champion somersault thrower of the world."

Yes, the circus was an enormous attraction, advertised for weeks in advance and talked about for the rest of the year. What was there else? The theatre. Between Colborne and King Streets in 1827, stood Frank's Hotel, an ordinary two-storey frame building. In the ball-room of this house the first theatre in York was extemporized, and performances were given of such plays as *Ali Baba and the Forty Thieves,* *The Lady of the Lake,* and *The Miller and His Men.* Soldiers from the garrison occasionally acted as supers.

The second theatre was the upper storey of a frame building on the north side of Colborne Street, west of the St. Lawrence Market. Performances were given here by a local amateur club; and here took place a "real-life" tragedy when Joseph Nolan was shot by Charles French, who paid the due penalty on October 23, 1828. That bleak occurrence killed the little theatre, and it was not until 1834 that another was opened. In order, perhaps, to lay any

possible ghost, the brothers Waugh, proprietors of a refresh-
ment room on King Street, opened the next theatre in a
Methodist Chapel. It too was on King Street but had ceased
to be used in 1833 after the completion of the Adelaide
Street Methodist Chapel. Here, in 1834, a panorama of the
Burning of Moscow was shown.

Both before and after the conversion of the Wesleyan chapel
into a place of amusement, theatrical performances were given
at times in an unoccupied barn-like building, on the north
side of Front street, a little east of Church street. Keating's
British Coffee House, a two-storey brick building, was a little
west of the theatre. This home of the drama was of frame.
The hall in which the performances were given was about
sixty feet long. There was no gallery. Seats were arranged
on the ground floor to accommodate between two and three
hundred spectators. Candles furnished the illumination of the
play-house. The prices of seats were half a crown for front
seats and 1s. 3d. for rear ones, Halifax currency. The pro-
grammes were plain slips of paper, printed with the names of
the players and their parts. The scenery was very crude, but
the acting was at times very good. Mr. and Mrs. Thorne played
comedy parts here in 1833, and on the nights when they appeared
the house was always crowded, Mrs. Thorne being an especial
favourite.

The next theatre was quite a building. It stood in the
rear of the lot at the north-east corner of King and York
Streets, near the old Shakespeare Hotel. It had a frontage of
30 feet, with the stage at the north end, and was about 60
feet long. The seats were ranged in tiers and it was
called the Theatre Royal. By that name it flourishes in
Walton's *City Directory* for 1837, and by that name its fate
was mentioned when almost the whole north-east corner of
the block was burned a few years later.

Whatever may have been the merits or demerits of the
Theatre Royal, in the public estimation, it evidently was ill-

thought of by the *British Colonist,* for in the issue of that paper
on September 4, 1839, we find the following: —

"Near the corner of York street and King street, in this
city, there stands a small tenement, which has been dignified
by the name of 'The Theatre Royal' and in confirmation of
this title the place has recently been taken possession of by a
party of strolling players from Yankee land. Any of our
readers who are curious can be at no difficulty to find it out,
as every evening the name is displayed in large letters over
the door, through the transparency of a huge lantern, 'Theatre
Royal.'

"It so happened, that on Saturday evening last, when passing
along with a friend, we were induced to enter, [the performance]
being, as we were informed, for the benefit of Miss E. Ince.
A benefit night at a theatre is generally expected to produce
something more than common, both in the shape of entertainment by the performers, and large receipts of dollars and
cents from the public who honour them with their company.
If any extra effort were made to please on this occasion, the
ordinary performance of these strollers must be very ordinary
indeed, and for the taste of Toronto, we trust that a somewhat
more than ordinary attendance took place on Saturday, as pit,
boxes, and gallery, seemed to be well filled.

"The performance commenced with what was styled in the
bills 'The much-admired farce of Nature and Philosophy, or
the youth who never saw a woman.' This farce may be
admired across the line, but neither in the sentiment, nor the
manner in which it was acted, was there anything to excite
admiration here; both the farce and the actors of it are altogether
too contemptible for criticism.

"An attempt was made by one of the company to sing a
Scotch song. It was noticed in the bills of the evening 'Scotch
Song, by Mrs. Lennox,' and we would beg as a favour of that
songstress, that she may never attempt the like again in this
place. Never before had it been our lot to listen to the beautiful
song by the Ettrick Shepherd, 'Cam' ye by Athol' so brutally
murdered. This was followed by an attempt to act the opera

of 'The Maid of Cashmere,' and it was but an attempt. Miss Ince danced tolerably well, and that is all that can be said in favour of the performance. By this time our patience was quite exhausted; we left, and immediately set to write this notice, lest by delay we might so far forget what we had witnessed as to do injustice afterwards to any of the company, by detracting from their just merits as players."

This kind of criticism is still familiar to those of us who read *Saturday Night* or listen to a radio review of recent films. Certainly, until 1849, when the old "Royal Lyceum" was opened, Toronto had no theatre of professional standing. Readers of Dickens will remember the theatrical company with which Nicholas Nickleby acted. Such performances, of such plays, attracted, amused, or annoyed Toronto theatregoers until the middle of the nineteenth century. The year 1852, when John Nickinson and his theatrical company came from Buffalo for a two weeks' engagement, marks the beginning of "the Legitimate" in Toronto. During the next half-century "stars" such as Henry Irving, Ellen Terry, Adelaide Neilson, Wilson Barrett ("The Silver King"), Genevieve Ward, Joseph Jefferson ("Rip Van Winkle"), Sarah Bernhardt and Lily Langtry appeared, and the theatregoing public, apparently, was always ample in number and generous in response.

There were other attractions in the decade 1850-60. Just to the west of the old Jail on Front street was an open space known as "The Fair Green".

On this green were held, till late in the "fifties", not only cattle and produce fairs, but also wild beast shows, and circuses; and occasionally it was also utilized as a mustering place for societies, who wished to make a demonstration by marching through the streets of the city.

One of the most notable, if not indeed the most notable of exhibitions held on the Fair Green, was that of the renowned P. T. Barnum in 1852. It was described thus:

P. T. Barnum's
Grand Colossal Museum and Menagerie

The largest travelling EXHIBITION in the World, being a combination of all the most popular and unexceptionable amusements of the age — enlarged and improved for the season of 1852.

A TEAM OF 10 ELEPHANTS

Will draw the Great Car of Juggernaut. A Baby Elephant only one year old and but 3½ feet high, will carry upon his back, around the interior of the immense Pavilion, the Lilliputian GEN. TOM THUMB. The magnificent cortege comprises 110 horses and 90 men. The Pavilion of Exhibition has been enlarged until it is capable of accommodating 15,000 spectators at once. The collection of living wild beasts includes the most splendid specimens ever exhibited in America. Among many others will be found

SIX BEAUTIFUL LIONS,
fresh from their native forests.

A SACRED BURMESE BULL,
from the Island of Ceylon, worshipped there by the Pagan Natives, and recently taken from an Idolatrous Temple.

A monster WHITE or POLAR BEAR! — of prodigious size and ferocity.

A magnificent ROYAL TIGRESS — the largest one ever captured alive.

AN INFANTILE CAMEL — only six months of age, the first one ever born in America, etc.

THE DROVE OF ELEPHANTS were captured in the jungle of Central Ceylon, by Messrs. S. B. June and Geo. Nutter, assisted by 260 natives, after a pursuit of three months and four days in the jungles. They were finally entrapped and secured in an Indian Kraal or Trap, of enormous dimensions and prodigious strength, where they were subdued. The calf elephant accompanies its dam, and was weaned on its passage from India.

A NATIVE CEYLON CHIEF, of high caste in his own country, has charge of the elephants, having accompanied them from Ceylon.

But for fear these attractions should not prove sufficient, it was advertised in addition to the above wonder, that the real genuine, original

GEN. TOM THUMB

is attached to this exhibition, and will appear, in all his performances, as given before the principal crowned heads of Europe, in his admired personations of Napoleon and Frederick the Great. The little General is twenty years of age, weighs only fifteen pounds, and is but twenty-eight inches high.

Then besides all the foregoing attractions there was

MR. NELLIS,

the man without arms, who executed his extraordinary feats of loading and firing a pistol with his toes; cut profile likenesses; shot at a mark with a bow and arrow; played upon the accordion and violoncello, etc.

And in addition to all these marvels a fine military band performed the most popular airs of the day, as the procession entered town, and also during the hours of exhibition.

Finally, the charge for admission was only 25 cents.

In the case of the Provincial Agricultural Exhibition, which held its first show in October 1846, admission was free. It was opened in Toronto, "on the grounds attached to the old Government House, several of the exhibits being located in the house itself." In the following year the Exhibition went to Hamilton, then to Cobourg, Kingston, Niagara, Brockville, returning to Toronto in 1852. "The Presbyterian Church (King and Simcoe Streets) stands almost on the spot where was the principal entrance to the fair-ground. Admission during the last two days was only twelve and a half cents — a York shilling." There were, however, sideshows for which another shilling was asked "and cheerfully paid", says the report.

At these provincial exhibitions almost every conceivable article used in Canada was exhibited, some of the exhibits being of a somewhat grotesque character. There were horses and cattle, sheep and pigs, poultry of all kinds and produce of every description. There were giant pumpkins and mammoth squashes, and a very good trade was done in selling the seeds of both these varieties of the vegetable kingdom. There were works of art in wool and in crayons FEARFULLY AND WONDER-FULLY executed in many cases. A favorite subject in wool-work was that of Abraham offering up Isaac. It was once remarked in reference to one of these artistic (?) productions, "That it was ugly enough to bring Abraham back again to protest against being represented in such a light." That happened now nearly forty years ago and much has been learned since then; while there is this to be said even for those hideously ugly pieces of fancy work, that they were done by young women who had little leisure and who had to deny themselves much needed recreation to do them at all,

which may serve in mitigation of sentence, but is no excuse. "Among the 'miscellaneous class' were exhibits of the following all but forgotten articles: — Melodeons, seraphims,[1] grain cradles and grape preserves. There was also a prize for glue.

It is easily understood that by 1857 the growing success of the Exhibition led to demands for suitable permanent buildings and a suitable permanent home. The first was supplied in 1858, when the corner-stone of the building known as the Crystal Palace was laid. This in July: the Exhibition was held there at the end of September.

The Palace was cruciform in shape, and from the inside presented a very handsome appearance. But outside the effect

[1] Seraphims, or Seraphines (the more usual name) were a free reed musical instrument invented in England by John Green in the year 1833, and superseded some twenty years later by the harmonium. Specimens lingered in some Canadian houses and small churches for another ten years.

was greatly marred by the flatness, or apparent flatness of the building. It looked as if some heavy weight had been dropped on the roof, crushing it down. The building from east to west was two hundred and fifty-six feet long and ninety-six feet wide. Its extreme height was only fifty-five feet. In the centre of the building, immediately under the dome, was a handsome fountain, the first of the kind ever erected in Upper Canada, which attracted a very great deal of attention and admiration from everyone who saw it. There were four minor jets of water rising from the central basin, figures of Chinese mandarins and the typical John Bull. From the central jet rose a column of water for some five or six feet upon which ever revolving was a gilt hollow ball, some six inches in circumference. This continued open for nearly a fortnight, and was very largely patronized.

It is necessary to add in reference to the last sentence, that "This" refers to the Exhibition and not to the hollow ball.

The opening ceremony was performed by the Governor-General, Sir Edmund Head. One or two sentences from his address find a response today.

"The prosperity of Canada; the unity of Canada; the life of Canada, depends on those inland waters, those great seas which pour down the St. Lawrence connecting us with the ocean and through the ocean with Europe and the mother country.

"The prosperity of Canada depends on the St. Lawrence, it is the life blood of the country. The all important thing for the future of Canada, for its wealth and national existence is its control of those great masses of water."

Soon after this the Exhibition settled down in one spot, in which it yearly breaks the previous records; and people enjoy themselves today as they did a century ago.

There have been other exhibitions in Toronto, notably one

in 1899 which was devoted to historical relics (books, furniture, pictures, etc.), held in Victoria College and accorded by the *Landmarks* a detailed description in more than ninety pages. This would be worth reprinting as a pamphlet; especially if it were found possible to record the present habitation of the exhibits. But although it can be classed as a re-creation of history it is a little late for our purpose. Let us go back to 1814 and to the record of an Assembly at York.

The bachelors of York, in the latter part of 1814, gave a ball at Frank's hotel. Even in its early days York was a very sociable place, small though it was, and naturally so owing to its isolation. The people of the government, the military, and a few of the more prominent merchants, made up a society which, although existing in a wilderness, had been reared in the culture and polish of Europe.[2]

The original manuscript of the preliminary arrangements for this ball is still in existence. Its first paragraphs are in the handwriting of Chief Justice Robinson. The signatures of the subscribers are autographs. This is a copy of the paper:—

At a meeting of the gentlemen of York, subscribers to the assemblies, Stephen Jarvis and George Ridout, Esquires, were appointed managers for the season, the sum to be paid by each subscriber to be three pounds, Halifax currency.

Subscribers are requested to call on Stephen Jarvis, one of the managers, to receive tickets on payment of their subscription.

First dance on St. Andrew's night, dancing to begin at half-past eight o'clock.

Delivered tickets to Dr. Powell, 12 dollars; J. Robinson, Esq.,

[2] The York Assembly had been in existence since 1805 at least. In that year a notice was published asking such gentlemen "as wish to become subscribers to the York Assembly this winter" to meet at Cooper's Tavern. This seems to indicate that dances had been given even earlier.

12 dollars; Mr. Lyons, 2½ dollars; Mr. Strachan, 12 dollars; Mr. Macaulay, 12 dollars; Captain Crittenden, six tickets; Mr. Gladin, 89th, 2½ dollars; G. Ridout, 12 dollars; F. S. Jarvis, 12 dollars; S. Jarvis, 12 dollars; L. Baker, 2½ dollars; Mr. Smith, 12 dollars.

We learn further that one lady was "richly attired in white satin with slippers to match, and wore a necklace and tiara of diamonds". Another lady "of great loveliness" wore black lace over an underskirt of crimson, with a rose at her waist and in her hair. *And* (a final note) the wine for the ball was bought of Quetton St. George & Co. — eight gallons of Teneriffe wine at forty shillings a gallon. That is "all we know [of the refreshments] and all we need to know" — as Keats might have written.

There were of course other dances held in "Muddy York"; at the old Red Lion, a few doors above Bloor Street, on the east side of Yonge, a hostelry whose owner advertised "the best strong beer at 8d. New York currency, per gallon, if drank in his house, and 2s. 6d. New York currency, taken out." The ballroom was on the second storey, an apartment about 40 feet by 20 feet in dimensions, and 18 feet high, with an arched ceiling. At each end there was a large chimney and fire-place; and, although it was then a long and muddy way from town, the entertainments given there were always well attended. People walked in those days . . . which naturally leads to a mention of the Orange Walk. This may be classed as a Diversion.

Orange "walks" on the Twelfth of July are said to have taken place in York, in 1820 and earlier. Records of early celebrations in the little town of York, as Toronto then was, are meagre. British regiments doing garrison duty in Upper and Lower Canada brought Orangeism to this country first, it is believed. But it was not till Ogle R. Gowan came to Canada from County Wexford, Ireland, that the Orange Association took form as an organization. The Grand Lodge of

British America, through his efforts, was organized at Brock-ville in 1830. The first Orange lodge in Toronto, Nassau No. 4, was organized in 1831. By 1833 York County had 1,000 Orangemen. At this date the Twelfth was annually observed.

The decision in 1834 to have no public procession was com-mended by *The Patriot* [newspaper]. Instead, a dinner was held, and it was thus reported by *The Patriot* of Tuesday, July 15, 1834: —

"That the enlightened of the Orangemen are men of good intentions, could never be doubted, and it is now evident that their influence and example have favorably impressed the great mass. It has been determined by the leading men of the great fraternity in Toronto, that henceforth there shall be no public processions or display, and in order to celebrate this gratifying concession to public opinion and thus put a seal upon their spontaneous and manly resolve, about thirty of them met at the Ontario House on Saturday last to partake of a friendly dinner. Some few guests were invited, of which number we had the honor to be one.

After the withdrawal of the cloth the following toasts pro-ceeded from the chair: —

1st. The King — and may he never forget the principles which placed his family on the British throne, of which principles we are determined ever to be supporters.

2nd. The Queen.

3rd. The Duke of Cumberland — our illustrious Grand Master — and the rest of the royal family.

4th. The Glorious, Pious and Immortal Memory of William the Third."

And thirteen other toasts, including one to "Our Fellow Subjects of every sect and of every creed". Unfortunately for the impression of general loving-kindness so generated, *The Patriot's* report continues:

His ex-Reverence of the Correspondent has given an article on the 12th of July, which is another item in the mass of evidence of the base malignity of his heart, but we cannot give him our attention till Friday. So foul a miscreant surely never before took type in hand.

In 1835 "some of the lower orders walked in procession" and the police court was busy during the whole of the next week with cases of assault and riot. In 1839

the *Christian Guardian* of Wednesday, July 17, refers to the celebration five days before as follows: —

"An unusually large Orange procession took place in this city on the 12th inst. The prohibitory letter of His Excellency the Lieutenant-Governor is stated to have been the reason of a larger assemblage than ordinary." Which is comfortingly Irish.

It would serve no purpose to take the reader year by year through similar reports. That for 1858 will serve: —

"The juveniles as usual," reports *The Patriot*, "amused themselves by setting off squibs and firecrackers, sometimes to the no little inconvenience of ladies who paraded the streets with a rather extended display of crinoline.

"As the procession was wending its way along Queen street, near William street, a row occurred, which at one time threatened to end more seriously than it did. Through some means a quarrel was stirred up between two parties, one of whom was an Orangeman and the other a Roman Catholic. Shots were freely fired, but though the contents of the pistols took effect in some instances, they did not result fatally. One man named James Brown, gardener to the mayor, was shot in the back. It is said the wound will not prove very serious. Another man named King, of the opposite party, was also wounded by a ball which passed through his cheek, carrying away some of his teeth and making a very ugly wound.

"A large body of police were called with guns loaded ready for action, for the disturbance was reaching alarming proportions. The armed constables were hurriedly driven from St.

Patrick's market, and with the help of the mayor order was restored. While open hostility ceased, knots of seven and eight gathered and discussed the affair in language none too temperate.

"A row also occurred on Victoria street, in which it was reported pistols were used.

"Temperance L.O.L., No. 301, dined that evening in its hall on George street."

Temperance! we ask you! To be sure there was a St. Patrick's Society, formed in 1836, with the object "of bringing together and uniting in bonds of friendship and unity natives of Ireland inhabiting this province"; but the Twelfth of July is no time for friendship and unity.

There was also a choral society formed in 1845, with the head of Upper Canada College as its President; but there is no information as to where it met, and after a few years it merged with the Philharmonic Society.

For twenty years, from 1852 to 1872, the St. Lawrence Hall was the centre of the town's indoor diversions. It was built on King Street east, on the site of the old red brick Town Hall or Market House, partially destroyed by fire in 1849.

Almost weekly for twenty years it was used for meetings: anti-slavery (with which it began), musical, theatrical, panoramas, costume-balls, concerts, meetings of protest against everything from vivisection to the Church of Rome, and, once or twice, Madame Adelina Patti. The hall was built to hold a thousand people; which did not prevent a newspaper from reporting (on the occasion of an Irish night) that "there could have been no fewer than two or three thousand persons present". In the spirit, probably. Twenty-four pages of small print, in volume three of the *Landmarks,* record the entertainments, recite the names of those responsible, and chronicle their success. Or the want of it. One of the last items to be recorded is: "On September 27th (1871) Jem Mace, the champion boxer of the world, together with a variety troupe, gave an exhibition of boxing with vocal

THE FIRST MARKET IN YORK

and instrumental music afterwards". If this strikes the reader with a sense of slight incongruity he will be repaid by attention to the next item. It is June 28, 1838, and Toronto is showing its loyalty to the young Victoria, as we have recently displayed ours (with some pomp) to the young Elizabeth.

The Queen's coronation took place at Westminster Abbey on June 28th, 1838, amidst great pomp and ceremony, and was not by any means allowed to pass unnoticed in Toronto. Here a grand procession of the firemen took place under the direction of the then Chief of the Brigade the late Mr. Thomas Denny Harris. The order of the procession was as follows: — First came the bands of the two local militia regiments, the Queen's Rangers and the Queen's Foresters, then the chief officers of the brigade, viz., T. D. Harris, chief engineer, Richard Woodsworth, assistant engineer, Robert Beard, David Paterson and James F. Westland, the first two of whom were chiefs of the Hook and Ladder Company and Toronto Fire Engine Company, and the latter was the secretary.

Following the officers was a fireman who carried a mace, gilded from top to bottom and surmounted by a lion. Then came two silk banners with emblematic devices, one having the word "Victoria" in its centre, surrounded by a wreath of the rose, shamrock and thistle, and underneath "British supremacy". The other banner had a representation of the British American fire engine on it, and the name of the company underneath the engine. Forty firemen were with the engine, which was gaily decorated. The firemen were arrayed in scarlet jackets and white trousers. These banners were painted by Alexander Hamilton. On the engine was a painting representing the death of Wolfe and the taking of Quebec. Then came two more flags, the work of Hart & March, and the hook and ladder waggon, followed by six axemen and twenty-eight firemen, then was borne the Royal Standard, and the rear was brought up by more firemen. The route of the procession was along Yonge street and King street to the Garrison common, where it dispersed.

How dull! an impotent and lame conclusion. Could there not have been a fire? The visiting Rochester firemen had one.

In the foregoing all these excitements took place in Toronto; but when city dwellers desired to be free from urban restraints they went over to the Island (as Londoners similarly placed are said to visit Paris). It will be a convenience in description to move on five years from 1838. In 1843 there were only three houses on the Island; and a few very primitive dwellings, mere cabins, used by the fisher folk.

Strictly speaking, the "Island" was not an island at all but a peninsula. It was not until 1857 or 1858 that the inroads of the waters of the Lake during a great storm caused what is now known as the Eastern gap, and converted the peninsula into an actual island. The first steamer that passed through this gap was the *Bowmanville,* on April 19th, 1859. Of the houses on the Island, the principal was a large, partly brick, three-storey dwelling erected by Lord Sydenham, in 1839, as a summer residence for himself, in consequence of Toronto at the time suffering from a visitation of that dread pest, cholera. This house, 50 x 40 feet . . . was built upon a layer of four-inch planks sunk about two feet in the sand, it being impossible from the nature of the soil to build a brick foundation. The lower storey was of brick; the second and upper ones were of wood. To the east of it was another small dwelling, occupied by the keeper of the lighthouse, James Durning, while about one hundred yards to the west was a third house, known afterwards as Parkinson's Hotel. These, the huts we have before mentioned, and the lighthouse were, until 1853, the only dwellings upon the Island. Between where now is Island Park, and the Eastern gap, were a great many trees, chiefly pines and Balm of Gilead. Exactly opposite the present Alert House is one of each of these trees, and this spot was a favorite rendezvous for picnic parties. To the east are several other scattered pines, much the same now as then, and from them one of the adjacent villas takes the very appropriate name of "The Pines."

In 1843 Louis Privat . . . took up his residence in the house built by Lord Sydenham, and opened it as an hotel. He was joined there in 1844 by his brother, Louis Joseph Privat, with his family.

But it was one thing to open an hotel; it was another to make it pay. So the two brothers decided that the one should "run" the hotel, while the other should devote his energies (and these were by no means inconsiderable), to obtaining visitors and customers to the same.

In furtherance of this object they purchased a vessel which had been running on the Niagara below the Falls to ply for passengers between Toronto and the Island. This, under command of L. J. Privat, they called the Peninsula Packet, but it is very doubtful if one person in a hundred who visited the Island by her means ever knew what her real name was, for from the mode by which she was propelled she was invariably known as "the horse boat," and by none other. She was by no means a very large vessel; being only sixty feet in length by twenty-three feet wide, and had what are now known as side wheels. These paddles were set in motion by two horses who trod on a circular table set flush with the deck in its centre. This table as it revolved worked upon rollers, which, being connected with the shaft, set the paddles in motion. The horses were stationary; the table on which they trod was furnished with ridges of wood radiating like spokes from the centre, which the horses caught with their feet, thus setting the table in motion. For some time the boat was worked with only two horses, but after about two years an alteration was effected in the arrangements, and in the vessel as well. Instead of two horses, five were introduced, and they walked round and round the deck, exactly as horses do when employed in working a threshing machine, and the vessel was set in motion precisely as such a machine is. A picture is given of the old "horse boat", remembered with affection by many residents of Toronto in the "forties" and

very early "fifties". This old vessel was, in 1850, taken off her route.

The Island afforded its visitors many other attractions besides the journey there, which, by the way, generally occupied thirty and sometimes forty minutes. Opposite the hotel was a merry-go-round and two large swings, the one to the east, the other to the west of the merry-go-round. The first was eighty feet high, the second but thirty, and all three were largely patronized by the younger portion of the Island's visitors. For the elders there was a bowling alley, known as "Ten Pin Alley," while to ensure instruction as well as amusement there was a small zoological collection consisting of a bear, wolf, a white deer, several racoons and two or three eagles. There was also a good deal of amusement of a somewhat miscellaneous nature. Every Queen's Birthday many of the sportsmen of Toronto journeyed to the Island for blackheart shooting. These were birds of passage of the plover tribe, who invariably were making their annual migration at this period of the year.

Another, though somewhat cruel, pastime consisted of trap pigeon shooting, wild pigeons being netted by bird catchers and sold to Privat for that purpose.

Besides these contests to test the prowess of marksmen, there was turkey shooting. This, it must be confessed, was very sorry sport. A turkey was tied and placed on an elevation about fifty yards from where the sportsmen (?) stood. Everyone who chose to enter, and pay a York shilling for each shot, was allowed to fire at the poor bird; the first who hit it became possessor of the turkey. This amiable pastime continued until the supply of turkeys was exhausted. There was yet one other occasional diversion, equally reprehensible but perhaps not quite so cruel as the one just mentioned. This was shooting a bear with a candle. A bear was purchased, (and forty years ago these were not difficult to obtain), and a man resident in Toronto used to give an exhibition of shooting this animal with a rifle ostensibly loaded only with an ordinary tallow candle. To see this performance a small sum was charged and those

who witnessed it went away believing the bear had met his
quietus solely through the force of the candle striking him.
They were not told, and probably would not have believed it
had they been so, that when the candle was put in the rifle a
bullet had preceded it, nevertheless such was the case. This
"sport" always took place in the winter and there was from
time to time an occasional fox hunt also, a fox being let loose
the night before to furnish the sport, and a very exhilarating
amusement was the result.

When the Privat brothers left the Island, they were succeeded
by John Quinn. Where their house stood is now covered by
the waters of the lake.

XI. THE LAKE AND THE ROAD

I. THE LAKE

Lake Ontario, whether liquid or solid, has always been reckoned among the assets of Toronto. Its own liabilities can be stated as a somewhat violent response to storms and as offering a convenience to enemy keels. But like the Hindu god it is both destroyer and preserver; along it the United Empire Loyalists first came to Upper Canada, along it Carleton, Simcoe, Sydenham made their way, and over it trade poured in upon a willing if scanty population. Here came the *Frontenac,* first steamboat on the lakes; here at an earlier date, Toronto lost the *York,* her premier merchant-man; and the first ocean-going vessel to be built on Lake Ontario (her name *The City of Toronto*) set out from these waters on her maiden voyage. For this chapter, the *Landmarks of Toronto* should rightfully be accounted water-marks.

In 1804 the sailing vessel *Speedy* foundered with all hands and "many of the leading inhabitants of York". Here is the account, as printed in the Canada *Gazette*:

The *Speedy,* Captain Paxton, left this port on Sunday evening, the 7th of October last, with a moderate breeze from the N. W., for Presque Isle, and was descried off that island on the Monday following before dark, where preparations were made for the reception of the passengers; but the wind coming round from the N. E. blew with such violence as to render it impossible for her to enter the harbor, and very shortly after she disappeared. A large fire was then kindled on shore, as a guide to the vessel during the night; but she has not since been seen or heard of,

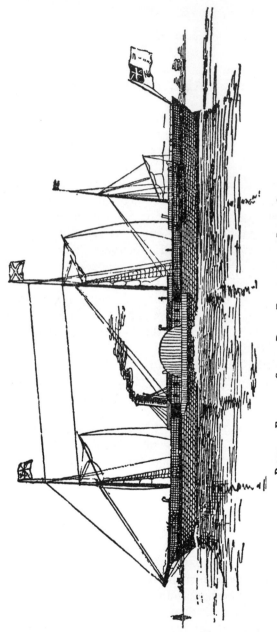

PIONEER ENGLISH STEAM BOAT *Frontenac* ON LAKE ONTARIO
170 ft. long, 700 tons

and it is with the most painful sensations we have to say we fear she is totally lost. Enquiry, we understand, has been made at almost every port on the lake, but without effect, and no intelligence respecting the fate of this unfortunate vessel could be obtained. It is therefore generally concluded that she has either upset or foundered. It is also reported by respectable authority that several articles, such as the compass box, hen-coop and mast, known to have belonged to this vessel, have been picked up on the opposite side of the lake.

LIST OF PASSENGERS

The passengers on board the ill-fated *Speedy,* as near as we can recollect, were Mr. Judge Cochrane, Robert I. D. Dray, Esq., Solicitor-General and member of the House of Assembly; Angus McDonell, Esq., advocate, also a member of the House of Assembly; Mr. Jacob Herchmer, merchant; Mr. John Stegman, surveyor; Mr. George Cowan, Indian in-terpreter; James Ruggles, Esq.; Mr. Anderson, student in the law; Mr. John Fisk, high constable, all of this place. The above named gentlemen were proceeding to the district of Newcastle, in order to hold the Circuit and for the trial of an Indian (also on board) indicted for the murder of John Sharp, late of the Queen's Rangers. It is also reported, but we cannot vouch for its authenticity, that, exclusive of the above passengers, there were on board two other persons, one in the service of Mr. Justice Cochrane, and the other in that of the Solicitor-General; as also two children of parents whose indigent circumstances necessitated them to travel by land.

STRENGTH OF THE CREW

The crew of the *Speedy,* it is said, consisted of five seamen (three of whom have left large families), exclusive of Capt. Paxton, who also had a very large family. The total number of souls on board the *Speedy* is computed to be about twenty.

Of the original murder that resulted in so many persons perishing, another volume of the *Landmarks* has this to note:

The name of the Indian who was on his way to be tried was Ogetonicut. His brother, Whistling Duck, had been killed by a white man, and he took his revenge on John Sharp, another white man. The deed was done at Bull Point, on Lake Scugog, where John Sharp was in charge of a trading post for furs belonging to the Messrs. Farewell. The Governor had promised, so it was alleged, that the slayer of Whistling Duck should be punished, but a twelvemonth had elapsed and nothing had been done. The whole tribe, the Muskrat branch of the Chippewas, with their Chief Wabbekisheco at their head, came up in canoes to York on this occasion, starting from the mouth of Annis creek, near Port Oshawa, and encamping at Gibraltar Point, on the peninsula in front of York. A guard of soldiers went over to assist in the arrest of Ogetonicut, who, it appears, had arrived with the rest. Chief Wabbekisheco took the culprit by the shoulder and delivered him up. He was lodged in the jail at York. During the summer it was proved by means of a survey that the spot where Sharp had been killed was within the district of Newcastle. It was held necessary, therefore, that the trial should take place in that district. Sellick's, at the carrying place, was to have been the scene of the investigation, and thither the *Speedy* was bound when she foundered. Mr. Justice Cochrane was a most estimable character personally, and a man of distinguished ability. He was only in his twenty-eighth year, and had been Chief Justice of Prince Edward Island before his arrival in Upper Canada. He was a native of Halifax, in Nova Scotia, but had studied law in Lincoln's Inn, and was called to the bar in England.

There appears something inevitable about the loss, something that recalls the classical Greek drama. Had the original murder—that of the Indian, Whistling Duck—been punished, after "white man's word" was given, Nemesis would not have claimed the lives of the leading lawyers of York. One only escaped: William Weekes, a popular barrister, who proceeded to Presqu' Isle on horseback instead of boarding the *Speedy*. But, that the tale of victims might be complete, Mr. Weekes was challenged to a duel in 1806 and died "on the field of honour". The murder of Whistling Duck was amply avenged.

We may now ask Time to return a few years and to allow a mention of the premier merchantman built in Canada. She was named the *York,* had been constructed on the river Niagara in 1792, appeared on Lake Ontario in the summer of 1793, plied for cargo until almost the end of 1799 and on the 29th of November encountered a severe storm. Later, she was noticed "sticking on a rock off the Devil's Nose", near the mouth of the Geneva *(sic)* River — where she became a total wreck and went entirely to pieces. This "Geneva River" was probably the Genesee.

The war of 1812-14 was conducted under sail, as far as the lakes were concerned; but scarcely was that war ended than peaceful rivalry turned to steam on both sides of the border. The Canadian product was the *Frontenac,* a side-wheel steamer, schooner rigged, of five hundred tons burden. The contract for building her was given to Henry Teabout, an American from Sacketts Harbour; and here is a description of her launching:

On Saturday, the 7th of September, 1816, the steamboat *Frontenac* was launched at the village of Ernesttown. A numerous concourse of people assembled on the occasion. But, in consequence of an approaching shower, a part of the spectators withdrew before the launch actually took place. The boat moved slowly from her place, and descended with majestic sweep into her proper element. The length of her keel is 150 feet; her deck 170 feet (the tonnage was about 700). Her proportions strike the eye very agreeably, and good judges have pronounced this to be the best piece of naval architecture of the kind yet produced in America. It reflects honor upon Messrs. Teabout & Chapman, the contractors, and their workmen; and also upon the proprietors, the greater part of whom are among the most respectable merchants and other inhabitants of the County of Frontenac, from which the name is derived. The machinery for this valuable boat was imported from England, and is said to be of an excellent structure. It is expected that she will be finished and ready for use in a few weeks. Steam navigation having succeeded to admiration in various rivers, the application of it to the waters of the lakes is an interesting experiment. Every friend to public improvement must wish it all the success which is due to a spirit of useful enterprise.

In 1817 the *Frontenac* was ready for business and newspapers tell of her setting out when "she moved with majestic grandeur against a strong wind."

Her commander was Captain James McKenzie, a retired officer of the Royal Navy. At first Captain McKenzie did not have over much confidence in his vessel, for early advertisements were thus qualified: "Steamboat Frontenac will sail from Kingston for Niagara, calling at York on the 1st and 15th days of each month with as much punctuality as the nature of the lake navigation will admit of." He soon acquired confidence, however, in himself and his boat, and announced his dates with greater precision.

Travelling in those days was expensive, compared with what it is now, as the advertisement of the Frontenac, which appeared conspicuously in successive numbers of the Kingston Chronicle, occupying the width of two columns, with a cut of the steamer at the top, will show. This advertisement in the Chronicle, April 30, 1819, reads: — "The steamboat Frontenac, James McKenzie, master, will in future leave the different ports on the following days. Kingston for York, on the 1st, 11th and 21st days of each month. York for Queenston, 3rd, 13th, and 23rd days of each month. Niagara for Kingston 5th, 15th and 25th days of each month. Rates of passages from Kingston to York and Niagara £3. From York to Niagara £1.

Children under three years of age half price, above three and under ten, two-thirds. A book will be kept for entering the names of passengers and the berths which they may choose, at which time the passage money must be paid. Passengers are allowed sixty pounds weight of baggage. Surplus baggage to be paid for at the usual rate. Gentlemen's servants cannot eat or sleep in the cabin. Deck passengers will pay fifteen shillings, and may either bring their own provisions or be furnished by the steward. For each dog brought on board five shillings. All applications for passage to be made to Captain McKenzie, on board. Freight will be transported to and from the above places at the rate of four shillings per barrel bulk and flour at the customary rate, delivered to the different consignees. A list of their names will be put in a conspicuous place on board, which must be deemed a sufficient notice, and the goods taken from the steamboat will be considered at the risk of the owners. For each small parcel 2s. 6d., which must be paid on delivery. Kingston, April 28, 1819." The *Frontenac* was subsequently burnt at or near Niagara about 1825. What was left of her hull was broken up, and the remnants of her machinery sold as old iron.

Another boat, the *Queen Charlotte,* was launched in 1818. She was the pioneer steamer on the Bay of Quinte and the upper reaches of the river.

The fare from the head of the Bay of Quinte to Kingston for the first season was £1 5s. currency, equal to $5; this included meals. The *Charlotte* was a very acceptable improvement in the navigation of the day. A few of the owners of sailing craft, perhaps, suffered for a time; but the settlers regarded her as an unmixed blessing. During the first years she was so accommodating as to stop anywhere to pick up a passenger from a small boat or let one off. She was not a commercial success until Gildersleeve became her commander; after that she paid well. She ran for many years, and was finally broken up on the shores of Cataraqui Bay.

The steamer Toronto was commenced at York late in the year 1824 or early in 1825. She was built at the foot of Church street, on the bay, and was of peculiar build, being constructed of half inch planks and the same shape at both ends. She is described by Dr. Scadding as being "A shell of successive layers of rather thin boards placed alternately lengthwise and athwart, with coatings between of stout brown paper, pitched." She ran between Kingston and Prescott a short time, afterwards to Toronto. She proved a failure, and after a few seasons disappeared.

In 1826 there were five steamboats on the lake "all affording excellent accommodation and the means of expeditious travelling." The enterprise shown was soon after extended. In 1832 the project of a steamer for the Holland River was suggested.

"STEAMBOAT ON LAKE SIMCOE," thus runs the advertisement, "Persons who feel interested in the success of this undertaking are respectively [sic] informed that Capt. McKenzie, late of the Alciope, who has himself offered to subscribe one-fourth of the sum required to build the proposed steamboat, is now at Buffalo for the purpose of purchasing an engine to be delivered at Holland Landing during the present winter. Capt. McKenzie, who visited Lake Simcoe last summer, is of opinion that a boat of sufficient size and power for the business of the lake can be built for £1,250. In order, however, to insure success it is proposed that stock to the amount of £2,000 should be subscribed and it is hoped that this sum will be raised without delay in order that the necessary steps may be taken on the return of Capt. McKenzie to commence building the boat with the view to its completion by the opening of navigation. The shares are twelve pounds, ten shillings each, payable to persons chosen by the stockholders."

The movement here initiated resulted in the steamer *Simcoe* which plied for some years between the Landing and the ports of Lake Simcoe. The *Simcoe* was built at the Upper Landing and after being launched, it was necessary to drag the boat by main force down to deep water through the thick sediment at the bottom of the stream. During the process, while the capstan and tackle or other arrangement was being vigorously worked, instead of the boat advancing, the land in considerable mass moved bodily towards the boat, like a cake of ice set free from the main floe. Much of the ground and marsh in the great estuary of the Holland River is said to be simply an accumulation of earthy and vegetable matter resting on water.

Some years later the Navy made a contribution to commerce.

On June 27th, 1836, there was a great public sale of naval stores at Kingston Dock Yard. Besides stores of every imaginable kind used in ship-building, the sale included one frigate, in frame, 56 guns; one ship, in frame, 22 guns; one brig, in frame, 14 guns, and one schooner, in frame, of 4 guns; also the *Cockburn* schooner, 70 tons, paid off in 1834, with her masts and spars; also the *Bull Frog,* tender, of 60 tons, with her sails and rigging in store; also ten gunboats in good condition, "as far as they are finished", to quote the exact words of the advertisement, besides "one old schooner and four old ships of war lying aground on the mud in the harbour", again to quote the same source. But besides this decidedly miscellaneous collection there were twelve boats, new and in use, from 14 to 32 feet, chiefly built of the best rock elm; and in addition were offered for sale six fire engines, three in good repair; and the other three the advertisement contents itself by describing as "repairable", which was a strictly non-committal statement. The papers of the day give no information how this sale resulted.

At any rate it was from odd materials that the *Ann Brown* resulted.

The *Ann Brown* was built about sixty years ago [i.e., in 838] at the corner of Front and Bay streets, by a day labourer, who worked at her in his spare time and in the evenings after his day's work was done. His wife lent him all the assistance she possibly could, and received the reward of having the vessel named after her. The vessel was launched from where she was built, for at that time the Esplanade was simply the bottom of the bay, and the water came right up to Front street. She was only about thirty tons burden, yet small as this appears now, she was considered a good-sized vessel then. She was rigged as a schooner, and, like all the schooners of those days, carried a square foretopsail and top-gallantsail.

For three years she traded successfully on Lake Huron and Georgian Bay with the Indians, but one night, when she was in the neighbourhood of Manitoulin Island, a squall struck the vessel. The captain was in the cabin at the time, but he abandoned the vessel in such haste that he left $500 behind him in the cabin locker. Together with his crew of two men he reached Manitoulin Island in the yawl boat. Next morning to their surprise they saw the schooner riding at anchor, bottom up, not far from shore. When she capsized the anchor had got clear of the cat-head, and the chain running out through the hawse-pipe, had taken firm hold of a boulder on the bottom, and so prevented the vessel from pounding herself to pieces on the shore. The vessel was righted without very much trouble and continued to trade with the Indians for some time. The captain found his $500 quite safe, and on the whole may be considered to have come off from the adventure very fortunately.

In 1850 the schooner, already considered an old boat, was sold for a stone-hooker; and in 1903 she was still afloat and water-worthy.

Each year from 1837, when the *Queen Victoria* was launched, added to the number of steamboats on the lakes. There were years of profit, there were also years of particular disaster.

On April 18th, 1840, a great fire took place at Kingston, which resulted in the entire destruction of the Ottawa and Rideau wharves, the steamer Cataraqui, the schooner Dora

Nelson, besides an immense quantity of goods, including 10,000 barrels of flour, pork and potash. The Lake Ontario Steamboat office was also destroyed. The fire was supposed to have been caused by sparks from the funnel of the American steamer Telegraph. An accident also happened to the steamer conveying the Governor General from Niagara to Toronto, in the middle of April. She got aground eight miles above the harbor, and His Excellency reached Toronto in a jolly boat after a row of eight miles. He left Toronto again for Kingston, on Friday, April 24th, on the steamer St. George.

An advertisement appeared in the Toronto papers throughout June, as well as in those published at Rochester, of cheap excursions on July 4th, by the Gore steamer, for the benefit of pleasure seekers. This aroused the wrath of the notorious "Bill" Johnson, known to fame as the hero of the Sir Robert Peel incident, and he, not for the first time, issued a proclamation. It appeared undated in the very first days of the month, and read thus: — "Wm. Johnson, Commodore, etc., Lake Ontario. Whereas, public notice has appeared in a Rochester daily paper, that the British steamer *Gore*, Capt. Dick, of Toronto, W. C., offers to make two pleasure trips from the landing at Carthage on the 4th inst. the anniversary of American Independence, and whereas it is well known that Dick and the owners of this boat are violent British Tories and bitter enemies of American Democratic institutions, but in order to fleece American citizens and fill their coffers with half dollars at their expense, they pretend to aid in the celebration of a day they abhor and detest."

The inhabitants of Rochester are therefore warned "if they value life," not to patronize these excursions, and so avoid, not only "the danger to be apprehended, but the disgrace and dishonor of countenancing and patronizing a party who hate Democracy and who have exulted and triumphed in the burning of the *Caroline* and murder of American citizens.

By command of his Excellency,
Benjamin Lett, P.C.,
On board the flagship Revenge off the Ducks."

This same Benjamin Lett was, almost simultaneously with the appearance of this silly production, arrested on a charge of attempting the destruction of the steamer *Great Britain.*

Early in June, about the 5th, just as the *Great Britain* was preparing to leave Oswego on her journey to the Canadian shore, a man brought on board a small box, containing three jars of gunpowder packed in wool, beneath which was concealed a lighted slow match. This box was placed with other baggage in front of the door of the ladies' cabin. A few minutes after the boat left the wharf the explosion took place which was not so destructive as had been intended, the injury being confined to the breaking of a few windows in the ladies' cabin and the blowing up of the skylight above. The boat put back immediately and the man who brought the box on board was arrested together with another man whom the former denounced as the chief instigator to the diabolical attempt. This man was "Bill" Johnson's friend, Benjamin Lett, and he was at once transmitted to Auburn, N.Y., county jail, but owing either to extraordinary vigilance on his part, or want of it on the part of his custodians, he made his escape when about four miles from his destination.

As in the case of Toronto's buildings recorded in the previous chapter, a pattern of destruction and construction establishes itself also upon the lake. Thus, in 1847, "the year of the fever", two new vessels were launched and one was sunk. The *Passport* and the *Magnet* were both advertised as the finest and fastest. "The owners of the *Magnet* considered their vessel the best on the continent" but they were, for Canadian steamboat owners of the day, fairly modest. They only advertised her at first as "the finest vessel on Lake Ontario". Her rival, the *Passport,* in 1849, while proceeding from Montreal to Kingston with a large number of steerage passengers — emigrants — encountered disaster.

It appears that the chief engineer of the *Passport* had recently been appointed to a better situation, and his successor not having been appointed, the boat on the night in question was in charge of the second engineer. Unfortunately at the time of the accident the second engineer had retired to his berth, leaving an inferior officer in command — he being, as afterwards appeared, an illiterate person, unable to read or write.

About 9 o'clock p.m. the *Passport* was off Lancaster (16 miles below Cornwall), the under deck being loaded with steerage passengers when the boat took the ground. Orders were given to stop the engine and back out; it appears that to do this, from the peculiar construction of the engine, the engineer should have opened one cock and shut another. He opened the first, but it is said neglected to shut the other. The steam in consequence rushed from the cylinder, through the hot-well, in among the steerage passengers — and the scene which followed may be imagined. The shriek which broke from the unhappy sufferers we are assured was frightful and was heard several miles off. The utmost consternation struck all on board, the character of the accident being for some time unknown; four persons jumped overboard, of whom two were saved, but it is feared the other two were drowned.

Capt. Bowen and his officers were most energetic, and the simple nature of the disaster having been ascertained and confidence somewhat restored, every exertion was made to relieve the sufferers. A surgeon came off from Lancaster to their assistance, and the scalded passengers having been brought on deck, it was found that 44 were severely injured. We are told that the scene during the night was horrible in the extreme; the cabin was strewed with men, women and children suffering the most frightful agony, and the shrieks of the dying rang throughout the night. After some delay the boat proceeded to Cornwall, by which time nine of the sufferers had expired. A coroner's inquest was held by Dr. McDonald and Mr. Dickson, and evidence taken — but we learn that no verdict was rendered, the enquiry having been adjourned.

This dependence upon the citizen *au naturel,* i.e., without a sauce (?) of education, was not sole and singular: here is another and similar happening, a few years later.

The *Propeller Banshee,* which must not, though, be confounded with the Royal Mail steamer of the same name, was wrecked in the St. Lawrence on September 14th. It is scarcely to be credited, but it is true nevertheless, that in descending the river at night the steamer was actually left in the sole charge of a man named Finnigan, who was at the helm. He went to sleep, and the steamer being left to her own guidance, ran ashore on Whiskey Island, on the American side of the river, about five miles below Alexander Bay. She struck a sunken rock, and in 20 minutes sank. Her captain's name was McCrea. The accounts of the disaster do not contain any mention of what the owners of the steamer had to say to him afterwards. It is, though, not probable that they were very complimentary in their remarks.

Even the best of captains, however, if "slightly overtaken", was capable of curious decisions.

One of Mr. Bethune's most trusted and faithful officers, and a great favorite (who shall be nameless), one time committed the great mistake of starting from Toronto to an American port an hour before the advertised time. It was supposed that he had been indulging too freely that morning, (which was most unusual, as he was practically a total abstainer), and although the mate and engineer remonstrated with the captain, it had no effect. The consequence was that he left his purser ashore and others of the crew. What was worse, an Englishman and his wife, who intended to go with the steamer on their way to England, and who had sent the nurse and children, including a young infant, to the boat in advance, discovered, when too late, that the steamer had left. One can imagine their feelings on learning the facts. Mr. Bethune, the proprietor, on being told the state of affairs, got ready another steamer which was in port, and started in pursuit of the runaway, overtook her, and transferred the crew and passengers. Fortunately the boat arrived at her port in time, and no harm came of the affair. The captain was suspended for the trip, but on returning to Toronto was reinstated, and such was the confidence reposed in him from his general unexceptionable conduct that his own promise was deemed a sufficient guarantee that the offence would not occur again, and it never did.

And while on the subject of captains, here is a picture of one who commanded a steamer of the Royal Mail Line.

There were in the fleet several old salts, originals in their way, brought up as regular seamen, having navigated nearly all quarters of the globe in sailing vessels. One in particular, Capt. Wm. Gordon, a brother-in-law of Capt. Thos. Dick, was a noted sailor of the old school, and had all the feelings and prejudices of his class against any innovation on the established rules of all sailing crafts, and a most thorough contempt of steam as a means of propelling power, which he said was a humbug, "a delusion and a snare." Mr. Bethune, at the time Capt. Gordon made his appearance in Toronto, was building at Niagara the steamer Admiral, and arrangements were made that Gordon should command her. In fitting it out he had the steamer rigged as much like a sea-going sailing craft as possible, two masts, large main and foresail, fore-topsail, square-sail, jib and flying jib, and a four-pound carronade mounted on the bow. The vessel was painted black, with a narrow streak of white around above her guards. All the Royal Mail steamers on the lake when built were rigged in the same way. The *City of Toronto* and *The Princess* had three masts, but after a time this rigging was found in the way and caused accidents, so they were changed, and reduced to only one mast and jib, and soon Gordon had the mortification of seeing his favorite rigging removed. He said "the owners were a set of lubbers, for what did they know about it, and who ever heard of a ship without masts!" Capt. Gordon was one of the finest and best hearted men possible, and a great favorite with the travelling public.

To conclude this mercantile section let the reader consider two ocean-going vessels built on the lake. First the *City of Toronto,* launched in 1855, "constructed entirely of selected upland white oak . . . an exceedingly strong and serviceable vessel". She was of 1,000 tons burden, with a length of 168 feet.

This was the first sea-going vessel built here, and, up to her time, the largest ocean vessel built in Upper Canada. Thousands witnessed the launch, which was not entirely successful, the ways spreading just as the vessel took the water. She was quickly floated off, however. After the launch a select party was invited to lunch on board the ship, and the Mayor (Hon. G. W. Allan) presented Mr. Hayes with a set of colours on behalf of the Council, as a public testimony for the firm's enterprise in originating a new branch of industry — ocean ship-building.

Owing to a difficulty in obtaining part of her equipment, it was not until the beginning of August that the ship left Toronto. Messrs. Hayes Bros. had built another sea-going vessel, the barque *Reindeer,* at Coldwater. The *Reindeer* and the *City of Toronto* were both intended for sale in the British market. They left Toronto in company, with cargoes of walnut. The *City of Toronto,* the larger vessel, having taken as much cargo aboard as the depth of the St. Lawrence canals would admit, completed loading at Quebec. She was to have been taken out by Captain Kidd, a veteran salt-water captain, but owing to some failure in arrangements, a Captain Clark took command of her. Besides her cargo of walnut, the ship carried several passengers.

The *City of Toronto* made a record run from Quebec to Liverpool, covering the distance in a little over two weeks. She then went into the timber trade, for which she was calculated, being fitted with bow and stern ports. On her second voyage, in the fall of 1856, when returning to Quebec for another cargo of timber, she was wrecked on the coast of Nova Scotia, and the greater part of her crew perished.

Ten years later, in 1865, came the voyage of the Brigantine *Sea Gull.*

"The Sixties" are looked back to by many vesselmen as the Golden Age of lake shipping. Those were the days, they will tell you, when every little lake port owned its fleet of sailing vessels, and lots of money was being made in the carrying trade. They will tell you of the many different vessels which were once the pride of the lake, and among these you will hear them mention the "brig" *Sea Gull*. She is remembered, not on account of her size, or her beauty, or her speed, for in none of these particulars was she remarkable, but because of a voyage she made, in the year 1865, down the river St. Lawrence and south-eastward, over the broad Atlantic across the line to Port Natal, in Cape Colony, South Africa. This voyage never was attempted before, or accomplished since, by a lake vessel.

The *Sea Gull* was built in Oakville, in 1864, by John Simpson, who with his brother built a great many of the once famous Oakville schooners, some of which are still afloat [in 1896]. The vessel was owned by John Murray, of Oakville, and Frank Jackman, sr., of Toronto, and was registered in this port. When she first came out she was a fore-and-aft centreboard schooner, of 201 tons register. These were her dimensions: Length over all, 105 feet; extreme beam, 22 feet; draught, when loaded, ten feet; when light, 4 feet 6 inches. She had the peculiarity of most Oakville vessels — her masts had quite a "spread." The raking mainmast was stepped rather far aft, and the foremast pretty well forward. She is said to have cost her owners some $15,000.

There was a brisk trade in those days between Toronto and Oswego, lumber and grain being carried down the lake and coal on the return trip. The *Sea Gull* was engaged in this trade for the first season.

In the spring of 1865 Mr. Davids, of Toronto, chartered her to take out a consignment of lumber, buggies and sundries to a man named Lysle, at Port Natal, South Africa. Alterations were made in her rig, to fit her better for her long voyage, and she was changed from a schooner to a brigantine, this rig being considered handier for use on salt water. She carried

fifteen different pieces of canvas, there being five square sails
on the foremast. Her crew amounted to ten men all told.
There were four men and two boys before the mast.

She left for Port Natal in June, 1865, and after a three
months' voyage, in which she met with no mishap, or, in fact,
anything at all extraordinary, reached her destination. She
crossed "the bar" at Port Natal under canvas, without the
assistance of a tug, a thing very seldom done. She excited considerable comment in that port by the length of her voyage,
and by the fact that she was the smallest vessel which up to
that time had entered the harbour, and the only Great Lakes
trader which had ever made the voyage. The cargo was
delivered to the consignee, and it might be mentioned that
the lumber was sold at the modest price of 8d. per foot. After
discharging her cargo, the *Sea Gull* lay in the harbour for
three months, waiting for a charter and making repairs and
alterations, for experience had taught the fresh water sailors
that several improvements might be made. Among the changes
was a reduction of eight feet in the height of the main-mast.

In January, 1866, the *Sea Gull* sailed for Boston with a
cargo of sugar, molasses, pepper, arrowroot, ivory and some
thirty-seven passengers, and arrived at her destination after a
voyage of ninety-eight days. There she discharged her cargo
and loaded flour for St. John's, Newfoundland, sailing from
that port in ballast for Sydney, Cape Breton, and there received a cargo of coal for Montreal. She came up light from
Montreal to Kingston and there got a cargo of wood for
Toronto.

In July, 1866, the *Sea Gull* arrived in this port after a voyage
of thirteen months and was placed on exhibition at Yonge
street wharf, where great crowds flocked to see her. The voyage
had been a very fortunate one; none of the crew was lost, the
vessel suffered no damage, and there were no mishaps whatever. Frank Jackman, sr., was captain, and his nephew, James
Jackman, mate. Captain May, a salt water sailor, acted as
navigator. About $9,000 was paid for the trip, and after all
bills were settled there was $2,000 profit. A sample of South

African rum was brought back, and kept on tap in the captain's cabin. Verily, a little of it went a long way — thousands of miles — and old marines declare it was strong enough to knock a man down.

After this voyage the *Sea Gull* continued for many years to earn money in the lake trade, until her eventful career was ended by fire in 1888.

This chapter would be incomplete without some mention of the Royal Canadian Yacht Club; although it is a little later in date than "Old Toronto's" general line, and there is little more than a beginning to record.

The society from which the present Royal Canadian Yacht Club has sprung was at first a boat club founded in 1850. Little, if anything, was done during that season or in the next, but in 1852 this society published its rules and regulations, and changed the name from Boat Club to that of the Toronto Yacht Club.

Prominent among its members were: Messrs. William Armstrong, C.E., John Arnold, Charles Heath, Thomas Shortiss, S. B. Harman (late City Treasurer); Dr. Hodder, Major Magrath, and Capt. Fellows.

The first meetings of the original promoters of the club were held in the office of Captain Fellows, commission merchant on Melinda street. There, seated on flour barrels, the club scheme was projected and was further matured at later conclaves held in a room over John Steel's saloon, which stood nearly opposite the present Academy of Music on King street. The first building used by the club was owned by Messrs. Gzowski and Macpherson and stood where the Union Station now stands. The first club house proper was erected on a scow and was moored just west of what was known as Rees' wharf. This house was occupied by the club until 1858 when it was found so seriously damaged by muskrats and heavy weather that it had to be abandoned. The club then purchased the wrecking steamer *Provincial,* which was fitted up as a club house and moored between Tinning's and Rees' wharves, opposite the Union Station. This was found to be a very unsatisfactory resting-place, however, as the vessel frequently contrived to get adrift. "Often," said Mr. William Armstrong, who kindly furnished sketches of these two floating habitations, "was I called up in the middle of the night with the information that she had broken loose, and then I had to go down and put in the rest of the night getting her fast again." This ship was occupied until 1869, when the club acquired a water lot west of Rees' wharf where they erected a commodious club house and substantial wharf. During the autumn of 1873 the club engaged for use during the winter months the premises now known as Club Chambers. In 1874 the property on King street adjoining the old Montreal House was purchased as a town club house. Here they remained till 1877 when a social union was effected with the Toronto Club, the R.C.Y.C. still retaining their water club house and their individuality as yachtsmen. In 1880, finding that they were being crowded out of an anchorage for their yachts, the club sold their water premises to the Grand Trunk and having obtained a suitable site on the Island erected their present club house. A city landing and boat house were secured at the foot of Lorne street and the steam yacht *Esperanza* was purchased to convey the members of the club to and fro. In 1889 the Royal Canadian Yacht Club and the Toronto Yacht Club (the latter of which had been in existence since 1880), effected an amalgamation. The Lorne street landing was disposed of and the new organization retained the club house of the Toronto club as their town headquarters and landing place.

II. THE ROAD

Yonge Street in the year 1800 was "a straggling waggon track, almost impassable to vehicles". It began at Queen Street, then called Lot Street and proceeded north, getting steadily worse. Trinity Square, in the modern *Street Guide,* is merely noted as "West from 258 Yonge, 3rd north of Queen". But the house of Doctor Macaulay, in what is

DON VALE HOUSE, 1870

now Trinity Square, "was long considered particularly remote and inaccessible and stories are told of persons be-
wildered and lost for hours in the adjoining marshes and
woods while trying to reach it. Justice Boulton travelling from
Prescott in his own vehicle and bound for Dr. Macaulay's
domicile was dissuaded on reaching Mr. Small's house at
the corner of King and Berkeley streets from attempting to
push on to his destination, although it was by no means late,
on account of the inconveniences and perils to be encountered,
and half the following day was taken up in accomplishing
the residue of his journey." Over such roads, when necessity
drove, the farmers came in to York; and the town's inhabitants were enabled to leave their native mud either in
their private carriages or by the public stage. Busy as
"the Coffin Block" at the junction of Wellington Street east
and Front Street used to be, it was best known in 1830 to 1835
in connection with William Weller's line of stages.

It was indeed a busy scene when the stages for Hamilton,
Kingston, Niagara and other points, loaded up with their
livery freight every morning and started on what would be
now considered a wearying journey.

How slow travelling was in the days of stage coaches may
be learned from the advertisements of the period. One reads
that "On the 20th of September, 1816, a stage will commence
running between York and Niagara. It will leave York every
Monday, arrive at Niagara on Thursday, and leave Queenston
every Friday. The baggage is to be considered at the risk of
the owner, and the fare to be paid in advance." In 1824 the
mails were conveyed the same distance via Ancaster in three
days. A post office advertisement for tenders, signed by William
Allan, P.M., reads: — "The mails are made up here (York),
on the afternoon of Monday and Thursday, and must be delivered at Niagara on the Wednesday and Saturday following,
and within the same period in returning." In 1835 Mr. William
Weller was the proprietor of a line of stages between Toronto
and Hamilton, known as "The Telegraph Line." In an ad-

vertisement he engages to take passengers through by daylight on the Lake Road during the winter season.

In 1847 *The Kingston Argus* comments as follows on Mr. William Weller's stages: "The Toronto stage now generally performs the distance between that place and Kingston in 28 hours, making a faster rate than has before been done except by express. This improved travelling cannot be attributed altogether to the good roads, but in a great measure to a determination of Mr. Weller to perform the distance in as short a time as possible."

In 1850 the following mail and stage coaches were advertised to leave Toronto, eastward, for Kingston: — The Eastern mail stage leaves the general stage office at the junction of Front and Wellington streets daily at 6 o'clock p.m.; Oshawa — another stage leaves the same office for Oshawa daily at 3 p.m.; Rouge — a stage leaves Stroud's, Market Square, for the Rouge, daily, Sundays excepted, at 4 p.m.; Markham Village — a stage leaves Arnott's, Clyde Inn, Palace street, daily, Sundays excepted, at 3 p.m. Westward, for Hamilton. The western mail stage by Dundas street, leaves the Hamilton and Lake Simcoe Mail Stage office, Liddell's buildings, Church street, daily, at 6 p.m. In winter a second stage leaves the same office for Hamilton via the Lake Shore road, daily, at 9 a.m.; Streetsville, a stage leaves Kellogg's, Colborne street, daily, Sundays excepted, for Streetsville, at 3 o'clock p.m. Northern for Holland Landing. A stage in connection with the steamer *Morning,* on Lake Simcoe, leaves the Simcoe stage office, Liddell's buildings, Church street, daily, Sundays excepted, at 7 o'clock a.m. and at 3 o'clock p.m. Another stage in connection with the steamer *Beaver* on Lake Simcoe, leaves the Western Hotel daily at 7 o'clock a.m.; Pine Grove — a stage leaves the stage office, Liddell's buildings, for Pine Grove daily at 3 o'clock p.m. There are also stages for Richmond Hill, Thornhill and York Mills, leaving the Market Square daily at 4 o'clock p.m.

Another manager of a stage line about the same time as Mr. Weller was Charles Thompson, who ran a northern line.

The stages were cumbrous affairs drawn by four horses, with delays at various points along the line. They were always crowded, and for this reason most of the people from Hamilton, Whitby, Cobourg and other places, who owned horses and carriages, preferred to drive to the capital in their own outfits and spend a few days here.

Mr. Weller's first advertisement appeared in the Upper Canada *Gazette,* January 14, 1830:

New Arrangement of Stages. — The mail stage between York and Kingston will commence running, agreeably to the winter arrangements, on the 7th day of December instant, leaving York and Kingston on Mondays and Thursdays at noon, arriving on Wednesdays and Saturdays, a.m. Books kept at the Steamboat Hotel York, and Kingston Hotel, Kingston. Extra[1] furnished for any part of the country on reasonable terms. All baggage at the risk of the owner. Wm. Weller, York: H. Norton & Co., Kingston.

But there had been earlier conveyances. In 1823 the *Gazette* contains "the first notice of a regular stage line during the winter from York to Kingston, via the Kingston road":

Stage Notice — J. Powers respectfully informs the public in general that he will run a stage on the road between York and Kingston during the sleighing season, and that no exertion shall be wanting on his part to give satisfaction to those who may please to honor him with their commands. Darlington, Jan. 6, 1823.

From York to Hamilton and Dundas became a much travelled road. In 1828 a second stage appeared:

A new line of stages has been lately established to run
_____
[1] i.e. a private conveyance by special arrangement.

through from Dundas to York, via Hamilton, three times a week. The proprietors are provided, we understand, with good horses and comfortable carriages for the convenience of travellers. The exertions they are making to add to the facility of communication in this part of the country will, we hope, be amply rewarded. Stage books are kept at Howard's Inn, York, and Jones', Dundas.

William Weller was also the hero of a spectacular episode. He conveyed

Sir Poulett Thomson (afterwards Lord Sydenham, who died in Kingston), the Governor-General, from Toronto to Montreal. This service was performed at a speed almost equal to that of the railway, being done at fifteen miles an hour from start to finish. Mr. Weller had a sleigh fitted up with a bed in it for the accommodation of the Governor-General. Weller himself took the box and reins. For this service he received $400, and the Governor also made him a present of a gold watch. Mr. Weller had made arrangements for the change of horses at short distances all along the road, and these changes were waiting ready harnessed at stated places. The horses were kept always at full speed. Mr. Weller and the Governor were the only occupants of the sleigh until the former became so exhausted that he could no longer hold the reins, when he took a driver with him, but he retained his seat on the box to the end of the journey.

This feat was performed on February 18, 1840. ("Probably the most rapid journey ever made in Canada over the ordinary winter roads." — *Life of Lord Sydenham*). The roads were frozen, so the going was good. The distance was 360 miles, which was travelled in 28 hours.

At its most prosperous period there were three lines of stages on Yonge Street. One was in connection with the steamers on Lake Simcoe, owned by Charles Thompson of Summerhill. Of one of them, the *Morning,* we learn: —

Great difficulty was experienced in fitting out this vessel. Her machinery had to be hauled up Yonge Street from Toronto on rollers, made from sections of tree trunks. Weeks were spent in the trip from the city.

But the end of the northern stage coach was approaching.

The fate of the stage line was sealed when, in 1853, the Northern railway was constructed. Up to that period all the passengers, baggage and mail between Toronto and Holland Landing had gone by stage. When the railway went through, the line to the Landing was discontinued. Mail was still carried as far as Richmond Hill by the bus line, which passed successively into the hands of John Palmer, a Richmond Hill hotel keeper named Raymond, William Cook, of the Yorkshire House, Thornhill, and John Thompson. This gentleman bought the line early in the seventies, and did not discontinue it until 1896, when the introduction of electric cars killed the business.

This could be the point at which to conclude, on a note of progress and electric cars; but we have two items of unfinished business. Concerning the Railway there is little to learn from the *Landmarks*. The Ontario, Simcoe and Huron Railroad Company, later known as the Northern Railway, was, at its beginning, an enterprise of the energetic Mr. F. C. Capreol.

The weather on the 15th of October, 1851, was beautiful. On that day in the presence of a great assemblage on the Esplanade, just west of Simcoe street, opposite the parliament buildings, Lady Elgin pressed her dainty foot upon the richly ornamented spade, and threw a little dirt into the handsomely carved oak wheel barrow which Mayor Bowes, who assisted in the ceremony, wheeled a short distance and then emptied. On this occasion Mayor Bowes was resplendent in a cocked hat, sword, knee breeches, silk stockings and shoes, with silver buckles.

The first locomotive for the new road was built at Portland, Maine. It was named Lady Elgin, and a photograph of it now hangs in the offices of the Northern Company. The Lady Elgin weighed about twenty-four tons. She had five-foot driving wheels and a 14 x 20 cylinder. She was what is technically

THE OLD GRAND TRUNK RAILWAY DEPOT

known as an inside connected engine, her works all lying under the boiler and out of sight. She was of too light calibre for anything but construction work and at that she was put after her arrival. Of all the men who had charge of the Lady Elgin during her existence the whereabouts of only one was known last year [1883]. That was Philip Warren, of Collingwood, then running a freight engine between that place and Toronto, and he had charge of the engine only a comparatively short time before she was finally side-tracked. Other engineers were William Huckett, Silas Huckett, Carlos McCaul, Chris Hildebrandt, John Legge, Josh. Metzker, Dan Sheehan and Dan

Bracken. They are all dead now. Before the railroad was opened the stages did all the business, and as steam travel took away the means of livelihood from owners and drivers, the company gave them positions on the road. The first accident occurred on the road on the afternoon of Sunday, July 16, 1853. A short distance south of Weston the engine struck a cow, throwing off the rails the coach, which rolled down a steep embankment, totally wrecking the car and severely injuring an Irish passenger and two brakemen, who were its only occupants. The baggage car was provided with chairs to do duty as a passenger coach for the rest of the trip and the train proceeded on its way only to strike a truck and go off the track again near Newmarket. The Lady Elgin was used for shunting until 1880, when the gauge of the road was changed.

First, however, this little engine had a taste of fame.

At 8 o'clock in the morning of May 16th, 1853, the first passenger train ever run in Canada, pulled out in the presence of a large crowd from the little wooden shed opposite the Queen's Hotel, which had been dignified by the name of station. The train was made up of the engine Lady Elgin, a box car and a passenger car. There was no ticket office, Alderman John Harvie, the conductor of the train, selling the tickets on board. The first ticket bought was by a shoemaker named Maher, living on east Queen street, who objected to paying a dollar to ride 30 miles. A dispute exists as to who was the engineer. It was either Carlos McCaul, of Parkdale, or M. Huckett. The destination of the train was Aurora. All along the route people turned out in great crowds to see the novel sight. Two hours after leaving the train whistled "Down Brakes" at Aurora. Mad Capreol's scheme was a great success. The first railroad excursion in Canada was on the Queen's Birthday of the same year.

In October 1856 the Eastern Division of the Grand Trunk Railway entered Toronto, running into the station at the Don; but a fire not long after destroyed eight locomotives, and in 1857, March 12, occurred the first serious accident, at the Desjardins Canal (between Toronto and Hamilton) where the loss of life was heavy. The real history of Toronto's railways began later.

One cannot end this chapter better than by a note upon the city's failure to come to terms with the river Don. Through the nineteenth century, but especially in the early years, ill-luck appeared to centre in that name. The river itself, the Don Bridge, the Don Road, and (later) the Don Gaol — were, all in turn, causing loss and vexation. Even the Don Mills were disastrously burned and never rebuilt. The river drowned men, the bridge was inadequate, the road was impassable, and the gaol carried its curse into the twentieth century. The sixth volume of the *Landmarks,* published in 1914, calls the river "A never ending Trouble"; and a letter in the York *Gazette* of July 4, 1807, calls attention to the impossibility of crossing the harbour "in all high winds". The printers of the *Gazette* agreed and say: "They would be happy to see some public spirited person set on foot a subscription for the purpose of erecting a bridge over Frank's creek, and the repairs of the causeway leading to Yonge street."

This brought results on April 1st:

The editors having been called upon by a number of gentlemen to request a meeting of such persons as might wish to subscribe towards erecting a bridge across that part of the River Don which separates the town and the peninsula, give notice that it is desired such meeting should take place tomorrow, at Campbell & Deary's Tavern, at 3 o'clock in the afternoon. They should be wanting in themselves and in their duty to the public were they not to give every encouragement and assistance in their power to so desirable an object. Humanity is interested in the laudable undertaking, and it may promote a more general subscription to state that for want of a bridge several lives (within their knowledge) have been lost. When

completed the peninsula will answer every purpose of an
extensive common to the owners of cattle; to those who may
use it for purposes of recreation, it furnishes a most delightful
walk or ride; as a race ground or place for field exercise, we
know not its equal; the sportsman will find a constant and
easy access to the best shooting ground, and the convalescent
might find health in an occasional excursion to the opposite
beach — and travellers or persons coming to market from
below would at all seasons find the town accessible, which to
them at present frequently is not, but at the imminent hazard
of life.

    Two weeks later we have:

THE DON BRIDGE: — The project of erecting a bridge
across the Don had evidently been well received, for the editor
waxes optimistic.

    "We have been favoured with a list of the sums subscribed
for the purpose of erecting a bridge across the Don, and have
the pleasure of informing those who wish to patronize the
undertaking that the subscription already exceeds one hundred
pounds. From the liberal sum given by Mrs. Gore an example
is offered to other ladies, and we may infer that his Excellency
permits that part of the demesne (the peninsula) to be rendered
useful to the community, whilst unappropriated to the particular
purposes for which it was reserved. When the requisite sum is
made up we will publish the names of the donors with pleasure."

    The first bridge over the Don at Queen street was built in
1803. It must have been swept away, hence a new bridge
was proposed.

    And on July 23, 1808, the matter receives advertisement:

DROWNED IN THE DON. — "Departed this life on the
20th Mr. Parshall Terry. His death was occasioned by his
getting into the River Don on horseback. By this misfortune
an exemplary wife and large, helpless family are left to the
care of the all-disposing Providence, and a resistless appeal is
made to the benevolence and sympathetic generosity of a

virtuous public. The particular situation of the road near the Don bridge calls imperiously upon the commissioners appointed by his Excellency for the particular care of the roads and employing the voted money for immediate repairs, as many lives are seriously threatened with danger by its present state, in consequence of the causeway being removed by an excessive flood. The place, when seen, suggests the nature of the required improvement, and as a part of duty we earnestly recommend it to public attention."

Parshall Terry essayed to ford the Don on horseback, at a point some fifty yards north of the present (1913) Queen street bridge. He was swept away, his body being afterwards found near the mouth of the river, but his horse reached the shore.

In 1823 we learn that York had hoped to build a bridge or bridges by public subscription:

On Friday evening last, pursuant to public notice given in the U. C. *Gazette,* a meeting of the subscribers and other inhabitants of the town of York was held at the house of Mr. Phair, in the Market place, for the purpose of taking into consideration the circumstances by which the Engineer has been placed by constructing a bridge (the charges of which were to have been defrayed by voluntary subscriptions) over the mouth of the River Don, when the following resolutions were proposed and adopted: —

That Mr. Edward Angell being duly appointed as Engineer to construct a bridge over the mouth of the River Don, according to a plan and estimate submitted to, and approved and signed by, a committee at a former meeting of the subscribers held at the Mansion House Hotel in the town of York, and having conducted himself in everything relating thereto with skill and attention, is honorably entitled to the further protection and support of the subscribers and of the inhabitants of the town generally, the funds already contributed being wholly inadequate to meet the exigencies of the undertaking.

However, a bridge must have been built, for in the *Gazette* of September 22, 1827 we read:

BRIDGES. — The Don bridge near this town is again in an impassable state; part of it gave way during the last week, and horses and carriages are now passed over on a temporary floating bridge on a toll being paid to the person who has erected that convenience. This circumstance has afforded the *Canadian Freeman* an opportunity of venting a little abuse against the magistrates. We have had occasion more than once to state that in such cases the magistrates cannot act in any other way than the law directs. If the system is bad the fault lies in the law and should be amended. As it now stands the following is the course to be adopted for making any necessary repairs. By George III, chapter 1, clause 12, the road surveyors must certify to the Quarter Session, and if then considered advisable by a majority, the former resolution may be confirmed and the work ordered to be done and paid for from the district treasury, provided the expense shall not exceed 50 pounds. From this it will be seen that the magistrates are limited in their authority, and cannot order the performance of any repairs that may exceed 50 pounds, and that if the expenditure of 50 pounds will not build it the only remedy is by application to the Legislature. We are willing to admit that the law requires to be amended, but while it remains as it is it is unjust to accuse any public functionaries with a neglect of duty.

The Old Don Bridge was erected in 1851; and over it, eight years later, was flung the body of Mr. John Hogan, M.P., for whose murder James Brown suffered death. In 1878 the bridge was swept away, and in the *Landmarks* the whole matter is thus summarized:

There have been many bridges over the Don. The first bridge was known as Playter's Bridge. It was higher up the river at the east end of Winchester street. Then there was the bridge known as Scadding's Bridge, which was there in the time of Governor Simcoe in 1794.

During the troubles of 1837 a number of those who took part in the Rebellion, under Col. Van Egmond,[2] set fire to the bridge and partially destroyed it. The damage was soon repaired, however, and the bridge continued in use till 1850 when, in a spring freshet in the early part of April, it was swept away. While this bridge was being reconstructed after the flood a boat known as the Cigar Ferry Boat was used in conveying passengers and vehicles to and from the city. The late Richard Tinning was enterprising enough to operate this ferry, but his enterprise (as it destroyed a good deal of the trade in ferrying people across the Don) aroused the anger of the 'longshoremen who had been doing this trade, and one night after the Cigar boat crew had left their craft, the boat was sunk in the east bank of the Don, near the Smith homestead. The craft was raised and was of service till the bridge was rebuilt.

Whether they came by lake, by river, or by road, the occasional misfortune, the "occupational hazard" that affected Toronto or "Muddy York" was never enough to prevent a majority of her inhabitants from living and thriving. That resilience persists, that spirit prevails; and long may it continue to dominate this country.

[2] More probably under Mackenzie and Matthews (see p. 117).

THE BOND HEAD INN, 1840

XII. YOUTH AND ITS EDUCATION

The native of Great Britain (whether his origins lay in England, Wales or the neighbouring Independency of Scotland), who migrated to Upper Canada towards the end of the eighteenth century, probably held with some fixity a belief in the value of education. This belief led, logically, to the view that those who by reason of youth were likely to be susceptible should have a rendezvous with education in its British form. Certainly that was the opinion of Mr. Richard Cockrel, of Niagara, the first schoolmaster in those parts and a qualified man:

"By observation and enquiry I am inclined to think that the education of youth is too much neglected in this Province. In some parts they have masters, in others none; and indeed those who have masters had almost as well be without them: I have since my arrival in this Province, had opportunities of conversing with several, and without exception found them mere novices in every branch of knowledge that is requisite to complete an English education. But here the cry will be against me and the stale but customary motto brought upon the carpet, viz. 'this is a new country and we must take such as we can get.'"

That this reproach is not mere rhetoric Cockrel proves by his note on the kind of person who takes up the occupation of a Teacher; "mushroom gentry", he calls them, and urges that "we find, now-a-days, persons filling the places of tutors, who have neither abilities nor address to recommend them, scarcely knowing B from a bull's foot . . . Hence we daily behold tailors, blacksmiths, coblers, worn-out livery servants, etc., etc., turning schoolmasters."

He was well in advance of his age in many ways; for instance, with regard to corporal punishment, he writes "I do not like the idea of stripes, and would never recommend them but when the strictest necessity required it."

The success of Mr. Cockrel's school may have led William Cooper into error. He seems to have felt that anyone could be a teacher (and it is remarkable how that idea persists). This notice appeared in the *Gazette* of November 3rd, 1798:

William Cooper begs leave to inform his friends and the public that he intends opening a school in his house in George Street on the 19th inst., for the instruction of youth in reading, writing, arithmetic, and English grammar. Those who choose to favour him with their pupils may rely on the greatest attention being paid to their virtue and morals.

A few months later, in July 1799, the Editor commends him:

We are happy in being informed that no person will be countenanced or permitted by the Government to teach school in any part of this province unless he shall have passed an examination before one of our commissioners, and receive a certificate from under his hand, specifying that he is adequate to the important task of a tutor. We conceive this piece of intelligence highly worthy of remark, as it will, in a great measure, prevent the imposition which the inhabitants of this country have hitherto experienced from itinerant characters, who preferred that to a more laborious way of getting through life. And on the other hand, the rising generation will reap infinite benefit from it, as it will tend to stimulate and encourage men of literary character to make permanent residence among us. Mr. William Cooper, teacher of the mathematics in this town has, not long since, passed an examination before the Rev. John Stuart, and received a license to teach school in this town, and it is to be hoped that all ranks of people will patronize so laudable an institution.

But alas, either Mr. Cooper did not obtain a sufficient
number of pupils or he came to the honest conclusion that
teaching was not his *métier*. In September, 1800, he advertises that he has received a licence to act as an auctioneer;
and in February, 1801, we read:

To be Sold by Auction. — On Monday, the 30th of March
next, at eleven o'clock in the forenoon, that commodious
and well situated house in Duke street, wherein Mr. Cooper
lately kept school, with the fifth of an acre of land thereunto
belonging.

William Cooper went on to be a very popular auctioneer:
what he was as a teacher we do not know (Alice, you
remember, remarked of the Duchess's baby, "It would have
made a dreadfully ugly child, but it makes a rather handsome
pig, I think").

For the youth of York home teaching was probably the
rule until about 1807, when

the Rev. Dr. O'Kill Stuart built a modest frame house as a
residence for himself on the plot of ground owned by him
at the south-east corner of King and George streets. At the
south-east corner of his house, and attached to it, he constructed a small low stone building, not much bigger than a
root-house. The stone walls stood in their native rudeness,
but they were afterward covered with a coating of clap-boards.
In this primitive school house the first public school of York
was established, and on the rolls of its pupils one may read
the names of boys who became rich and celebrated men and
of girls who blossomed into the belles of the growing capital.
The school was called the Home District School, and it was
opened on the first of June, 1807, by the Rev. Dr. O'Kill Stuart,
who taught there several years.

Contemporary records show that the first names entered
on its books were those of John Ridout, William A. Hamilton,

Thomas G. Hamilton, George H. Detlor, George S. Boulton, Robert Stanton, William Stanton, Angus McDonell, Alexander Hamilton, Wilson Hamilton, Robert Ross, and Allan McNab. Among the girls' names are many afterward distinguished in the society of Upper Canada. The Rev. Dr. John Strachan, afterward first bishop of Toronto, succeeded Dr. Stuart as incumbent of St. James' in 1813. The Home District School came to an end, and in its place Dr. Strachan established the District Grammar School.

The illustration shows the Rectory after it had become a general store. The small stone building on the left of it is York's Home District School.

And now there enters education, personified by Dr. Strachan. He had been a teacher since the age of 19.

In 1799, a young man poor in purse, but rich in a well-trained mind, he came to Upper Canada and took a tutorship in a Kingston family. In 1807, mainly through his exertions, an act was passed establishing a grammar school in each district of the province, and very soon three superior schools were started at Cornwall, Kingston and Niagara, and later at York and other districts of Upper Canada. These schools were for pupils of both sexes. Dr. Strachan's Cornwall school is famous and on its books were the names of very many celebrated in the annals of Upper Canada. So successful was his work here, and so well was he beloved that, in 1833, forty-two of his former scholars presented him with an address in which they say: — "Our young minds received there an impression which has scarcely become fainter from time of the deep and sincere interest which you took not only in our advancement in learning and science, but in all that concerned our happiness or could affect our future prospects in life."

In reply Dr. Strachan said (in part):

"It has ever been my conviction that our scholars should be considered for the time our children; and that as parents we should study their peculiar dispositions if we really wish to improve them, for if we feel not something of the tender relation of parents toward them, we cannot expect to be successful in their education. It was on this principle I attempted to proceed." While Dr. Strachan was in the height of his success as a teacher at the Cornwall school — the fame of which had spread not only through Upper Canada but also through the lower provinces — Lieutenant-Governor Gore in . 1812 offered him the parish of York. The clerical income was small and there was no parsonage. But the Governor added the chaplaincy of the troops at £150 a year, and as a still further inducement held out the promise of establishing a school. Dr. Strachan accepted the offer, and on August 2nd, 1812, the first Sunday after his arrival, he preached a sermon on the war before the Legislature in the parish church. It was not long before a district grammar school was established at York after the model of the one at Cornwall. For a time before the erection of the new building, an obscure frame building of the most ordinary kind on the north side of King street, just east of Yonge street, was occupied as the school house. Soon afterward a large field almost square, containing six acres, filled with huge pine stumps and small ponds of water in which crayfish were abundant, was set apart. Through the middle of this field from north to south ran a shallow swale where water collected after rains. The whole field was covered with the natural herbage that usually grows upon clearings. This block was designated College square, the block south of it being termed Church square and the reservation to the west of that Court House square. In the minds of those who laid out these plots the expectation was that they should remain ornamental pieces of grounds or small parks surrounding the buildings and the institutions for which they were set apart. The College Square was bounded on the south by Adelaide street, on the north by Richmond street, on the east by Jarvis street, and on the west by Church street. These are the modern names, Church street being the only one of the four that has retained its original nomenclature; Adelaide was formerly Newgate street, because the jail stood near it. Richmond was Hospital street and Jarvis was first Nelson and then New street. The new District Grammar School building stood at the southwest corner of this lot, 114 feet from its western and 104 feet from its southern boundary. The rest of the block was the playground of the school. The building was a good sized frame structure, fifty-five feet long and forty feet wide, of two stories, each of respectable altitude. The gables faced east and west. On each side of the school were two rows of ordinary sash windows, five on the ground floor and the same number on the floor above. At the east end were four windows two above and two below. At the west end were five windows and the entrance door. The whole exterior of the building was painted of a blueish hue. Within on the first floor, beyond the loggia, was a large square apartment. About three yards from each of its angles a plain timber post helped to sustain the ceiling. At about four feet from the floor each of these quasi-pillars began to be chamfered off at its four angles. Filling up the southeast corner of the room was a small platform approached on three sides by a couple of steps. On this was a desk about eight feet long, its lower part cased over in front with thin deal boards. On the floor along the whole length of the southern and northern sides of the chamber were narrow desks set close against the wall with benches arranged at their outer side. At right angles to these running out on each side into the apartment stood a series of shorter desks with double slopes and benches placed on either side. Through the whole length of the room from east to west between the rows of cross benches there was a wide vacant space. The walls and ceilings and desks and seats were all of unpainted pine of a yellowish hue. During school hours this room presented the usual aspect of a school interior. The ruler of this place was Dr. John Strachan. The Rev. Dr. Bethune, afterward Bishop Strachan's successor in the Episcopate, came to York in 1819 as assistant teacher in the Grammar School. Of his first visit to the school, after describing it as a capacious wooden building standing on an open common, a little in the rear of St. James' churchyard, he says: — "on entering it for the first time with the reverend principal on a bright September morning fresh schoolboy feelings were wakened up at the sight of forty or fifty happy young faces, from seventeen down to five years of age. There was a class of only two in Greek, who took up Horace and Livy in Latin, and there were three Latin forms below them, the most numerous and sprightly reading Cornelius Nepos. None were much advanced in mathematics, and, with the exception of the senior two, had not passed the fourth book of Euclid. Everything was taught on the same plan as at Cornwall, but at York the pupils were much less advanced and the head master rarely took any share in the actual work of instruction. I had had the opportunity of seeing both schools, and though the glory of the former was never approached by the latter, still there are reminiscences connected with the school at York more fresh and lively than could be awakened by the more celebrated one at Cornwall." On public days when examinations were being conducted or debates were going on, the exercises were held up-stairs in a long room with a partially vaulted ceiling on the south side of the building. At the east end was a platform. Everybody in town used to attend on these occasions, from the Lieutenant-Governor down, especially the parents of the scholars. Dr. Scadding, who attended this school, has preserved many facts in regard to it from which much of the information in this article is derived. At the examination on August 7, 1816, John Claus spoke the prologue in which he advises Governor Gore, then at the head of affairs, to distinguish himself by attention to the educational interests of the country.

Reading through the programme of "Examination exercises" it is evident that there is a great deal of recitation and declamation to a very little examination.

In the prologue pronounced by Robert Baldwin (in verse) the administration of Hastings in India is eulogized, Sir William

Jones is apostrophized in connection with his Asiatic researches, the Marquis of Wellesley and the college founded by him at Calcutta suggests the necessity of a similar institution in Canada, and Sir Peregrine Maitland, who was probably present, is told that he could immortalize himself by establishing such an institution. The epilogue is a doggerel on United States innovations in the English language. For the greater part the examinations were conducted orally. Parliamentary debates were of frequent occurrence. On ordinary occasions these took place in the main school room, but on public days they were held up-stairs. These debates consisted of the delivery of speeches, somewhat abridged, which had been made in the House of Commons. The object aimed at in Dr. Strachan's system of education was a speedy and real preparation for actual life. He himself knew from experience how early a youth may enter upon the serious work of life, and he summed up his object in the following sentence spoken to his pupils: "The time allowed in a new country like this is scarcely sufficient to sow the most necessary seed, very great progress is not therefore to be expected; if the principles are properly engrafted we have done well." He was continually impressing upon his scholars the fact that the learning acquired at school was only the foundation and that they themselves must lay the superstructure. There was a system of mutual questioning in classes which stimulated thought and research. In the higher classes every boy was required to furnish a set of questions for his classmates on the understanding that he should give the correct reply in case the answerer failed. Then there were rhetorical contests for which one boy challenged another. Dr. Strachan was a strict disciplinarian and well he needed to be, for his scholars were continually thrown in contact with Indians, half-breeds and bad specimens of French adventurers. Flogging was rare and only resorted to in case of obstinacy, wanton cruelty or some word or act of immorality. For lesser offences the punishments were varied and frequently suggested themselves, for in everything Dr. Strachan had freed himself from routine and he wished his scholars to do the same. He might sentence a boy to stand against a post with his pockets turned inside out, or he might make him kneel for a few minutes or stand with outstretched arm holding a book. An apple or marble brought out during school hours would likely result in the exhibition of the contents of the pockets. A boy once giving an audible twang on a jewsharp during work hours was compelled to stand up on a desk and play an air for the entertainment of the school. Of sports during play hours there were not so many as now. Mr. Clarke Gamble says that cricket was wholly unknown, and that ball was the most popular game, both among the boys and girls, the former playing with a ball as hard as it was possible to make it, and the latter with a soft ball. In the winter of course snow-balling was in high favour. Once a year, before the mid-summer vacation, a feast was allowed in the school room, to which all contributed. Dr. Scadding remarks that it was some-times rather a riotous affair. The District Grammar School received its appellation "The Blue School" from the fact that it was painted blue. This was not done until 1818, for in that year Dr. Strachan advertised a course of popular lectures on natural philosophy at two guineas the course, the proceeds to be laid out in painting the District School. Apropos of this, Gourlay in his "Sketches of Upper Canada" remarks: "Schools and colleges, where are they? Few yet painted, though lectures on natural philosophy are now abundant." Mr. Samuel Armour, a graduate from Glasgow University, was first appointed as assistant and then succeeded Dr. Strachan as master of the Grammar School. He was an ardent sportsman and when flocks of wild pigeons flew over the town and guns were popping and banging on every side he could scarcely restrain himself sufficiently to attend to his classes.

Mr. Armour was succeeded by Dr. Thomas Phillips, who, in 1830, was appointed Vice-Principal of Upper Canada College. The history of Upper Canada College is pretty well known. This will be only a sketch.

The Old Richey Terrace

In 1827 the charter of Upper Canada College was granted by George IV, when Sir Peregrine Maitland was second Governor of Upper Canada. In 1829 Sir John Colborne succeeded Sir Peregrine Maitland, and he proceeded to establish the College. In 1829 tenders were called for the erection of the building on King street west, in York, (Toronto), in the block bounded by Graves (Simcoe street), John, Adelaide and King streets. During the erection of these buildings the College classes were opened in the old blue school, the Home District School, which stood in the square directly north of St. James' Cathedral block. The land was known as "College square." In January, 1831, the new buildings on King street west being ready, the classes were removed, and the "old blue school" was dismantled, but afterwards, in 1836, was reopened as the Home District School.

In the Upper Canada *Gazette* of December 17, 1829, this advertisement is printed: — "Upper Canada College, established at York. Visitor, the Lieutenant-Governor for the time being. This college will open after the approaching Christmas vacation, on Monday, the 8th of January, 1830, under the conduct of the masters appointed at Oxford by the Vice-Chancellor and other electors in July last. Principal, the Rev. J. H. Harris, D.D., late Fellow of Clare Hall, Cambridge. Classical Department; Vice-Principal, the Rev. T. Phillips, D.D., of Queen's College, Cambridge; First Classical Master, the Rev. Chas. Mathews, M.A., of Pembroke Hall, Cambridge; Second Classical Master, the Rev. W. Boulton, B.A., of Queen's College, Oxford; Mathematical Department, the Rev. Chas. Dade, M.A., Fellow of Caius College, Cambridge, and late Mathematical Master at Elizabeth College; French, Mr. J. P. De La Haye; English, Writing and Arithmetic, Mr. G. A. Barber and Mr. J. Padfield; Drawing Master, Mr. Drury. Signed, G. H. Markland, Secretary to the Board of Education." Sir John Colborne on his arrival in Upper Canada was fresh from the governorship of Guernsey, one of the Channel Islands. During his administration there he had revived a decayed public school now known as Elizabeth College. Being of opinion that the new country to which he had been transferred was not ripe for a university on the scale contemplated in a royal charter which had been procured he addressed himself to the establishment of an institution which should meet the university wants of the community.

Naturally the system upon which the new Upper Canada College was modelled was that which was then adopted in most of the great public schools in England. The classes were first opened on the 8th of January, 1830, in the building on Adelaide street, which had formerly been used as the Home District Grammar School. Here it continued for more than a year. In 1831 the institution was removed to the site which it has since occupied, opposite Government House, what was originally a very broken piece of ground denominated Russell Square. In the message of the Lieutenant-Governor to the Legislative Assembly in 1831 it is stated that from the original grant of land by the Crown 66,000 acres had been set apart for the support of Upper Canada College and Royal Grammar School. The management of Upper Canada College was from its foundation in 1829 until March, 1833, under the control of its own board of directors and trustees, when by an order of of the Lieutenant-Governor it was transferred to the council of King's College, and by the Act of 1837 was incorporated with and formed an appendage of the University of King's College, subject to its jurisdiction, and it thus remained until the first of January, 1850, when the University Act of 1849 came into force, which, while declaring that the College was an appendage of the University, conferred upon it the management by its own council, subject to the authority of the head of the University, as to the disallowance of any statute or rule; also with an Endowment Board.

Two notes can be added, as they relate to early scholars. First, Dr. Scadding,

who was the first pupil whose name was entered on the books of Upper Canada College when it was opened in 1830. He

was also, as has been previously stated, the first head boy
of that institution, and also, it is believed, the first of its alumni
who entered either the Universities of Oxford or Cambridge,
and also the first Upper Canada College boy who took holy
orders in the Anglican church, and in due course received
his degree of D.D. from his university. He entered Upper
Canada College, as has been stated, in 1830, and in 1834
matriculated at St. John's College, Cambridge, as an under-
graduate. In 1837 he obtained his degree of B.A., and that
of M.A. three years later. Returning to Canada in 1838, he
was ordained successively deacon and priest in the Anglican
church, and until 1847 was one of the clergy attached to the
cathedral church of St. James, Toronto. In the same year that
Dr. Scadding entered into holy orders (1838) he was appointed
third classical master at Upper Canada College; at a little
later date he became second classical master, and about 1842
first classical master. Dr. Scadding continued uninterruptedly,
from 1838 until 1863, as a master at the college, resigning
in the latter year, when he turned his attention wholly to
clerical and literary labours.

Throughout the volumes of the *Landmarks* Dr. Scadding
finds frequent mention; and his book *Toronto of Old* is
continually quoted.

There was another excellent type of youth which attended
Upper Canada College.

These were men of action, often the sons of soldiers and
themselves destined for the service of arms. Such was the
eldest son of Colonel Wells who resided in "a large, two-
storey, rough cast house, overlooking the city, on Davenport
Hill, some few hundred yards from where now runs Spadina
Road." The father had won the Gold Cross for Distinguished
Service at Badajoz; the son did gallant service in the Crimea.

It is related of him that when a boy at Upper Canada
College, during the troublous period of 1837, he organized and
drilled a company of cadets drawn from the pupils attending

that school. These embryo warriors were not armed with anything more formidable than broomsticks, nevertheless it is on record that they offered their services to Sir Francis Bond Head "to assist in the suppression of the rebellion." It is almost needless to say that the offer was declined with thanks.

As for the University, that is also outside our limits. Two paragraphs may recall to Torontonians what very few care to remember.

Buildings have their vicissitudes as well as men, but was ever design of builders more completely thwarted than that an edifice intended for the home of the Muses should become an asylum for the insane, and instead of the smooth flowing measures of Homer and Virgil should resound with the cries and wailings of mad women. As early as 1791 and before Governor Simcoe had left England to take charge of his newly created Canadian province he suggested to Sir Joseph Banks, president of the Royal Society, the desirability of "a college of a higher class" in the colony. Of course at that time scarcely any students could have been found to attend the college if it had been established, but something of provision was made for its existence at a future day by the grant for such a purpose of a large portion of public land. In 1819 Gourlay thought the province still unprepared for a college, but suggested that batches of twenty-five students should be annually sent from Upper Canada to the English Universities, and supported there at the public expense. An elaborate model of a great educational institution was prepared, but when the time came to establish the University of Toronto it was rejected, and the work of drawing up a new plan was given to Mr. Young, a local architect. Only a part of one of the buildings of the plan was ever erected. It is shown in the illustration in the *Landmarks,* and is only a wing, the intention having been to extend the building several hundred feet to the westward. The wing had a frontage of from sixty to seventy-five feet. It was built of beautiful white cut stone. It is being torn down as the new Parliament buildings go up and the material is used in their construction. This building was not long used as an educational establishment; indeed about 1856, and for some few years afterwards, it was converted into a branch of the Provincial Lunatic Asylum.

Let us now glance at some of the little "schools" that rose and endured for awhile and uncomplainingly perished: at least, no complaint survives.

In 1815 the *Gazette* introduces a lady:

Mrs. Lancaster respectfully informs her friends and the public that she will open a school on Wednesday, the 1st day of November next, at Mr. J. P. Post's, jnr., new town, for the accommodation of children, where reading, writing and needle work will be taught by her.

The "new town" comprised the dwellings west of George Street which is now Toronto Street. Mrs. Lancaster was one of the first ladies to set up a school, but she was soon followed by others. Here are advertisements in 1822:

"York, Upper Canada, under the patronage of the Rt. Honourable Lady Sarah Maitland, and the principal ladies of Upper Canada. Mrs. Cockburn, (successor to Mrs. Goodman), respectfully announces to her friends and the public, that she will commence her school duties on the first Monday in June. Mrs. Cockburn submits to their inspection, her school terms which she trusts will be found moderate that parents will be enabled to give young ladies the requisite time to the desired acquirements. Terms per quarter, for education in the English language grammatically, history, geography, the use of the globes, with plain and fancy needle work, 2 pounds, writing and ciphering 10s, the French language 1 pound, drawing and painting on velvet 1 pound and 10 shillings, for board and lodging 8 pounds 10 shillings.

"Music, dancing, flower and card work are also taught in the school, and charged moderately.

"Mrs. Cockburn will receive a class of little children from 4 to 7 years of age, for £5 per quarter each, entrance one guinea.

"Every lady to provide a table and teaspoon, knife and fork, sheets and towels, and to pay for her own washing.

"Three months' notice is expected before any lady leaves the school; the terms of tuition to day scholars are the same as to boarders, with half a guinea entrance."

In this issue is also the advertisement of a Mr. Hughes, who was a land surveyor, and was also willing to act as tutor. He advertises thus: "Education. — Christopher Hughes, Deputy Surveyor, begs leave to acquaint his friends and the public that he has commenced land surveying, and by unremitting attention to his duty hopes to merit a share of public patronage. Orders sent to Mr. Howard's, York, Mr. Flake's, Yonge street, and to the Rev. Mr. Ginkin's, of the Township of Markham, will be attended to. N.B. — C. H. would engage as a private tutor in the family of a gentleman in the town of York or its vicinity, when not employed in surveying. His system of education comprises reading, writing, arithmetic, bookkeeping and declamation, geography, use of the globes, elements of euclid, algebra, and all the minor branches of the mathematics."

About this time we learn of the existence of the Market Lane School. There was a Masonic Hall on Market Lane (now Colborne Street). It was the first structure in York that had a cupola.

This appendage at the western gable, supported by slender props, was intended for the reception of a bell, which, however, was never supplied. On the outside of the building, at the western end, was a staircase leading up to the Masonic Hall on the second floor. In the hall were held the first meetings of the first Mechanics' institute. Here, too, were delivered the first popular lectures, among the lecturers being John Fenton, for some time the parish clerk of St. James' church. So early as 1820 the Masonic Hall bore a weather-beaten appearance.

The lower part of the building was used as a school-house, known as the Market Lane school. The masters were successively Mr. Stewart, Mr. Appleton and Mr. Caldicott. Of these the best known was Thomas Appleton, a good teacher and a kind man, held in equally high esteem by the pupils and their parents. Mr. Appleton was afterward master of the central school, and there for a time Mr. Fenton was his assistant. The teachers' seat was at the right of the door as one entered the building. Plain wooden benches and desks of the most primitive fashion were the accommodations provided for the scholars, of whom there were about thirty, in the year 1822. There were no buildings between the school-house and the bay, and from the windows the boys and girls could watch the vessels coming and going. Among the pupils of the school in 1822 was young McMurray, who afterward became Bishop of Niagara. His father kept a little huckster shop in a small frame building on the south side of King street, midway between Yonge street and Leader Lane. While a school boy the future bishop was a page in the House of Assembly. On leaving Appleton's school he for a time went to Dr. Strachan's school. He was afterward sent to western Canada as a missionary, and while there took for a wife an Indian woman. A brother of Bishop McMurray also attended the school. He became a watchmaker. George and Gardner Bostwick, and their sisters, May and Margaret, were pupils, as were also Alfred and Thaddeus Patrick and their sisters. The belle of the school was Margaret Fair, the daughter of landlord Fair, the successor of Mr. Frank in the management of Frank's hotel, and afterward the proprietor of a hotel on King street. Pretty Miss Fair married a worthless fellow, and became so reduced in circumstances that she was obliged to take in washing. Her brother, Bob Fair, was also a scholar of Mr. Appleton's. In the Mackenzie rebellion he joined McGrath's troop, and was thrown from his horse, near the Don bridge, and killed.

Two other schools that flourished about 1830 were Miss Hussey's Day School and the Toronto Academy. The City

Hall now stands where Miss Hussey taught but her school was long remembered. She had the reputation of being an excellent teacher, kind as well as strict, and "She always kept some kind of lunch on her table for any pupils that might be hungry." The school was given up in 1854.

Toronto Academy stood at the back of the four brick buildings that preceded the old Queen's Hotel; and its first Principal (in 1846) was the Rev. Alex. Gale, a celebrated Presbyterian pastor. The *Landmarks* has this to say about one of his pupils:

There was one female pupil at this school, a girl remarkable for her aptness at mathematics and classics, Miss Jane Gale, daughter of Rev. Alex. Gale, the principal. This young lady afterwards married the Rev. Mr. Ingliss, of Hamilton. Miss Gale had extraordinary ability, and it was nothing uncommon for her father, when some of his friends were at the house, to hand his daughter a difficult Greek or Latin author, and request her to translate at sight, which she did with the greatest ease. In mathematics she was phenomenal, and an intricate question in mental arithmetic, that would require an ordinary mind four or five minutes with pencil and paper, would be answered by her in a few seconds. Miss Gale had a brother, Mr. James Gale, who at one time was a teller of the Commercial Bank of Hamilton, and he likewise had considerable ability.

Education for ladies also included the fine arts. Madame Harris had a dancing school under the patronage of the Countess of Dalhousie — a school that flourished for years. And in 1831 "one of the most fashionable and best conducted schools in York" was opened. Here is the advertisement:

BOARDING AND DAY SCHOOL

The Misses McCord beg leave to announce to the inhabitants of York and in its vicinity that they will open on Monday, the 18th inst., a boarding and day school for the education of ladies. The system which they propose to follow will be found different from the plan generally pursued; but as it is one which is now adopted in the most respectable seminaries in Great Britain and Ireland, and one by which they have always taught, they have experienced the satisfaction which it has inevitably given, and feel confident that on trial it will be approved of here. They therefore hope to merit a share of public patronage. Terms can be known by applying at their house in George street. York, July 7th, 1831.

All these schools appear to have been respectable, reasonably well managed and reasonably successful; but there must have been others of a different hue. A celebrated school was the Central or National school, situated on the north-west corner of Jarvis and Adelaide streets.

Mr. Appleton was one of the first teachers at this school, and at a later date Mr. Spragge. In the Central the girls were upstairs and the boys downstairs. The entrance for the girls was by the side stairs, running up the north side of the building from Jarvis street, or New street. The entrance for the boys was through a big gate on Adelaide street. The lower floor of the Central had large folding doors, so that the two rooms could be thrown into one. Mr. John Fenton, a literary genius of the day, was at one time Mr. Appleton's assistant teacher here. Between the boys attending the Central school and the boys of the Grammar school, difficulties, of course, arose, and on many occasions feats of arms, accompanied by considerable risk to life and limb, were performed on both sides, with sticks and stones. Youngsters, ambitious of a character of extra daring, had thus an opportunity of distinguishing themselves in the eyes of their less courageous companions. The same would-be heroes had many stories to tell of the perils to which they were exposed in their way to and from school. Those of them who came from the western part of the town, had, according to their own showing, mortal enemies in the men of Ketchum's tannery, with whom it was necessary occasionally to have an encounter, while those who lived in the east of the town, narrated, in response, the attacks experienced or delivered by themselves, in passing Shaw's or Hugill's brewery.

In George Walton's directory for 1833 is the following advertisement: "York Central or National School at the corner of Newgate and New streets. His Excellency, Lieut.-Gov., patron. His Excellency being desirous that the course of instruction at this school should include all the branches usually comprehended in a good English education, has directed that it be conducted in the following manner. Boys' school, First Department, Joseph Spragge, master, English, reading, writing and arithmetic on the principles of Ball & Lancaster; Second Department, J. T. Wilson, headmaster, English, reading, writing, arithmetic, English grammar, bookkeeping, elements of geography. Girls' school, Rebecca Sylvester, mistress, English, reading, writing, arithmetic and drawing. Scholars are to pay $1 per quarter. No family to pay for more than two children at a time whatever be the number attending. Parents are requested to send children regularly in as neat and decent an order as their circumstances will permit. Free tickets of instruction to children of parents who cannot pay may be had of Archdeacon John Strachan, or Lieut.-Col. Joseph Wells. Received instruction in year ending April 30, 1833, boys, 402, girls, 235. At present in actual attendance, boys 200, girls 138."

About this date also (1833) we read of Boyd's Commercial Academy on Bay street.

Hundreds of the boys of Toronto received their tuition at the hands of Mr. Boyd. He was an excellent teacher, one who commanded not only the respect of the people at large, but of the pupils, who were so carefully looked after by him in their younger days.

In the *British Colonist* of the 29th December, 1841, appeared the following advertisement in regard to Boyd's school: —

"The annual examination of this flourishing seminary took

place on the 26th inst., in the presence of many respectable inhabitants of this city. The Lord Bishop of Toronto, assisted by Rev. W. T. Leach, and Robt. Baldwin, Esq., had the kindness to examine the different classes . . . The school numbers nearly one hundred and thirty pupils, boys and girls, the children of substantial tradesmen and residents of Toronto . . . Mr. Boyd was complimented by the Bishop on his great merit as a teacher, and on the superior skill and unwearied diligence which he manifested in conducting so large a school."

Bay Street at this time was *the* fashionable street, and near Boyd's Academy the Misses Skirving had a ladies' school, very popular for fifteen years — and, later, part of a city shirt factory.

In 1832 there was a meeting of the subscribers to the Infant School — a short-lived attempt at early benevolence. This meeting was called by the Rev. James Harris, from Belfast, first pastor of Knox Church. Its fate is unknown.

The next for note is a Catholic school.

About the time of the Mackenzie rebellion a humourous and clever Irishman by the name of Denis Heffernan came to Toronto. He was a slight, dark-complexioned man about five feet ten inches in height. His family and connections were good, and he himself had been well educated, was an accomplished scholar and one of the best mathematicians of his day. Shortly after coming to Canada he was one day thrown from his horse and picked up for dead. The fall injured him internally but, although he did not die, he recovered only after several years of illness, which drained alike his strength and his purse. On partially regaining his health he decided to turn his accomplishments to account and become a school master. Accordingly he opened a private school in his residence, which he owned. This was a two-storey frame house on the south side of Richmond street about one hundred feet east of Church street. The house was a common enough looking structure standing on the street line. It was about twenty feet front with a gable. The door was on the east of the front and beside it was one window. Upstairs was one window and also a small one in the attic. These were the only windows on the street front. There were two rooms upstairs and two on the ground floor, with a small extension which served as a kitchen. It was in the front room, upstairs, that he opened his school about 1839 or 1840. It was a mixed private school, and although Mr. Heffernan was a Roman Catholic, among his scholars were some Protestants. In 1841 Mr. Heffernan had about twenty pupils, most of whom were boys. Mr. Heffernan was installed as teacher in the school-house in the fire hall lot. He could scarcely be called a pedagogue, for he rather drove than led his pupils through the intricacies of rudimentary learning, reading, writing, arithmetic, grammar, spelling and geography being all the branches taught.

In 1843 another Irishman started a school, which lasted until 1848. His name was Hart and the school and residence was on the west side of Church Street nearly midway between Queen and Richmond Streets. Thirty or forty pupils, all boys, attended during its best days.

The school room was arranged in a peculiar fashion. The master sat behind a high desk on one side with his back to the wall. Around the other three sides were ranged one continuous row of benches with desks in front of them. On these benches the boys sat, every one with his back to the master and his eyes to the wall. By this method of arranging his pupils he could watch every boy's movements unknown to him, and frequently when two boys were racing pens across the desk he would quietly descend from his perch, and stepping on tip-toe across the room, would suddenly seize each by the shoulders, greatly to their consternation. English branches and Latin constituted the course of study at the school. Mr. Hart was very attentive to his duties, very humourous, and although very passionate at times, was rather a favourite among the boys. He seemed to live in constant dread of his wife, a tall, lean, angular and wiry-looking woman. A switch of nine tails was his weapon of punishment. It was his habit to mention how many blows — pandies, they were called in the school-room vernacular — the convicted boy was to receive. The customary number was eight, four on each hand. John Dixon used to give great amusement to the boys and great vexation to the master by his argumentative resistance to punishment by the cat. After dodging and squirming to avoid the blows, he would dispute the count until the master became so confused and enraged that he would give him two or three extra cuts with the stick end of the cat, but John invariably beat him on the count. With all his supposed cleverness as a master the smart boys would outwit him. One gave him every day for three months the same problems worked out by the Rule of Three. School hours were from nine to twelve and from one to three except on Saturdays, when the boys were given a half holiday. The plank sidewalk in front of the building was used for marbles, peg-tops and other school-boy amusements. The elder boys, nearly every one of whom owned a rooster, indulged in the more advanced sport of cock fighting in the adjoining field of Mr. Jarvis. The lane at the south of the house was the battlefield, and here nearly every day a pugilistic encounter took place. On several occasions J. Dalrymple, after a truant's trip of a week, was brought to the school-room by his mother, tied hand and foot and in a cart. These were red-letter days for the master, who would superintend his disembarkation with great glee, rolling up his coat-sleeves, flourishing his instrument of torture and calling out in exultant tones, "Bring him in, bring him in by the nape of the neck till I give him a taste of the flail."

Knox College was instituted in 1844, after "The Disruption", and Dr. Gale and the Rev. Henry Esson taught there. It was then a purely theological institution with no power to grant degrees. A school for youth that is closer to our purpose was founded in 1851: St. Paul's Church Grammar School. The Principal was the Rev. John G. D. McKenzie and the school was conducted in the basement of his private house. The intention was that it should be a training school for Trinity College, but about 1854 the idea was abandoned and Mr. McKenzie gave up teaching.

It is time that someone asked about the training of these teachers, and indeed, some time before this, a commission appointed to enquire into the state of education in the Province of Upper Canada had reported in scathing terms.

Respecting the District Grammar schools which had been established under the Act of 1807, they recommended that there should be uniformity as regards the system, that all teachers should pass an examination as to their fitness (the state of education in the province can be imagined when it was necessary to make such a recommendation), that where the number of pupils in each school exceeded 30 an assistant should be engaged, that all school houses should be built on a uniform plan, that there should be a certain number of free pupils, and that all schools should be systematically inspected.

Respecting Model schools they also made many recommendations for their improvement in the system of study and the subjects to be taught.

Regarding Normal schools the report was most emphatic. "No plan of education can be efficiently carried out without the establishment of schools for the training of teachers," and their recommendation was that the Central school in Toronto should be a Normal school, with others to be added as occasion might require.

The commissioners invited opinions from many of the leading men of the day on the question of schools and their teachers, and it is worth while to give brief extracts from the replies of some of those who were consulted. Mahlon Burwell wrote: "I cannot conceive anything more wanting in efficiency than our present system for common school education." Rev. Robert Murray, who was the first Superintendent of Education for Upper Canada, wrote, describing it as, "The present wretched system of education." Then, suggesting a remedy, he continued:

"It appears absolutely necessary, to ensure the efficiency of a system, that men of education, who themselves have had large experience in the education of youth, should be appointed to superintend the whole system."

Bishop Strachan, speaking of the bill drawn up by Mr. Mahlon Burwell, whose opinion has just been quoted, said: "The Common School Bill drawn up by Mr. Burwell appears to be an able performance . . . It is based on true principles."

The last opinion that it is necessary to quote is that of the Hon. P. B. De Blaquiere. He was even more emphatic than was Mr. Burwell, saying: "The present condition of teachers is truly wretched, and reflects great disgrace upon the nation."

This was the state of educational matters when Upper and Lower Canada became united in 1840.

A School Act was passed the same session applicable to both provinces, only to be repealed in 1843 as being wholly unworkable in the lower province, and separate acts were passed for each province, and on them was implanted a scheme to apply to both Upper and Lower Canada for public and common schools, with a monetary appropriation of £50,000, or $200,000, in aid of their support.

In a letter to Mr. I. G. Hodgins, of Toronto, the Hon. Isaac Buchanan, writing under date April 11th, 1882, thus tells how it came about that such a very large sum was obtained from the public exchequer. He wrote: "This first attempt of mine to get an endowment for education (out of the clergy reserve fund) failed, as there was no responsible government then. But five years afterwards, when my election for Toronto had carried responsible government, and before the first Parliament met, I was talking to the Governor-General (C. Poulett Thomson, Lord Sydenham). He felt under considerable obligation to me for standing in the breach when Mr. Robert Baldwin found that he could not succeed in carrying Toronto. He spoke of Canada as 'a drag upon the mother country.' I replied warmly, for I felt sure (as I told him) that if we were allowed to throw the affairs of the province into regular books . . . we would show a surplus over expenditure. His Excellency agreed to my proposal, and I stipulated that, if we showed a yearly surplus, one-half would be given as an endowment for an educational system. Happily, we found that Upper Canada had a surplus revenue of about £100,000 ($400,000) one half of which the Parliament of 1841 laid aside for education, the law stipulating that every district council getting a share of it would tax locally for as much more, and this constituted the fund of your educational system."

The first Council of Public Instruction was appointed in 1846, headed by Egerton Ryerson, D.D., Chief Superintendent of Schools.

The first Normal School was on King street west, in the old Government House, the stables of which were fitted up as a Model School. In 1849, when the Government returned to Toronto the Normal School was removed to the Temperance Hall, on Temperance street, and in 1852 removed to the present buildings in St. James' square.

And here our enquiry into the education of youth might rest, even though a postscript concerning Mrs. Forster's school at "Pinehurst" is essential. The *Landmarks of Toronto* calls Mrs. Forster "one of the most accomplished of schoolmistresses and charming of women." Her school, from 1853 to 1866, was the equivalent of Havergal or of Branksome in our own day; and many prominent Canadians sent their daughters to be educated at Pinehurst.

Celebrated, too, were Miss Macnally's school, on the north side of Wellington Street, and Miss Macartney's school on King Street west; but we cannot give space to either. For an epilogue it must be "Arms and the man I sing" — the man — Alexander Muir, author of "The Maple Leaf Forever", poet, teacher, athlete, Imperialist and public speaker. The ninety pages that *Landmarks of Toronto* devotes to him cover all these attributes, as well as his birth and parentage, with part of the history of Canada. Here we can but give

"PINEHURST"

Mrs. Forster's Ladies' School, Head of John Street

extracts to prove two points: that Muir was a man of unusual powers and a schoolmaster of extraordinary ability.

In the pioneer days throughout Upper Canada, the settlers who were anxious that their sons and daughters should receive the rudiments of education were not particular as to credentials in the selection of a dominie.

The old preceptor may have been a man of many trades and callings. In some parts of old Upper Canada the first school teachers were those who had been regimental schoolmasters, and many of these were excellent teachers and disciplinarians.

Other men who were well up in the art of keeping the rod in pickle for unruly boys were of a class who had no particular calling, save and except that they had received the rudiments — "the three R's" — in the old land, and after years perhaps at the desk or in the shop, ventured across the sea, ready to take up, as men are to-day, the first occupation that came their way.

While some of these early pioneers who tutored the youngsters of the backwoods, had not much knowledge of educational principles, they did their best under very trying circumstances, to give value for the three or four shillings per quarter that fond parents were called upon to pay for the tuition of each pupil, for there was no stated salary.

The pioneer pedagogue was, to a certain extent, a bird of passage. He boarded round with the families of the youngsters under his charge. His popularity with his pupils was an uncertain quantity. His creed might be "No larnin' without lickin'," or he might be an angel in temper with a stock of moral suasion always on hand. History records that of this latter class the examples were few and far between.

It is said that an old teacher, talking to a mother who found fault with the backwardness of her children at school, said: "My good woman, it's not my fault; what your children require is not a teacher, but a wild beast tamer," and at his remark the mother sighed and said no more.

John Muir, Alexander's father, taught in a log school built in 1817. It was known as school section No. 1, of Scarboro, and the nearest village is Agincourt. Twenty years later, Alexander Muir taught in the same school. He began to teach in 1853. He had excellent credentials as a possible wild-beast tamer; could clear over six feet at the high jump, was a noted cricketer, a champion at quoits and of great physical strength.

Alexander Muir received his early training in the father's school, and in the late forties he entered Queen's College, Kingston. The books of the registrar of Queen's College, Kingston, show that he entered that institution in 1847, when he was 17 years of age. His place of birth is given as "Scarborough, Scotland," and his father's occupation as a "farmer." The entry that Alexander Muir was born in "Scarborough, Scotland," is certainly an error. There is no place of that name in Scotland. The registrar of that date evidently mixed up the place of residence with the place of birth.

Mr. Muir attended college during the sessions of 1847-50 and received the degree of B.A. in April, 1851.

He taught the rural youth of Scarboro until about 1860 and then became Principal of the Leslieville school — a one-room school, a township school until 1870. One of his pupils wrote of him:

"Alexander Muir's method of teaching was his own. He followed no monotonous stereotyped form, and that was the charm. Children loved to go to school because he made them love him by his kind and entertaining disposition. Some days he would treat us to some chemical experiments, as for instance, one cold day in winter when the old box stove would be red hot, he would explain to the wondering scholars how salt and snow would freeze water on a chair by the stove. Another time he would send several boys outside on the road to dance and kick up, while inside he would with the camera and a ray of light through the keyhole of the school door, show the amazed scholars on the white wall beyond the figures of their dancing playmates outside. The wonders of animal magnetism would be illustrated by some experiment, or how electricity could be generated by friction and attract bits of torn paper, etc., to it. These experiments the children would practise at home, to the wonder of their friends and parents, so that Alexander Muir not only taught a school, but a whole countryside. The pupils to Leslieville school came from Todmorden, The Plains, East Toronto, Norway, and as far east as Scarboro town line.

And at our games and sports Mr. Muir always took part, relating for our emulation, deeds of jumping and running done by some wonderful person, and as the fame of his own prowess was the proud possession of every scholar, small wonder that in our eyes he was a wonderful man, and the little red schoolhouse enchanted land."

He left Leslieville in 1870 and took charge of the Jesse Ketchum school on the Davenport Road. He left there in 1872 for the "Common School" at Newmarket. The Yorkville children and friends gave him a complimentary concert, a gold medal (but that was for rowing), a family Bible and the following address:

Dear Teacher, — We are all very, very sorry that you are soon to leave us. You have been so kind and have taken such pains to explain our lessons and make them pleasant to us, that we feel deeply thankful, and have learned to love and prize you very highly as our teacher.

You have shown your deep interest in us, not only in the usual school studies, but also in your endeavors to plant in our minds the more precious lessons of truth and virtue, so as to make us, as far as you could, good boys and girls, as well as being good scholars.

We love you also because you have been so gentle and patient with us, also your patience, by us, has too often been tried. We have also been very thoughtless and very inattentive, for which we are now very sorry.

Will you please accept from us, the pupils of the Yorkville Central school, this copy of that Holy Word of God, out of which you have so long and so faithfully taught us, your pupils?

May you be spared for many a year to read and to enjoy those sacred pages, and to teach them to others when you are removed from us.

And now, dear teacher, we must say good-bye.

Wherever you go may you find scholars who will love you better and give you more pleasure than we have done, and may all happiness and prosperity attend you, and if we do not meet you again on earth, we hope and pray that we will all meet around the throne in heaven.

Your affectionate friends,
The Pupils of the Central School, Yorkville.

In his next school it was the same.

Everyone, young and old, in Newmarket loved Alexander Muir. He always had a cheery word and a handshake for those who greeted him, and his familiar figure as he walked along the street, wearing for headgear a Glengarry cap, ornamented with a silver Scotch thistle, and the tails flying — he looked the typical Scotsman, just as they appear to-day in the little village of Lesmahagow in the land where he first saw light.

Mr. Muir was a staunch Presbyterian. While in Scarboro he took a deep interest in the services, and was always ready to promote the welfare of the church, either by leading the choir or telling good stories to the little ones in the Sabbath School.

Alexander Muir was a teacher far in advance of his time. He had a natural inborn psychological sense that most teachers have to acquire and many never attain. Some people have a natural gift in dress and color combination; others have to study for effects. So it was with Muir's teaching — always equal to the occasion.

He could read a boy's mind as an open book and deal with him according to his individual needs. There was rarely if ever a truancy while he was teaching in Beaverton, because there was always something doing in his school, and if a boy missed a day he was sure to be sorry for it when he returned.

Here is where his great foresight counted the most. This sitting in a monotonous school-room, watching the clock (we did not have one in Beaverton), was the great lacking in by-gone school days. The modern thought in teaching is to keep the child busy, not only mentally, but physically, as well, so we have added to the curriculum, manual training, domestic science and art and many subjects, all tending to the natural development or "sending the whole child to school."

All through Mr. Muir's teaching there were these little incidents creating interest, concentrating the attention, banishing monotony. Yes, indeed, a teacher in advance of his time.

The bigness of Alexander Muir stood out above all else in that old school; bigness of frame, of voice, of character. These were the traits that made the boys fear and love him. He was not a whipper. The boys did not know what it was to have Alexander Muir thrash them.

"I don't want him to muscle me,"[1] was the way they put it when asked why they behaved.

Perhaps enough has here been made of a shining career that closed in 1906. This was a great man and a great Canadian: a teacher in advance not only of his own time but possibly of ours.

[1] To pick the boy up, hold him at arms' length, and shake him.

APPENDIX

THE PLUNDERED LIBRARY

The question of the library destroyed by the Americans is complicated by the fact that many historians assume it to have been the parliamentary library. There is certainly a confusion of terms—in the journals of the House of Assembly when the restoration of the parliamentary library is discussed, the term used is "Public Library for the use of the Legislature". The evidence of Dr. Strachan, however, seems conclusive. In an open letter to Thomas Jefferson, quoted in Middleton's *Municipality of Toronto,* vol. I, p. 122, he writes,

"In April, 1813, the public buildings at York, the capital of Upper Canada, were burnt by the troops of the United States, contrary to the articles of capitulation. They consisted of two elegant halls with convenient offices for the accommodation of the Legislature and the Courts of Justice. The library and all the papers and records of these institutions were consumed. At the same time the church was robbed, and the Town Library totally pillaged. Commodore Chauncey, who has generally behaved honorably, was so ashamed of this last transaction that he endeavored to collect the books belonging to the Public Library and actually sent back two boxes filled with them, but hardly any were complete."

This clears up the confusion between the Parliamentary and the "Town (Subscription) Library" and makes it fairly evident that the books returned had not been taken from the former. In the York *Gazette* of October 14, 1815 is printed the following notice:—

"A meeting of the subscribers to the Toronto Library is to be held on Tuesday next, the 17th inst., at 2 o'clock, at the Church in York, to take into consideration the disposal of such books as are now remaining of that Library.—Thomas Scott."

We have no direct information as to the action, if any, taken by the subscribers; but seven years later a corner of the curtain is lifted. The Treasurer of the little library, William Allan, writes in 1822 to the Chief Justice, William Dummer Powell:—

York 11th Sept. 1822

Sir

There has been in my possession ever since 1815—Several Books belonging to the Toronto Library that was Established here on 9th Dec. 1810—Which was taken away by the Enemy at the Capture of York on 24th April 1813, and afterwards in part returned by order of Commodore Chauncy, and which are not only An incumbrance to me but they are most likely (illegible) from being kept so long Shut up as there is now four of the Gentlemen here out of *Five* who were chosen Directors at the Original meeting in *1810* I must beg that some determination may be made respecting them either to have them sold by Auction (as many of the volumes are now wanting)— or otherwise that I may be freed from any longer charge.

I have the Honor to be

(etc.)

W. Allan, Treasurer To the
Late Toronto Library at York.

Directors chosen at
the meeting in 1810—
The Honble Chief Justice
The Honble Thos Scott
Mr. Wood
The Solicitor Genl
then I believe was Mr. Justice Boulton

The Honble Chief Justice Powell

Draft of answer in William Dummer Powell's handwriting

York 19 Sept. 1822

Wm Allan Esq.

Sir
    Your letter of the 11 Instant on the Subject of the Toronto
Library Books which have been so long an Encumbrance to
you, should have been earlier attended to, but my mind has
been engaged. [?] I do not think the Directors would choose
to give any order therein without a notice to the Subscribers to
attend a meeting for that Purpose—the assize week which will
commence on the 12 October may be a proper season to collect
the greatest number and if you will advertize in the Gazette a
meeting of the Directors & Subscribers for the purpose to be
on Wednesday on that week, I doubt not some order will be
adopted to relieve you & defray any Charge attending the
Custody or delivery [?] of the Books.

Those books must have been an encumbrance, for William
Allan inserted a notice in the Upper Canada *Gazette* of September 19, the very day on which Judge Powell's reply was sent
to him:—

"A meeting of the directors, and those who were subscribers to
the Toronto Library, that was established at York in December, 1810, is requested on Wednesday, the 16th of October,
at two o'clock at De Forest's Hotel, to take into consideration
the disposal of such of the books as now remain, belonging to
the said library, in the possession of W. Allan. W. ALLAN,
Treasurer.
    N.B. Any persons having in their possession any of the books
belonging to this library are requested to send to W.A."

And finally, on December 12, 1822, the remainder books pass
into other hands. Thomas Mosley, auctioneer, deficient in legs
but with a serviceable tongue, advertises:—

"Custom House Sale . . . on Saturday the 21st of December—four chests of tea, two kegs of tobacco, 18 boxes of raisins . . . Also several volumes of books in the best order, that formerly belonged to the Toronto library, in this town."

For much of the above information the Editor is indebted to Toronto's Chief Librarian, Dr. C. R. Sanderson, and to Miss L. E. Loeber, on the Staff of the Reference Department. Grateful acknowledgment is made herewith.

A SELECTIVE INDEX OF PROPER NAMES